31st Dec 2015

For Lesley ——— .

ACCoRDiNG
to my
ANGeLS

thank you for being part of my journey

with love and twinkles

Alison Knox

BALBOA
PRESS
A DIVISION OF HAY HOUSE

Balboa Press books may be ordered through booksellers or by contacting:

Balboa Press
A Division of Hay House
1663 Liberty Drive
Bloomington, IN 47403
www.balboapress.com
1 (877) 407-4847

Print information available on the last page.

ISBN: 978-1-5043-4391-6 (sc)
ISBN: 978-1-5043-4392-3 (e)

Balboa Press rev. date: 11/20/2015

ACCORD

verb

1. to be in agreement or harmony; agree.
2. to make agree or correspond; adapt.
3. to grant; bestow: to accord due praise.
4. Archaic. to settle; reconcile. noun
5. proper relationship or proportion; harmony.
6. a harmonious union of sounds, colors, etc.
7. consent or concurrence of opinions or wills; agreement.
8. An international agreement; settlement of questions outstanding among nations.

idioms

9. of one's own accord, without being asked or told; voluntarily: We did the extra work of our own accord

Source ~ www.dictionary.com

Foreword

The first question I ask any budding author writing their memoir is 'Who are you writing this for?' Sometimes we are called to write for catharsis and our own healing. Sometimes our story needs to be told to heal others or to inspire them and to let them know they are not alone. Alison's story has many layers. On the surface it is the story of her encounters with angels. In the layers beneath it is the angels who are telling their stories and giving us insight into their world. The angels know for sure whom they are writing for – they write through Alison to the ones that need, and are ready, to hear.

If you are drawn to read this book, the chances are you have already encountered angels in some form or you may have experienced Alison's work. You might still be sceptical or even confused about angels – do they really exist? Are they just a figment of your imagination?

My first encounters with Alison and her angels were at a Mind Body Spirit fair in Newark. I sat in on Alison's talk and what really stood out was the matter of fact way she talked about them, like they were friends who had just popped in for a cuppa. There was no wafty, new-age, airy fairyness about them or her. There was a good dose of realism, even cynicism, in her words.

Having known Alison, and her husband Martin, for a number of years, I can vouch for the fact that these really are 'everyday' angels. And perhaps this is the first lesson they want us to learn. While we depict them as ethereal winged creatures, they are in fact every day, matter of fact beings. They come in many forms from ideas to solid humans. Not all angels are sweet and fluffy either. Sometimes they are our nemesis.

One of the stories that Alison tells had a most profound effect on me – and on many others who have heard me retell the story. It is her story about the grey men in suits who made her sit on her hands but forced her to stand in her truth. She quotes the passage from

Hebrews 13:2 "Be not forgetful to entertain strangers: for thereby some have entertained angels unawares" in realising, years later, that these men were perhaps angels in disguise; pushing her to the edge, making her face, and stick up for, her true self.

This story was one of my 'aha' moments.

It struck me that I too had experienced this – a boss who made me redundant from a job I no longer loved but was too attached to to leave. For a decade I had seen him as the devil ejecting me from the company I loved. Reframing him as an angel, that gave me the impetus to fly on my own, released and healed that energetic wound.

Alison will talk of 'channelling' the angels and as a writer and artist, I know and understand this isn't some woo-woo idea or something that she believes makes her particularly 'chosen' or special. All creative people will tell you that their best work comes *through* them not *from* them.

When Alison says, "*There is no script, save that which is already engraved upon my soul, through my own experiences and understanding as my Truth. Everything is channelled to me and through me. Words and images bypass the brain and emerge fully formed and untainted by my own 'ideas' onto the page. It is all done, according to my angels' directive. The angels speak for themselves through my paintings.*" she is speaking a truth that many (if not all) writers and artists experience.

What emerges is often a source of wonderment to us. In these moments we are the pen or the brush and 'something' greater than our physical self is doing the writing or the painting. We may or may not articulate our work as being divinely guided or directed by angels. Some may use the word 'muse' instead. Some still struggle with the angst of thinking they must do it themselves, having not learnt to trust or tune into their higher consciousness.

Whatever; this work is most certainly a calling and Alison has stepped up to the plate in accepting hers. That she wasn't looking for 'it' or the angels, but they found her anyway, and that her journey with them has unfolded from what she describes as "*a perfect point of absolute ignorance, a totally blank canvas!*" makes her statement "*I am an artist, working directly with the most powerful, potentially transformational and healing of angelic energies,*" all the more real and true.

Alison's angel artworks have, over a number of years, sought homes in our house. They have come in varying shapes and sizes. Two particular angels have a special resonance and have been working their magic with us.

I first encountered 'Yes' Angel in Alison's studio when it was barely birthed, the paint still wet and not even finished. Yet I knew as soon as I saw it that this was to be my angel. I had no idea where the money would come from or how this angel was going to come into my life but I knew at some deep visceral level it would come to pass.

And so it did. Some months after this first encounter with Yes, my then fiancé had a windfall. He called Alison to ask if "Yes" was still available. It was and Alison duly delivered it.

Yes has helped me say 'yes' to accepting and naming myself as a writer and as an artist. Yes also helped me say 'yes' to my fiancé in the next step on our journey together. The giver of this beautiful gift is now my husband.

We married in 2014 in the church of St Michael and All Angels in my home village in Lincolnshire. Alison was my best woman and Martin was Paul's best man. Alison created an artwork of Archangel Michael to grace the church for our wedding ceremony. Michael has played a significant role in our lives since that day. Where "Yes" has encouraged us to take steps toward the unknown and unimaginable, Michael has helped us cut loose the bonds of what holds us back.

Alison and I share a love of Kahlil Gibran's 'The Prophet'. When he writes of children he says:

"Your children are not your children.
They are the sons and daughters of Life's longing for itself.
They come through you but not from you,
And though they are with you yet they belong not to you.

You are the bows from which your children as living arrows are sent forth."

It has always struck me that creative work, especially divinely guided creative work, is akin to the children that Gibran speaks of, and that as artists, we *are* the bows from which our creations as living arrows are sent forth into the world. It is not for us to know what gift that creation will bring to its recipient or reader, just as we cannot (and should not) dictate what our child will do or who our child should be.

Angels have many gifts to deliver. Creative work is just one of their channels of communication. Many healers and Lightworkers use Alison's angel artworks as tools, to support and amplify their own work with clients and patients. Some angel artworks are happy to simply enhance a home environment by radiating their positive energy from the mantelpiece.

There are many gifts in stories too. Have you gained most of your inspiration, hope, comfort, encouragement, prompt to action etc. from hearing or reading someone's story or their thoughts? Were your thoughts stirred with 'I could do that'? 'Thank God, I am not alone?' 'If they can do it, so can I?' Isn't that how it happens? Something we read or hear or see prompts us to think or do?

In sharing her stories through this book, Alison and the angels are sharing their gift. Someone is waiting to hear it. Someone is waiting for inspiration, for hope, for comfort, for encouragement, for their prompt to action or for the spark that ignites their fire.

Maybe that someone is you.

Dive in!

Your angels are waiting for you.

Tina Bettison: Writer, Broadcaster and Artist ~
Be'love'd Art From My Heart

~ INTRODUCTION ~

"The greatest thing a human soul ever does in this world is to see something, and tell what is saw in a plain way. Hundreds of people can talk for one who can think; but thousands can think for one who can see."

John Ruskin: Modern Painters 1856

According to my angels, they had been looking for me for a long time. . . I, however, had assuredly not been looking for them.

They found me anyway.

Everything since has unfolded from a perfect point of absolute ignorance, a totally blank canvas!

Today, I am an artist, living and working directly with the most powerful, potentially transformational and healing of angelic energies.

This, my very personal account of an incredible, magical journey, is often shared openly at my public talks and workshops, and through my website newsletters and Facebook postings.

There is no script, save that which is already engraved upon my soul, through my own experiences, and understanding as my Truth.

Everything the angels wish to share is channelled to me and through me. Words and images bypass the brain and emerge fully formed and untainted by my own "ideas" onto the page or canvas.

It is all done, according to my angels directive.

The angels speak for themselves through my paintings. They touch the soul at a deeply profound level and are "experienced" rather than simply "seen".

Of course, the visual images, and written words, are often beautiful, breath taking, but the true impact of their presence is felt at a soul level once a connection has been established.

Many Lightworkers and Healers use my works as tools, to support and amplify their own work with clients and patients. Other times the angels are happy to simply enhance a home environment by radiating their positive energy from the mantelpiece or a handy wall space.

Angels have many gifts to deliver, it is not for *me* to know or reveal what those are.

There exists a precious bond between angel and human where such things are shared, intimately, when the moment is perfect.

If you were to ask "*What will the angels do for me*?"

The truthful answer is "*I don't know*". . . that is between you and your angel.

I am not in the business of "selling" angels . . . I can only put a price on my skill as an artist and allow you to purchase the finished art.

I work from the heart with LOVE not sentimentality.

My angels are often emotionally challenging and can be very direct.

We work together, in accordance, under the flag of "EVeRYDaY ANGeLS" because that is exactly what they are and what we do.

There are no days off.

By entertaining them, my life has changed accordingly.

So, it is time for me to write the story which I have been living out, and telling; even though it is yet un-ended, I can tell it so far, in a plain way.

In sharing these stories with you, I am filling in some of the gaps that time doesn't usually permit me to share in public arena.

Each experience can be taken on its own or supported by another which then grows into a bigger expanded awareness. There is always a beginning, a middle and an end.

The angels can speak for themselves, but sometimes it is hard for you to hear. It is easier if I tell their story through my own.

Why?

Because this is part of my purpose.

Why me?

Why not me?

I honour the angels by working in accordance, simply doing what is asked of me, as best I can.

I don't always know the "*nuts and bolts*" but I trust implicitly that the work will be undertaken to the highest possible standard, to the highest good.

This book is no exception, my lack of experience as a writer will not stop me doing what has to be done!

Maybe I do not know everything there is to know about angels, but they do know all there is to know about me, and in the knowing, still they seek my services.

I have to work with the information I have available at the time, in the moment of calling. If I prevaricate, waiting for things to be perfect, to have all the t's crossed and i's dotted, then trust me, I would not be typing this now, and you would not be reading it.

Here is a great and simple truth. . . it is always the perfect time, and if it is not, it simply won't happen.

Trust to that.

I do.

~IN OR OUT? ~

"If you want to find out, you have to go in"
Danielle La Porte

Angels may call you to your Purpose, and you will hear the call exactly when you are ready to hear.

♥Can you be open of heart and clear of vision?
♥Can you commit to the path, no excuses, forever, whatever?
♥If it looks like it needs doing; can you do it.?
♥Can you embrace the stranger?
♥Can you leave your comfort zone?
♥Will you look for the open doors and check which way they swing?
♥Will you do your best?
♥**Discern. . . discern . . discern.**
♥Will you ask for help if you need it?
♥Do you love what you do; do what you love?
♥Can you accept that Spirituality is not a race or a competition?
♥Can you accept that once you know; you cannot un-know?
♥Can you accept that much of this defies rational explanation, nevertheless, it is?
♥Are you prepared to meet your detractors with alacrity and compassion?
♥Do you understand that the road less travelled is that way for a reason?
♥Can you accept that you cannot take everyone with you?
♥Are you ready to pack your own parachute?

Can you?
Will you?
Do you?

That's your work.

As a child I was never very good at doing what was asked of me.

According to my Mum, she would often have to administer a sharp clip around the ear 'ole to get me to pay attention. It could take two or three polite "asks" before the clip had to be delivered. It is no different now, the angels still have their work cut out for them and sometimes it takes a little longer than they would like for me to "get it".

Many of my Life Lessons have had to be of the "clip around the ear" variety. Some, sharper than others!

It is absolutely my understanding that we are all tested throughout our life on our commitment to our purpose. Often, those things which we hold most precious are the very things chosen to test us the most, to shatter and break us, then to help put us back together again. Often it is our misplaced fears that hold us back from that which we most desire.

We so desperately want "in" but we are scared and don't quite know how.

How we view our life experiences determines how we move forward. Attitude is the greatest factor. How do you respond to life? Sometimes those unlearned lessons have to be dealt again and again, and still we do not "get it" or understand.

For me, for many years, my professional career success and my status and standing within it, was my measure of self worth and value. It was my excuse to keep me from finding, facing and embracing my true self.

For others it may be their children, elderly parents, domestic life, health, financial wealth, addictions or sexual behaviours, whatever, but for me it was definitely my "job" that kept me a stranger to myself.

We tend to define ourselves by things which are outside of us. Ego plays a big part in our choices and often leads us by the nose into dangerous choppy waters. When we flail around and start to drown, we wonder how this could have happened! Where were our angels when we needed them? Probably they were closer than we could ever have imagined.

Here, I'll need to shatter any sentimental illusions you might hold about the purpose of angels.

I hate to do it so early in this book, but I'll risk it!

Angels are not here to do your dirty work for you! They open us up to a greater awareness of our own innate capabilities and show us the way.

When you call on your tame "parking angel" what actually happens is that you simply bring yourself into a greater state of awareness of your environment, you pay more attention and notice subtle things like reversing lights, a slight movement in a car starting its engine, or an exhaust blowing, you simply see what was anyway available to you. When you are busy or stressed this sudden manifestation of the perfect parking place feels like a miracle. I am sure we have all done it. I assure you, angels have got bigger fish to fry, and we humans are perfectly capable of finding our own parking spaces.

In my experience Angels do not "fix things", they are not the ones with magic wands! What they do, is to empower us by showing us our choices. There are no "right" or "wrong" choices, just choices. We will always get there in the end; it just takes longer with some of the choices we make. Sometimes we have to go backwards to go forwards. The "best" choice often feels the hardest and the most challenging.

Divine intervention, is often a shift of our own consciousness which allows us to see from a clearer, higher and very different perspective. The Angels can help set us up for that perfect moment, but it is we who choose to take the leap or make the move.

Or not.

In my understanding, Angels are here with us now, upon this Earth plane, to help us restore the balance between humanity; nature; the elements, and the Earth itself. They exist to help bring us closer to our Truth, to help facilitate our greater purpose, and to show us better ways of doing what has to be done.

Angels are, first and foremost, beings of Light. Pure vibration. Energy imprints. They have no physical form. They are awesome, magnificent, ineffable, powerful, dynamic, and extraordinary. Capable of challenging as well as reassuring, they can bring peace, comfort, hope, love, bliss, insight, unity, harmony and balance. (To mention just a few of their gifts.)

Angels are essentially the messengers, connectors between the earthly and heavenly realms.

In Latin, the word Angelus means 'messenger'.

Angels present themselves in ways we can best accept and understand, they appreciate that we need points of focus, whether that be a painting, a sculpture, a little white feather, a carved crystal, or a little frilly dolly. They understand that we, as humans, feel we are comparatively weak, undeserving, feeble things and we need to feel our safety and comfort in these matters. So, they seek to remind us of our own power and magnitude, our infinite capabilities and above all else to celebrate our humanness.

Sometimes, when necessary or appropriate they can "hi-jack" a human body and infuse it with their light vibration and energy. So, from time to time, angels are able to appear to us in human form. I know I have witnessed this many times, even if sometimes I haven't instantly recognised them for who they were.

I am often asked how to go about making a direct connection with the angels.

Well, my answers may be disappointing.

I don't have all the answers, only my own experiences.

As it happens, I don't believe I am any more special or unique than anyone else, but what I do know is that to experience this gift requires committed work.

Let us imagine this experience of connection to be like any other gift, be it a musical talent, artistic ability, athleticism, dance . . . whatever. There is a point at which the gift is recognised, and either we can embrace, hone and nurture it, and through dedicated practice and commitment to it, become proficient, excel with mastery over whatever that gift may be.

How unwilling are you to be distracted from your purpose?

It is the difference between a regular bloke who enjoys kicking a football around the park with his kids and the footballing superstar David Beckham (although I am sure he enjoys kicking a football around with his kids too). That man made a choice to do what he does, and I feel sure that was not without some personal sacrifice, despite all the trappings of his luxurious lifestyle.

This kind of commitment of purpose invariably requires a degree of sacrifice.

We so want to find out, but we are scared to go in.

When you thought you were drowning; no doubt your angels were throwing you the life raft of "choice" and you were assiduously ignoring them. Perhaps you had a different life raft in mind?

This is our human trait to put expectations on outcomes, to want so badly, yet reject so abjectly when the gift is delivered. Perhaps the packaging didn't look quite as we expected it to?

To accept the Gift requires commitment.

Joan of Arc said, 'I die for speaking the message of the angels'.

I trust my sacrifice will not be as ultimate as that of Joan!

There are many ways to "die" for your Truth and purpose. Often that simply means giving up your old non serving patterns, behaviours, and comfort zones. New values form and tolerances change. It is necessary to risk losing some part of what was, to engage with what is, and what will be.

So, I ask the question of you, are you ready to "die" for your Spiritual Self?

In one of my workshops the angels ask us "What is dying to be born?" It is always a big, tough question, but so rewarding when the answers come, borne on the wings of the feeling.

So, let me ask you; where are you in terms of your commitment to your Truth?

Rather than attend to your spiritual development, do you choose to slump in front of your TV watching some soap opera with a large glass of Pinot Grigio, all nice and comfy cosy?

Do you forgo (yet another) spiritually nourishing workshop, because the kids/grandkids/husband/best friend want you to do something for them?

Did you ignore that heart expanding e-mail about the special channelling Webinar because you have a pile of ironing to do?

Have you cancelled yet another event related to your own spiritual growth because you thought you better pop over to see your sister because she is having a bad time of things right now.

You must be starving!

Spiritually starving!

Excuses, excuses.

All this stuff is very worthy, BUT it has to take a back seat . . . sorry, but that's the way it is.

If you want the divine connection, you have to be prepared to risk disappointing a few mortals rather than disappoint a single angel.

Remember how when you get aboard a plane, they do a safety demonstration? They instruct "In an emergency, oxygen masks will appear. Apply your own before you try to help anyone else" It's the very same principle . . . you cannot help anyone if you have abandoned yourself.

Once I had made my choice; this is how it had to be.

I am not saying that any of this was easy.

It wasn't.

I lost a few along the way.

It soon sorts out the wheat from the chaff in your life.

When you have had this kind of awakening, there is no going back. You cannot suddenly change your mind and un-know what you know.

Those of you who are parents may recognise the feeling that there are times you would like to give those kids right back, but you can't, so your life as you knew it necessarily becomes very different in order to accommodate a different set of priorities. You meet different people, outside of your original social circle, and you find your interests and tastes change, your tolerances shift, your awareness increases and so necessarily, your life changes. Subtle or dramatic, change is inevitable.

In my experience, Angels are woven into the very tapestry of our lives. They are present and prevalent whether we choose to see or acknowledge them or not.

Imagine a radio receiver, tuned to a certain frequency. Sometimes it may be in tune and you hear it loud and clear and sometimes it is not, all you get is a lot of crackling and static. The fact you find it hard to get a clear signal would indicate you need to retune your radio. Did you even upgrade to digital? There are hundreds if not thousands of stations broadcasting out there, you cannot pick them up simply because you are not tuned in. That doesn't mean those broadcasts don't exist, only that *you* are not in tune with them.

When you tune in to the higher frequencies you suddenly get clear, instant and intelligent connection.

That is how I find it is with the Angels.

It helps to find the right teacher to guide, support and mentor you, and to have the right people around you to maintain your new, higher frequency.

I encourage you to be discerning about the company that you choose to keep.

A supportive energy around you makes all the difference. You will be surprised where your support comes from. It may not be from those you expect. Be patient, and non judgemental with those who find it hard to accept what you are doing and how fast you are moving; change feels scary.

Seek out those who inspire and fire your spirit.

There are many fine teachers out there who will give you ways of connecting with angels. There are beautiful rituals you can do to call the Angels in, special places you can go to be in their energy, incense can be burned, crystals can be consulted, retreats can be undertaken, but it is all pointless unless you are willing to be open, sometimes it can feel like you have been cracked open, and to give yourself over absolutely to whatever has to be done.

Please do not ask the angels to show you your life's purpose then turn your nose up "What? That old thing? Again? . . . hey. . .hang on, what else have you got for me?"

The Gift, may be something we have lived with all our lives. Mine was my art.

I was never shown the nuts and bolts of what was to be done, I just got a sense of purpose and as best I could, I rose to the challenge.

I confess, when I was first availed of my own purpose, I balked, not knowing how this could be possible, it was so far removed from my day to day experience it seemed highly unlikely.

Would you like to know my purpose?

"Through my work, the Light of Humanity and the Light of the Divine are unified"

How would you feel if you were told that on day one of your journey?

I confess when I was given that strange and beautiful insight, by a beloved Teacher, I had no idea what it meant, yet. . . I knew it to be true.

I'll explain more of this later, I promise.

So, despite my ignorance and total lack of knowledge, I just stepped up to the mark and did my best.

Why me?

Because I said "YES".

I was in.

I delivered on my promise.

I LOVE what I do.

It was not always so.

There is a Zen proverb ; "*Before enlightenment, chop wood. After enlightenment, chop wood*" . . . yep!

So, please, don't say "*It's all right for you . . .*" as though my life has been totally pink and fluffy all the way along. Far from it! My life is as commonly domestic as anyone else's. I have the same things to worry about, the same bills to pay, a marriage to attend to, the same laundry to wash, the dog to walk and my bees to manage. I shop, cook the dinner, make the beds and generally juggle my life. Occasionally, I chop wood too!

Same as it ever was and ever will be.

I have made it my business to meet those who inspire and educate me, I have given up the stuff that serves no purpose.

I have stayed up all night working on what was asked of me, (this very book, I finished writing the first draft whilst on holiday in Turkey in 2012) .

There have been times when I have driven miles to deliver what was required of me, I have risked the displeasure of my nearest and dearest as I have forfeited the normal family stuff to meet the critical celestial deadlines.

I have lost friends when we no longer shared common interests and activities.

I have given my time, my heart and my resources to upholding what has been gifted to me. I have actively sought ways to share my knowledge, to teach others what I know, and to bring EVeRYDaY ANGeLS into public domain. I keep my angels accessible, I am still within easy reach of anyone who is prepared to call or email me.

I am still 100% sane.

Part of my work is to tell this story.

Within these plainly written words, subtle Divine Keys are imprinted to open and release, empower and inspire, reassure and comfort, as well as challenge and provoke.

Just choosing to read this book will already have triggered a response deep within your soul.

When you have finish the book, please, just sit with it for a while. Focus on the cover. Run your fingers over it, flick the pages and feel the air moving across the edges of the pages, listen to the sound it makes. Let the vibration stay with you as the words settle deeper. Pay attention to what sticks with you. Make notes, scribble on the pages, fill it full of "post its", pass it to your friends, share it with colleagues. Dip in and out of the chapters and let the words you need, find you. They will settle within your heart.

Writing this book has been a process of enlightenment.

I have had to go delving back into old diaries and cross reference dates and experiences. Many of those experiences were actually happening simultaneously although it felt to me as though they were sequential, with greater time lapses between events. The conscious mind can be very deceiving on such matters. As far as possible I have told the story in the order that it happened. I know people do like the order of time frames and points of reference. I apologise now if the adventure takes a few sharp twist and turns and backtracks. It feels rather like an aeroplane recalculating its flight path to get to its destination safely, it has to veer and tack; veer and tack, to stay on course.

Where possible and relevant, I have given dates, but really it is of no consequence. Time means nothing in this work: today meets yesterday whilst tomorrow slips silently into last night a week on Tuesday. Weeks give birth to months, to slip through the fingers like the proverbial sand; before you know it another year has "poofed" away.

For purposes of privacy I have been discreet with names.

Grab yourself a cuppa of your favourite brew, have a cheeky biscuit, slip into your comfy slippers, settle down and make yourself feel at home.

Relax into a warm embrace of the Divine, and I will tell you my story, according to my angels.

~ BEFORE ANGELS ~

Chapter 1

~THE GREATEST GIFT~

"The greatest gifts you can give your children are the roots of responsibility and the wings of independence"

Denis Waitley

I'll be honest with you at the outset; I was never out looking for angels. There was no prior interest, frankly; I could take them or leave them. I didn't disbelieve, but I had no awareness.

They found me anyway. Their ignorant host.

Now, isn't hindsight is a wonderful thing?

From my vantage point of where I am now, I can see so clearly the moments of connection, the crossroad points, the choices and the interventions.

The choices are interesting, (we will come on to those again later), but I never saw them in that light at the time. I just felt that life was giving me a hard time of it. Sometimes, it felt like an absolute pasting!

Oh, and the other thing I may as well tell you now, before we really get started into this; I never had any religious framework in my life. We just were not a religious family.

My parents brought us up to be decent human beings, respectful of the world we lived in and grateful for what we had. That was probably enough. My only experience of churchgoing was as a very small child starting school in Scotland, my infant school was Presbyterian, and I have fond memories of hymn singing and saying prayers by rote. It was years before I realised that God was not actually named Harold. . *"Our Father, who art in Heaven; Harold be thy name. . ."*

Learning without understanding is always a bit risky!

I am the eldest of five.

Gaynor is my next sibling in line, then Steve, then Rick, then Elaine. We were born with approximately a year between us all, in succession, to young but enthusiastic parents. My sister Gaynor and I were born in Liverpool, Steve in Denham in Middlesex and Rick and Elaine in Dundee, Scotland. Dad was still a student when we were kids and we moved about quite a bit before we returned to live in Widnes in the late 1960's.

Mum, stayed at home to raise us until I was in my early teens.

My parents chose to teach us independence. They gave us our wings. We were encouraged to be exactly who we are. I do not remember any "exam pressure" or being pushed into anything particular as a career. We all passed 11 plus, as it was in those days, without much fuss or fanfare. We were all bright. I was not academic.

As adults we have all made very different life choices, but we are all doing exactly what we do best, and as far as I can tell we are all happy doing it.

So, as a child, with very little material riches available, it often fell to me to entertain the younger ones, my creative thinking was honed quite early on. We may have had very little money, but were abundantly rich in love, support and freedom of expression.

At school, I was popular and easy going, I had a small circle of "best friends". Never academically brilliant, I had a tendency to default to the art room at the merest whiff of a maths test, (yes, even though I passed 11 plus!) I was often to be found painting or drawing when I should have been getting to grips with protractors or trigonometry.

I always knew that art was my thing.

My choices, as presented by my Careers teacher, were limited. I could have gone to work at the crisp factory, the soap factory, the shirt factory, or the Ford motor factory. The world of Widnes was a very limited oyster!

I determined to go to Art College; and made it my business to get there.

At 16, with just about enough qualifications to get me in, I enrolled as a Foundation student at Warrington College of Art.

There, I found my bliss.

I was encouraged to study all forms of art including ceramics, life drawing, photography, sculpting, painting and sketching. It was not particularly radical, experimental or alternative, more about learning the right way and the right tools. It was such a joy to be able to hone my raw and embryonic skills as an artist.

I fell in love with it instantly.

There, I also found and fell instantly in love with the man who was to become my husband, Martin. He is my Soulmate and my Eternal Beloved.

Having successfully completed my first year of Foundation Course, I wanted to apply to Trent Polytechnic in Nottingham (now Nottingham Trent University) for a BA (Hons) degree in Fashion and Textiles. Unfortunately, my school exam results were insufficient to get me into Polytechnic and so I had to make a supreme effort to upgrade my meagre qualifications. I enrolled at the local Tech and retook some really boring subjects which I can barely recall now. As I mentioned, I was very determined.

Most significantly, I was to meet Martin's mum, Valerie. As well as being a talented embroidery artist and textiles designer in her own right, Valerie taught dressmaking and needlework at a local girls High School. To my eyes Valerie was the epitome of chic with her shiny dark brown bobbed hair, husky voice and trendy clothes. She drove a sexy Toyota Celica car and drank gin and tonics (although not at the same time). Valerie offered to cram me through an "O" level course as an external student to gain a precious extra qualification in a subject that might even be remotely useful. Her faith in me, and her dedication to making sure I had the tuition I needed, inspired me to go for it. We spent many a Sunday afternoon making dirndl skirts and strange blouses in the sewing room. Poor Martin suffered the indignity of having to wear a few of my "creations" (no. . . not the dirndl skirts or blouses, but I did rustle up some smashing tweedy trousers and a cheesecloth shirt!) .

The hard work paid off, my application to Trent was accepted and I was on the road to becoming a "Fashionista"

Three years later, armed to the teeth with a fashion fabulous First Class BA honours degree and plenty of 80's style attitude; I was ready to take on the world!

And so, my journey began.

I had no idea just where it was going to take me.

After I left college, I worked at a succession of design jobs in the fickle world of fashion, which had brought me swiftly to what was going to prove a pivotal point in my life.

Even then, the Laws of Attraction were unwittingly at play and I just so happened to be in the right place at the right time talking to the right people who were looking for someone to fill the right job.

As one of "Thatcher's Children", I carved a brilliant career for myself, a sharp upwardly mobile swathe, right through the 1980's and into a position of extreme power and glamour working in Buying Office of one of the UK's then sexiest and most successful fashion retailers on the High Street. I was employed by one of the most iconic Retail Gurus of the time.

Whilst still only in my early 20s, I was consistently promoted, seemingly without effort or planning, until ultimately I reached the heady heights of Board Director, at the ripe old age of 29.

My wonderful job, and all its marvellous trappings, meant everything to me. As well as earning a very good salary, there were loads of perks. I experienced international travel; First Class of course. I was regularly wined and dined by eager suppliers. I enjoyed a generous clothing allowance. I had a flash and sexy company car, plus the services of a Driver (not flash and sexy but a very good bloke!), and if I really had to get there superfast . . use of a company helicopter.

That was how it all looked on the surface.

In reality it was often very stressful, lonely, tiring and disorientating, but, never the less, I loved it. I had the energy, blind faith, and courageousness of youth to just jump in there and go for it. I felt invincible. There is a lot to be said for "ignorance on fire"

My job had become the thing by which I defined myself. It was how others defined me too; my success was, by association, their success.

Friends and family were nothing less than encouraging in all I did and all I achieved.

It felt wonderful! Sometimes.

If you had asked me in those days, "*Who are you?*" I would not have fundamentally understood the question.

"I" was what I "did" and who I worked for.

I was very fortunate to be working for a man, and a Company, who had true vision and passion for the business, and he attracted others to him with the same potential. My brightly plumed colleagues were very much birds of a certain feather who definitely flocked together.

As time went by, a few years down the line, I began to realise I was increasingly leaving my "arty" self behind.

My role was becoming less about creativity and more about the dreaded "number crunching, team management, and the seemingly endless restructuring of departments. The size of my departmental ££££ budgets would make your hair stand on end!

My trusty Filofax was filled with back to back "meetings".

I had no wiggle room.

Remember, I had been a scribbly kid, not particularly good at the academic stuff, and I had always assiduously avoided "numbers" having struggled with maths at school and spectacularly gaining an "unclassified" CSE Commercial Maths. Somehow, I had managed to manoeuvre myself into the very thing that I had always hated, and now it was becoming my main focus.

I was scared.

The strain started to tell.

I often felt sick and panicky as I drove into work (in my big flash company car!) and became paranoid that I would be "found out". I dreaded that my bosses and colleagues would realise I was actually rubbish at my job, I would be out on my ear in disgrace. I felt like a fraud. I was displaying classic "imposter syndrome".

There was no one to confide in and nowhere to run to.

Failure was never an option. There would be no show of weakness.

To cope, I simply became harder edged and cleverer at hiding behind my brittle mask of capability. There was no amnesty, no opportunity for me to put my hand up and say "I can't do this". Not without consequences. This realisation was my big demonic secret that I lived with, day in day out. This was the Truth that roared and mocked and poked at me at night when I tried to sleep my way through yet another bottle of Nytol.

I became very resourceful. I learned to surround myself only with people who were good at the stuff I wasn't. I chose my teams carefully.

This job that I had loved so much was becoming my living nightmare.

One night, far from home; alone, in yet another faceless 5 Star hotel room, something extraordinary happened.

On my bedside table I found a small innocuous torn slip of paper, just a scrap really. It would have been easy to have missed it, or just picked it up and put it in a waste paper basket. But it was so out of place in that pristine environment, something made me look at it.

The words typed upon it were so beautiful.

"From this dark, cold hotel room, and the endlessness that you fear.
You are pulled from the wreckage of your silent reverie.
You're in the arms of the Angel; may you find some comfort here . ."

I picked it up, read and reread the words, and then wept like I had never wept before.

I had no idea where the tears came from, but the feeling was animalistic and raw, far deeper than anything I had ever understood about myself.

It was cathartic.

For once, that night, I slept soundly.

It never occurred to me to find out where that scrap of paper came from, or who wrote those words. I just accepted it, and it meant something inexplicable to me.

Yes, of course I kept it. I still have it.

Years later, in the company of angels, I was driving somewhere in my distinctly less flash "twinkle wagon" and I caught a few bars of a song being played on the radio. Incredibly, I recognised the lyrics as the same as those written on my treasured scrap of paper. It was from a film called "City of Angels" and the track is called "Angel" by Sarah McLachlan. You can easily find it on Youtube.

The words still move me.

Ooops, back to the story!

After 6 years of living in the fast lane, the company I worked for had new management. My original boss, the visionary mentor, had been ousted in a Boardroom coup. This had changed the lay of the workplace landscape rather dramatically. The new management team who stepped in had a very different agenda, they were not visionary, they were very much the "nuts and bolts ".

Of course I gave it my best shot.

My best shot was not good enough.

My position was summarily made redundant.

After 6 years of upward mobility. . . that was it!

Thank you, and goodbye!

I was just 30.

I had no idea what to do, or how to handle it.

To be fair, and I must be fair; the whole thing was managed admirably by the company. They treated me with great respect and supported me very well. The payoff package was more than generous. There was no mud to be slung in either direction. The decision, I was assured, was one of "economics" not "personality" or ability.

Platitudes didn't help stop me feeling as though my whole world had collapsed.

I cleared my desk, and called my husband, Martin, to tell him my news.

I cannot remember much after that. I was numb.

Everything I had believed in, everything I had defined myself by had gone.

Friends and family did not know how to react. This was the early 1990s and redundancy was not a common experience, not in my field of work anyway. Every day, I expected the phone to ring and for my ex-boss to tell me they had made a HUGE mistake! I truly believed that they would beg me to come back, tell me how much they had missed me and offer me double my previous salary!

Yeah!! As if!

I was deluded.

What this meant was; I had no interest in looking for another job. I wanted my old job back, and I was prepared to wait for it to be returned.

Of course a very generous redundancy package had softened the blow considerably. I had never had so much money in my life! I managed to fritter it all away during the course of the next year.

My priority had been to rebuild, as best I could, some semblance of what I had before.

I set myself up as a "Consultant" with no clients, no business plan, and no vision.

I took on a very nice office space, hired a PA, bought myself a shiny new car, and one for my PA too just in case she needed to pop to the post office or something!

I built a castle on sand.

What was I thinking???

My world had suddenly become very small and very cold.

I just wanted normal reinstated.

♥ According to my angels : I was not living my truth.

This had of course been an angelic "set up", a way for me to extricate myself from something that was no longer serving my highest good.

As I had become increasingly stressed with my "fabulous" job, it had taken me ever further away from my, as yet unseen, destiny.

My fears of losing my job were always on the basis of being found lacking, not quite good enough, caught out as a "fraud", incompetent and incapable. I was heading straight for that self imposed reality as the fear created more fear and soon I would become paralysed by it.

Ashamed, I was no longer capable of loving my work. When love turned to fear, I was already lost.

The angels had to step in and steer me back onto the right path.

My "life's purpose" would remain unfulfilled because I had not yet acknowledged that I even had one.

To help me out, the Universe conspired to give me a neat "get out" in the form of a redundancy.

Of course I didn't see it that way at the time.

I could have made a clean getaway if I chose to do so. The financial side was taken care of, and I had been offered, and flatly rejected, outplacement counselling. Had I not been so stubborn and deeply ashamed, perhaps I would have handled things differently.

What I chose to do; was spend the redundancy money on things which made me feel less diminished, to fill a loveless void, to boost my shattered self esteem, to paper over the gaping holes in my ego.

In my Consultancy, I had nice plants, a lovely PA and a coffee machine. I read an awful lot of glossy magazines, and I did a lot of "lunches".

Everything was an act of desperation.

For a while, the angels must have simply rolled their eyes and indulged me, to let me work it all out for myself. As of course they do, and they must.

Chapter 2

~ INDIA ~

"If I were asked under what sky the human mind has most fully developed some of its choicest gifts, has most deeply pondered on the greatest problems of life and has found solutions, I should point to India."

Max Mueller

In the midst of all my self pity, misery and confusion, I was offered a tiny window of hope, and opportunity, which came in the rather unexpected form of an invitation to teach on a short term contract at N.I.F.T (National Institute of Fashion and Textiles) in New Delhi, India. A full time lecturer had not able to fulfil their obligation. I was merely an emergency plug in.

The pay was rubbish.

I said "YES!"

Of course I had been to India before as part of my previous incarnation as the Fabulous Fashionista, I had stayed in some lovely places. Mostly First Class and 5 Star.

That was not quite what this experience was to be about.

I was to provide a series of lectures on fashion marketing and branding to the regular day students and then to a group of paying adults as a kind of "night school". My visit had been advertised in the local paper, and the classes were immediately fully subscribed.

Let me be honest; I had no idea what I was doing.

From somewhere deep within, I managed to dig up my enthusiasm, alacrity and joie de vivre and fuelled by those meagre scraps I jumped into the deep end via Air India!

Let's say this experience totally blew the doors off all my preconceptions and expectations.

I had truly entered another world. My life back in England held very few useful reference points for my temporary life in India. I had to re-evaluate my attitudes and behaviours to be of any use what so ever in my new environment.

The generosity of spirit and heart from those who had no reason to offer me anything, was humbling. I was welcomed with open arms, embraced with warmth, included in the most holy of celebrations, invited into the private homes of many of my students, offered the best hospitality from everyone I met.

For the first time in a long while, I truly felt at one with myself and with my colleagues and new found friends.

The accommodation was charming and adequate. The Ambassador Hotel was a small privately owned place with its own flock of vultures perched in the trees in the pretty gardens with an immaculately manicured lawn.

My appointed Driver was a cheery if terrifyingly ambitious "boy racer" of at least 80 years old, behind the wheel of a traditional Ambassador (the old Morris Oxford model) which seemed to be impervious to the maelstrom of traffic and random animals encountered en route to college and back.

At the hotel, my request for toast as a breakfast option was greeted with gentle mirth and kind tolerance, as barely crisp squidgy slices of white bread were proffered with great ceremony in a small golden basket by a gloriously turbaned gentleman of unfathomable years (possibly related to the boy racer). Each morning he would secrete a

Alison Knox

hand written message of joyful optimism, a famous quote or religious text, under the toast. It always made me smile. I wish I had kept them.

Every day was an adventure, full of exciting unfamiliar sights, sounds, flavours and fragrances. I was thrilled by the vibrancy and the colour, the energy and the joy.

Conversely, of course there was dire poverty, disease and deprivation woven into the fabric of day to day life, and the grace within that, brought me up short in terms of my own misery. It helped me to see, and to feel gratitude for my own life. I was able to put things into a better context.

I would qualify this extraordinary time, as amongst the best experiences of my life.

I feel it humanised me again.

I was, and still am so very grateful.

♥ *According to my angels: I had to leave my comfort zone for a while.*

Sometimes we need to be taken totally out of our comfort zone, especially when we already feel uncomfortable and out of sorts.

To have to operate in a new and challenging environment, among strangers with unfamiliar customs and circumstances so different to ones own, can be just the catalyst needed to move into a new way of being.

The angels must have been rubbing their hands in glee when this opportunity came up, they may have even conspired to help it happen. It just needed me to see it for the opportunity that it was.

I did.

Despite my nervousness and lack of teaching qualification, I took up the challenge and enjoyed a period of exploration and huge personal growth.

The trip stretched me as a person, as a human being, giving me a very different perspective on things, my life in particular.

It was wonderful.

When I returned home I saw my sad little "business" for what is really was; a sham.

It all looked very nice, but it was not a business.

The castle built on sand had no foundation, and it had crumbled already.

It had simply been a handy refuge for a battered ego.

If life presents you with this kind of random opportunity, respectfully pay attention. It may hold some really important experiences for you.

Chapter 3

~ MOVING ON ~

"In everyone's life, at some time, our inner fire goes out. It is then burst into flame by an encounter with another human being. We should all be thankful for those people who rekindle the inner spirit."

Albert Schweitzer

Almost a year had soon passed and despite my interlude in India, I was becoming increasingly unbearable. Martin, my gorgeous and totally supportive husband was long suffering and tolerant. Friends had got tired of listening to me whining and family couldn't bear to see me de-throned, defrocked and miserable. My shame was their shame, so it seemed.

I was so damned miserable, self obsessed and probably clinically depressed. It was very hard to get out of the Corporate mentality, I was still institutionalised.

As is often the way, fate stepped in and took a chance with me. A job had been advertised in local newspaper, a friend had showed it to me and urged me to apply. She felt it would be "perfect". I was not so sure. The job spec sounded altogether rather too lowly for the likes of "moi" and, it was based in the industrial heartland of Birmingham.

This was a family owned Fashion House, headed by a patriarchal Jewish refugee. It was far from cutting edge or sexy, but it was a solid well respected business.

They needed a Design Director.

Despite myself, and without any other options on the horizon, I sent my application.

I got an interview.

I confess I didn't exactly make much effort. My credentials were brilliant, my reputation went before me. I felt I had nothing to prove.

The Managing Director seemed to like me. He wanted to show me around the factory.

The design team was small and very "hands on", not at all like the huge department of designers I had left behind. After informal introductions to the team, as "an interview candidate" we all shared pleasantries about fashion stuff and people we knew in common and touched on the vagaries of the industry and put the world of frocks to rights. One of the designers, who unbeknownst to me, would have the final veto of my appointment, was to become my best friend, a true ally, and to remains so to this day.

Her name; Athena, as in, the Greek goddess.

To my great surprise, relief and mild horror, I was offered the job, subject to, undertaking a full medical examination. Apparently, this medical was no great shakes, typical protocol relating to company pensions or insurance or something. I was able to attend with no health issues, bright eyed and bushy tailed, full of beans!

Suffice to say, being in rude health, I was not expecting the look on the doctors' face when he retracted his speculum from my nether regions asking "When did you last have a smear test?"

I knew it was in recent history because I was very good at that sort of thing.

The doctor looked unconvinced. "Well, I don't like the look of you. I want you to go and see a specialist colleague of mine tomorrow."

He was not really prepared to say more, but his tone of urgency told me it was not good news.

An immediate appointment was made, and off I went to see the nominated specialist.

Martin accompanied me, as we realised the tests might leave me a bit wobbly, and anyway a bit of moral support would be very welcome.

I was not ill. There was no pain. I had no symptoms of anything untoward.

What was there to worry about?

Martin was very quiet.

The specialist didn't like the look of me either.

Martin became even quieter.

I was sent to the Queens Medical Centre in Nottingham for a colposcopy. (if you want to know what that is, then Google it. . . it's not much fun!)

It was there; in a small unprepossessing consulting room in the colposcopy clinic that I was dealt the hard bald fact; I had cervical cancer.

Martin was now ashen.

The Consultant confirmed; I had not just some dodgy, unpleasant precancerous cells; not some vague suspicious lump, but "You have a fully formed and seemingly virulent cancer".

So there!

I was stunned.

My priorities had suddenly swung from "Poor me I don't have a job" to "Poor me I have a life threatening disease".

Actually, I was livid, how very inconvenient. I was just about to start a new job.

A single second in time can change everything.

Something inside me accepted that this was how it was, and so I had better find a way of dealing with it.

Martin was visibly shaken, and my immediate priority was to keep him from panicking.

♥ According to my angels : I must be reduced to ashes for my fire to be rekindled.

When it came to my cancer, I now realise that I was still not listening, not paying attention.

I was still very lost to myself.

So, the job in Birmingham was shown to me, I needed the experience despite my ego saying it was "not good enough".

I had to get over myself.

To be reduced to ashes.

Fierce love had to be deployed.

It was absolutely necessary .

You have to pay attention when cancer is around, especially when it is around you personally.

My responses to the experience would pave the way for the future. Choices, made now, would determine how soon I would see my "gift" and how readily I would embrace it.

Alison Knox

I do believe that the cancer experience was "softened", with a form of damage limitation, I only hurt as much as was necessary for me to feel it was real.

How could I have known that within these dire circumstances would be the shining jewel of a gift in the form of my best friend Athena. I truly feel we have shared many lifetimes together, subsequently our spiritual paths have been very intertwined and my life would feel a smaller place without her in it.

Chapter 4

~ I YIELD TO FEAR ~

"Ask not that events should happen as you will, but let your will be that events should happen as they do, and you shall have peace."

Epictetus

The wheels of the great National Health Service quickly rolled into motion and before I knew it I was ensconced in a neat hospital bed on a public ward.

I had never been ill before. In fact I was not convinced I was now. A few pains or physical evidence would have been good confirmation at this point because, for all I knew, the doctors could have just been making all this up!

As a very robust child, I had missed out on the traditional childhood illnesses and ailments, tonsillitis, appendicitis, broken limbs, cracked skull etc etc. All those things prepare you for adulthood and help you to understand what it feels like to go into hospital and endure traumatic pain.

Powerless, I had a sense of simply having handed myself over.

Resistance was futile.

I had to resign myself to the circumstances.

Other people held all the keys here. I felt incidental in my own lifescape. I no longer had any control of what was happening and that was such an unfamiliar experience for me. Until recent times, I had always felt very much in "control" and frankly, I quite liked it that way.

Right now, I was very afraid.

I was very afraid of everything.

This was uncharted territory. I feared the efficient brusqueness of the nurses; the seemingly over zealous use of needles; the festive arrangement of drips, like Christmas garlands; the other patients, with all their horror stories, so keen to share them with the "new girl"; the unidentifiable food; the ridiculous bedpans; the possibility of dying a messy and undignified death involving tragic paper pants that looked like J cloths.

Oh yes. . . I was very afraid!

One of my first visitors to the ward was Athena, the Greek Goddess.

There is a saying that goes "A friend for a reason, a friend for a season, a friend for a lifetime"

When someone is in your life for a REASON, they have come to assist you through a difficulty, they may seem like a godsend, and they are! They are there for the reason you need them to be. Then, unaccountably on your part, or at an inconvenient time, this person will say or do something to bring the relationship to an end. Sometimes they die. Sometimes they walk away. Sometimes they do something to force you to take a stand. Our need has been met, our desire fulfilled, their work is done. Be grateful and accept it is time to move on.

Those who come into your life for a SEASON, because you need to share, grow, or learn. They bring you some particular experience. They may challenge or encourage you to do something you would never have considered before. They may give you an unbelievable amount of happiness. It is totally genuine, and you should enjoy it but, only for a season. It is not a forever relationship.

LIFETIME friendships teach lifetime lessons: things you must pay attention to and build upon. They are part of your emotional foundation .You accept the lesson, love the person, and put what you have learned to use in all other relationships and areas of your life.

Athena was to prove to be a lifetime, and beyond, kind of a friend. We had known of each other professionally in the fashion industry. Athena was a brilliant knitwear designer. We had met up again briefly at my recent interview with the company in Birmingham. It was she, who had the final call on the decision to employ me. Incredibly, the job had been left open for me, in the full knowledge that I was to be out of action for a while, and I was invited to join the team as soon as I was ready. I was even to be paid sickness benefit whilst I was recovering! What a blessing that was to prove to be.

Athena had turned up, a vibrant vision with her flame red hair and lips, armed with an array of very strange nightwear, a vast selection of voluminous gowns, with leg of mutton sleeves and capacious frills and furbelows. These; she assured me, had been loaned to her when she went into hospital for a hysterectomy. She thought they might be useful.

Athena's personal experience of a similar operation was a great blessing to me and she was able to share some practical survival tips. Most memorable, was her advice to drink plenty of peppermint tea as it helps with the wind! She was right!

All the way through, Athena was going to be there for me with her robust good humour, challenging nightwear and sound advice. The Universe has ways of bringing those people we need into our lives. I am still not sure about the nightdresses though!

The Consultant and the operating team came to see me in relays. Each one telling me in turn, with great detail, what part they were going to play and how they couldn't really give me much hope to go on .

I prayed that the surgeons scalpel would not be as blunt as his words. He told me straight, he could not give a prognosis. The cancer seemed to have come from nowhere, it had progress fast, virulent and aggressive. It was a mystery.

Until they got inside my body and had a good rummage around, they would not know how far things had spread, whether I would need chemotherapy or radiotherapy and indeed if I would live or die.

Each successive conversation with the surgical and nursing team left me more fearful, anxious and disorientated.

When my husband, Martin, arrived to see me, I saw the fear behind his eyes. It was not a pretty sight. I knew he had been given the same news.

I put my bravest foot forward and tried to console him that everything would be alright and I was feeling just fine. Nothing for him to worry his pretty little head about about. It was probably the biggest lie I have ever told him. He knew it was a lie.

Martin had never really seen me anything less than robust and confident. Even through the redundancy I had been careful not to give too much emotional stuff away.

I never shed a tear in front of Martin, or anyone else for that matter, my stiff upper lip was rigid!

We never really talked about the emotional impact of any of this. I just wanted "normal" back, and in my normal world I didn't do tears or weakness.

Normal had become very important to me.

The last year had been tough on Martin too.

He had endured seeing me spiral in ever decreasing circles of painful regret and mourning over my "lost" job. I had faced up to my friends and family with brazen stoicism which spared them all the truth of my despair, grief and fears. He had witnessed my pathetic attempts to resurrect something that never was. Martin knew I did not take interference with good grace, even when it was kindly meant. He just let me get on with it, steadfast, and there if I needed him.

Sorry Martin, I am not sure I was very grateful at the time.

Now this!!

Cancer!!

♥ *According to my angels; In crisis, I must yield to my fears.*

Why was I so surprised?

My lifestyle had been running on empty, and the residual dregs of fear and emptiness for such a long time.

Before the redundancy I had lived with stress on a daily basis.

Not only did I have a fast paced job, with endless international travel and very little time for any consideration for my health, but I was forever yoyo dieting, eating pre packed frozen meals at irregular times, drinking a few too many glasses of wine on a regular basis, and taking very little exercise. I had thrown my hormones into confusion by taking a convenient contraceptive pill without a break for far too many years.

For the previous twelve months, I had been struggling to come to terms with loss and grief without seeking help or counsel. This was a kind of self sabotage. I was never going to recover on my own, and I had no idea how or who to ask for help.

I do believe that this response was my body's way of forcing me to slow down and pay attention to how I was living my life.

It was a very tough call, and a very big lesson.

Fear had created crisis.

Crisis often brings opportunity.

Chapter 5

~ A VISITOR ~

"Be not forgetful to entertain strangers, for thereby have some entertained angels unawares"

Hebrews 13:2

The evening prior to the surgery, eventually, when Martin and Athena had long gone home and the medics had stopped prodding and poking at me, I had another visitor.

I was sitting up in my bed, feeling a little desolate and abandoned.

The ward was busy, and open, but my bed had screens around it, so I was able to enjoy some privacy. It had been such a shock to me how little privacy we had. Our personal business seemed to be public property, even a trip to the toilet required permission and report to the nursing staff. There was no dignity involved.

At this stage in the proceedings, I had not been allowed any pre~ meds .They needed me to be alert for the final signatures of permission on the never ending paperwork.

Suddenly, I was aware that a man had approached my bed.

A very lovely man.

I cannot describe him in any great detail. He could have matched the description of any number of hospital staff. He wore whites. He had short dark hair, and smooth olive toned skin, his manner was gentle and very assured.

Politely, he sat down, at the foot of the bed, paused, and looked up directly into my eyes.

In his presence I felt calm, centred and at peace.

He asked "How do you feel right now Alison?"

Despite his beneficial impact on my sensibilities, I told him "Terrified!!"

"Tell me, of what are you fearful?" he continued with a calm level voice that held me stilled.

I stuttered, unsure of myself, and then it all came out, tumbling and splashing like a dammed up river. The fear, the shame, the dashed hopes, the worry.

Then I said simply. . . . "Death"

Totally un-phased by my outburst he asked "What makes you fearful of death?"

That slowed down the tirade, because quite frankly I didn't know.

I had absolutely no measure.

I had never even felt traumatic pain. As a child I had whooping cough, but I don't think that qualified as traumatic.

I know I didn't feel ready to die, that there were "things" I still needed to do. Don't ask me what "things", I have no idea, it was just a feeling. I had no experience of death or of dying so how could I judge?

We talked.

We talked for what appeared to be hours, about me.

I had never talked like this to anyone before. He was totally present to me, and he saw me. It was a new experience for me.

All my hopes, dreams, joys, loves, fears . . . everything that had ever needed talking through were opened up, examined, expressed and released.

This lovely, gentle man, allowed me to unburden all my "stuff" completely without judgement. His warm compassion and sensitivity struck me quite profoundly. It felt strange but wonderful.

I was relieved.

This conversation was different.

This was strengthening to me.

This is what we shared.

"Death is a birthing process. When a child is within the womb, it is first an embryo, a simple mass of cells, yet it has a "life" an existence of sorts. As the embryo develops it takes on another form of existence, it grows into a recognisable life form, a baby now capable of certain movements and feelings. The foetus becomes a sentient being within the mothers womb. It has a life, an existence within an environment that supports it, nourishes it, nurtures it, and provides for it everything that it needs to survive and thrive. In due course that existence must end, as the child is delivered into another existence, through the process we call birthing. To the baby, this can be deeply traumatic and painful as it can also be beautiful and gentle. The experience depends on how that process is handled by those around it. If that baby were able to speak of its experience, it may describe the process as a death. It has transited from one state of being into another, it now exists in a physical dimension. This baby must adapt and adjust to its new existence in order to be "alive.

What we may call death; the process from the physical into the non physical again is simply another birthing stage. It too can be traumatic, painful, difficult, or gentle, beautiful, comfortable, depending on the circumstances and those involved at the time of the process.

It takes a lot of energy to die well, as indeed it does to be born well, it is important that those around the process understand this.

There is nothing to fear.

Death is a process of birthing into Light."

When his words had walked me to the other side of my fears, and we had naturally reached the end of our conversation he told me something, quite assuredly.

"*You will survive this*"

I heard myself say "*Thank you*"

Who was I thanking? and why?

Even the Consultant could not give me that assurance.

Then . . .

He simply asked me, "*Do you trust*?"

I heard myself say "*Yes!*"

In that moment of saying "Yes" the residual fear lifted, palpably, it was gone.

And so, it seems, had the lovely man.

How strange?

I thought it was a bit odd. I would have liked to thank him for spending so much time with me, for making me feel so much better about everything, restoring my confidence and giving me hope. I did wonder if perhaps he had been a hospital Chaplain or one of the Volunteers.

I was transformed from a quaking mess to blissfully relaxed.

A nurse came by to check on me and so of course, I asked her about the lovely man.

Who was he? Where had he scooted off to so sharpish?

The nurse looked a bit perplexed, and assured me that she had only just popped her head around the screen about five minutes before, just to check I was okay, and there was no-one with me.

I told her, she must be mistaken, he had been with me for hours, putting my world to rights. "No love, honestly, you were just sitting up in bed looking peaceful so I left you alone for a few more minutes. You looked so happy"

We threw the conversation back and forth for a while and eventually agreed that it didn't really matter who he was. It was how he left me feeling that mattered.

I felt at peace.

I was ready to face what lay ahead and to face it fearlessly.

♥ *According to my angels: I must face death in order to face life.*

Hindsight is a wonderful thing.

It never occurred to me at that time that this "lovely man" might in fact be an angel.

At this point, I had no awareness of angels and as I said at the outset, I was not, nor am I now, religious. I had no framework of belief of any sort to hang my hat on.

This kind of experience was totally unfamiliar to me. I had never felt that kind of total peace before.

I do now absolutely believe he was an angel.

For a long while I simply had him down as a very welcome "do gooder".

Even now after all these years the sense of him stays with me. His calmness; his stillness; his compassion and yes, his "loveliness". Moreover, I do believe he was Samael, often acknowledged as the angel of death.

How do I know it was Samael?

Years later, when I had access to references and resources regarding the Angelic Realms, the name of Samael was shown to me, and through time and distance I FELT his name upon my soul. Yes, it was written within a printed book, but my heart lifted it out from the page and showed it to me, and I embraced it.

It is as simple as that.

I knew him.

I realise, that in his presence I was able to communicate my deepest fears around death to him, and he responded with such clarity and assurance. This gives me the confidence to attribute that experience to him.

Now, when I say his name, Samael, within the context of that experience, I feel him as I felt him then.

I was able to look at him.

He held my gaze with his own steady eyes as we spoke.

The next time we meet we will know each other and there will be no fear on my part.

As I am now; I have no fear of death, my own or anyone else's. I feel I can be there, as he was for me, and let death be birthed in with love, grace and compassion, as one would a newborn child. It is an honour to do so for another soul.

The question he put to me regarding "Trust" was a much bigger and profound question that I could have possibly imagined at that time. It was not just about that moment, but about everything that was yet to come, and has been ever since.

Everything I am, everything I do, all my work is based upon that word. TRUST.

We are always sent the messengers which are the most appropriate for the circumstances and our state of mind. In these dire circumstances there would have been no point sending me some great feather backed "hunk" blowing a trumpet, wearing a long white robe and a glowing halo. Noooooo. . . that would have added massively to my fear quotient and I would have hot footed it out of that place in my hospital gown and J cloth pants as fast as you like!

I doubt I would be writing this book now!

Chapter 6

~ RECOVERY~

Blessed are the cracked, for they shall let the light in."

- Groucho Marx

Samael, the compassionate angel, was absolutely right. I did survive.

This experience had cracked me open and shown me aspects of myself that I had never acknowledged before. The Light could finally start to infiltrate.

I have vulnerability. I have fears. I have pain. I have loneliness. I have courage. I have resilience. I have trust. I have people who love me and whom I love in return.

I am not invincible.

The cancer required a Wertheim hysterectomy, involving the complete removal of the womb, the cervix and a few other intimate bits and bobs which I won't trouble you with right now. Most crucially, the radical surgery, terrible as it was, did the trick.

There was no need for chemo or radiotherapy.

The surgery required my flesh be cut hip bone to hip bone and I was rattling with drips and tubes, which I could hardly bear to even look at.

The pain was so excruciating, I was allowed a self administered drip of morphine which barely touched the sides of my agony. I almost wrestled the nurse to the ground when eventually I had to be disconnected, you can apparently get addicted to that stuff!

Athena was right about the wind . . . my internal organs had been inflated with air, like a balloon, for surgery, and it all had to be released again. Peppermint tea was a life saver. My voluminous nightwear billowed around me like a galleon in full sail.

I had to wait 10 days before I got that news. It was cause for great celebration. The nurses and patients alike came to congratulate me and to share my relief. I think we marked the occasion by removing some of my bandages.

There was still a long way to go.

The experience of being in hospital was hugely challenging.

I was totally vulnerable and reliant on others for everything, including the most fundamental and intimate requirements. For a while I had to use a catheter that went in through my navel, so I was rigged up to bags and pipes and tubes. In order to have a shower, which was indeed a luxury, I had to put all the paraphernalia in a plastic carrier bag and hang it on a hook on the shower wall. It seemed to take forever, but the precious moment of feeling that warm, cleansing, water hit my parched and wrinkled body was indeed heaven. I bore the indignity of having the attendant nurse do the dousing, for the simple pure pleasure of the moment.

The whole reliance issue was difficult for me.

Comparatively, the loss of my autonomy felt worse than the loss of my reproductive organs.

As well as Athena and Martin, I was regularly visited by my very elderly next door neighbours, Jean and Colin. They were a cheerful and lively couple who became a lifeline to the outer world.

Each day, they would amiably potter into the ward with freshly washed nightwear, trashy celeb' magazines, large impractical tropical fruits and bottles of luridly colourful squash.

They took it upon themselves to look after Martin, cooking him meals and baby sitting our young dog Minnie whilst he was at work and struggling to accept what was happening to me.

When I came home, they made a point of looking in on me in every day, and encouraged me to take mild exercise, mainly pottering up to the local shops with them. I was a pathetic sight; with a pensioner on each arm for support, it took hours to shuffle the length of the high street and all my strength to carry my small purchase home.

I developed a new respect for the elderly and infirm.

I came to love these people as good and dear friends. Of course I had seen them before, as neighbours to say hello to, but never truly *seen* them.

Now they were my guardian angels right next door.

How things had changed.

Within a few weeks of being home I was declared fit enough to attend a friend's wedding. It was a grand event and I was a little nervous. The last time she had seen me I had been her dynamic, boss. Now, I was a little old lady, bent double and shuffling slowly.

I found it very hard to concentrate. My focus was on taking the next step or next breath. I was still in some agony and taking heavy duty painkillers.

Social interaction was difficult. Normally, I was an absolute chatterbox, always with something to say. Now, I could just about hold sentences together. At the wedding dinner, we were seated on the "friends" table and I was placed next to a man who was "big" in the fashion industry. He knew all the hottest up and coming designers and was involved with a chain of very smart shops. Ordinarily I would have been in my element and hung on to his every word, if indeed I had not been giving him chapter and verse of my own. I remember vividly, my struggle to maintain my interest in what he was saying,(and he had plenty to say), and then the crushing moment when he turned away from me, finding my company boring.

I literally got the "cold shoulder". In my defence, I told him that I was still on heavy pain killers and my concentration was poor. This went no way to appease him and I was written off as a "no one".

It did my fragile confidence no good at all and I could do no more than sit there looking at the back of his lovely Vivienne Westwood jacket, mocking me.

How the mighty had fallen.

I must admit, what had rather taken me by surprise in all of this, was other people's reactions to the dreaded "C" word.

For all the love and support I received, there were also those who ran in the opposite direction as fast as they could. I was shocked how many times the phone was put down in haste when I shared my news, or the excuses quickly made to cut the conversation short. It was as though I became some kind of contagious social pariah. I quickly learned to read the fear in others and to choose my words carefully.

An ex work colleague phoned me to tell me her exciting news. She sounded very odd, kind of cagey, about the fact she was pregnant for the second time. It took me a few minutes to understand what she was actually trying to tell me. When I tackled her on her strange vagueness, she admitted she was trying to spare my feelings knowing that now that I would be unable to birth any children of my own. The embarrassment in that moment, for both of us, was dreadful. I don't believe I had given that aspect of the situation much thought, but of course it was true. I would now, never be a mother to my own child.

I had never really given the prospect of children a second thought.

I had always been too busy being fabulous! In fact, I had never even properly discussed the matter with Martin. There had always been an unspoken agreement that "We don't want kids". We had never really had to do much thinking about it. There had never been any undue pressure or encouragement from family or chivvying from well meaning friends. Those who knew us would realise a child would not fit into our lifestyle very easily. It had been hard enough to accommodate a small dog and a couple of cats. So the tricky question of parenthood had been answered for us really.

There was a finality to it that left no room for sentimentality.

I honestly never suffered the pining or urges for a child, and could always look into a pram with complete emotional safety.

♥ *According to my angels: In order to grow my spiritual Self, I must slow down my physical Self.*

Once the cancer was revealed, the physical body would have to slow down and so the ethereal or Light body could be worked upon.

I believe the timing of this cancer operation was no co-incidence.

It was 22nd November 1991.

In 2001 exactly 10 years on to the day, my first angel painting would come.

At this particular juncture, we were still a long way off.

In order for me to prepare, knowingly or unknowingly, for the awakening that was to come in 2001, there would need to be some necessary adjustments to my non physical self.

These subtle but profound invisible changes could then be accounted for by instigating some visible changes at a physical level, and one way to ensure that this could happen, would be for me to be taken out of my conscious state deeply enough for the work to be done. This may sound like absolute nonsense. . . I appreciate that. However,

I was undoubtedly subtly different after the op', and any noticeable changes in me could be attributed to "she's never been the same since she had the . . . you know . . the c.a.n.c.e.r". It would allow change to be readily explained.

This recovery process was indeed miraculous.

Here is what I learned.

♥*The cancer had been spotted in time and dealt with surgically.*
♥*There was no follow up treatment needed.*
♥*The healing process was incredible: physically, mentally, emotionally and spiritually.*
♥*I had learned many lessons about myself, many of my attitudes had changed, particularly my ability to ask for and accept help with good grace.*
♥*Gratitude came into it and goes along way.*
♥*The realisation and acceptance that I was not always in control.*
♥*That I did not have the roadmap and the instruction booklet.*
♥*That physical pain can be endured and survived.*
♥*That being loved unconditionally does help.*
♥*That being weakened can strengthen.*
♥*That I was no longer who I had been, but was getting closer to who I actually am.*

Chapter 7

~ THE WITNESS~

"The only way to discover the limits of the possible is to go beyond them into the impossible."

-Arthur C. Clarke

My recovery was indeed astonishing. I had stepped right back into "normal" as soon as possible, and before I knew it, I was driving to Birmingham every day having started my new job in January 1992.

For the next few years it was necessary for me to attend the hospital on a regular basis for check ups. Initially, I had to go once a month, but it was eventually reduced in frequency to once every three then once every six months. These visits served to remind me of the fact this had actually happened to me. I had quickly emotionally disengaged from the experience as life seemingly picked up where it had left off. The check ups were almost an inconvenience. The woman who had undergone the trauma of losing her reproductive system at the age of 31, was somebody I used to know, I no longer had attachment to her or what she had been through.

One day, in the Spring of 1994, I had been for my regular hospital appointment and had for some reason chosen to walk back from The Queens Medical Centre. It is a good 4 miles from home, along a busy inner ring road, so this was a rather odd thing to choose to do.

It must have been about 2.30 in the afternoon as I approached a large traffic island en route.

I was aware of some sort of commotion going on in the layby near to a bus stop. I could see a tatty white commercial van parked up, and a group of aggressive youths pushing and shoving someone, who turned out to be an elderly gentleman.

It looked very nasty.

As I drew nearer, I noted there were quite a few people at the nearby bus stop just standing there!!!! Faces blankly turned away ignoring the whole scenario!!

Something came over me.

Something far bigger and braver than I, and I found myself stepping around the van and into the road to approach the centre of the fracas.

The elderly man was pleading with the youths, and I could see his broken spectacles lying in the road, his face was bloodied. As though on autopilot, my physical body moved towards him. My actions felt no longer to be my own. I had become a witness to my own Self.

Firstly; I leapt into the road and retrieved the broken spectacles and handed them back to the elderly man, in doing so, I stepped between them all and asked calmly "Is there a problem here?

I was looking directly into the hardened eyes of the most aggressive of the youths. He told me some half baked story about this "idiot" having driven into his car at the roundabout and then driving off. He had apparently cornered him at the layby and now wanted immediate financial compensation for the damage to his car.

Ignoring for a moment the terrified victim, I actually reached out and took hold of the hand of the aggressor . . . . what was I thinking??? . . . quietly and calmly I asked him to show me the damage.

We walked together, hand in hand, over to a small pimped up hatchback car, parked just behind the white van. To my untrained eye it looked fine and shiny enough. No sign of any damage. Hmmmm?

The rest of the gang had now foregathered and were keen to corroborate the story and support their mates outrage at the disrespectful insult that had been meted out by "white van man".

Once again I took the hand of the aggressor and walked back over to the van where the victim was still catching his breath. I then took hold of his hand too. . . . (Oh don't even ask!!! I had no idea what came over me!). . . I suggested to the "van man" that as he was so obviously the source of the problem, perhaps he should take responsibility by phoning the police.

He squinted at me, through broken lenses, as though I was mad! I held my ground, stayed absolutely calm and still, and continued to hold their hands, like small children.

In those days, mobile phones were not so common, so I ushered the pair of them over four lanes of busy traffic to a public phone box where I pushed "van man" inside and instructed him to make the 999 call to the police, and then I nonchalantly leaned on the door of the booth so he was secured inside. I hoped he would understand my motives without me having to explain.

I remained coolly attached to the very large paw of a very large and confused guy who was suddenly looking extremely bewildered.

I distracted him by asking about his car. What make? What model? How fast? How long had he had it, all stuff that appealed to his ego and had him suddenly chattering away like we were old pals. I planned to keep him busy until the police arrived. If he did cotton on to what I was doing, and make a bolt for freedom, then at least I had a good description of him and his mates, and his car too.

Most importantly, "van man" was safely ensconced in the phone box.

Within seconds we heard sirens, and a couple of police cars pulled up, I gave an inward sigh of relief and an outwardly cheery *"Oh good, this will all soon be sorted out then!"* and without further ado, whisked my new found friend back over the road and delivered him into the waiting arms of the law and their very keen looking dogs.

An ambulance had arrived, all blue light flashing and sirens wailing, and I saw "van man" being stretchered away.

I didn't even know his name.

The whole gang were quickly rounded up and after giving my name and address and statement to the Officers, I continued my walk home.

To my surprise a police car was waiting for me on my driveway. I wondered what they could possibly want, I felt I had done my bit.

Over a nice cup of tea in my kitchen, the officers explained the truth of the situation to me.

What I had witnessed was called "highway robbery" a form of extortion. The gang, who were well known to the police, had earmarked the van and driver and forced him off the road on the pretext of the claim that the van had hit their car. It hadn't. The gang had demanded money with menaces from the driver who had refused. He had agreed to swap insurance details, but that is not what these guys wanted. They wanted money, they needed it for drugs. When the driver refused to cooperate, they tried to help him see sense by knocking the living daylights out of him with baseball bats (they were found on the back seat of the car later!). The van driver was apparently so badly injured, he was at that point on a renal ward on a kidney dialysis machine at the hospital. By the way, did I know that the guy I was holding hands with was a trained boxer??

Oh!?

The police wanted my witness statement, which I was able to give. What I couldn't give them, was an adequate explanation or reason why I had intervened.

The best I could offer was that I had just done what was needed in the moment. I hadn't considered the potential consequences.

I am pretty much an average woman, 5ft 6" tall, average weight, of average strength, average courage and not given to picking fights with drug-dealing highway robbers.

The officers assured me that my calmness and lack of fear had obviously taken them all by surprise and the robbers did not know how to respond.

Fortunately, a passing motorist had seen the whole thing and had phoned the police. They were on the way even before "van man" made his emergency call.

I was asked to appear in court as witness for the prosecution.

I agreed that I would.

♥ According to my angels: The new, improved "Alison" needed to meet her Self.

My understanding of what actually happened here is this.

I was being tested, for my future suitability for purpose, and called as a witness to my own Self.

In that moment, I was actually outside of myself, it was as though I were watching a film or a TV show. I could see it all unfolding but I had no connection with it. I had temporarily exited my physical body.

My physical body was now being used as a vehicle of angelic intervention.

It was not "me" holding those hands, nor "me" that diffused the anger and rage in those people. The angel now operating within my physical body did all that.

I had felt no fear, no fear at all.

Many months later I once again encountered the "gang" by accident on the train.

We were all on our way to the court hearing in Leicester. As soon as I saw them my heart almost stopped. I could not tear my eyes away, and although I desperately wanted to hide, there was nowhere to go. However, I need not have worried, they walked straight past me, oblivious. This small ordinary woman in her bright red coat was not the same person who had spoiled their fun that day.

I; was not who or what they saw.

When I arrived in Leicester, I gave them all a wide berth and made my way into the Witness Room.

I was reunited with "van man" for the first time.

He was now in a wheelchair, looking very fragile.

I went over to say hello and he looked at me blankly "Who are you?", he demanded.

Explaining my part in the horrific events and he looked at me hard and sidelong "No!" he declared incredulously "That was never you . . . you are far too small!"

He went on to assure me that there was no way I could have tackled that group of thugs. His rescuer had been a "big strong person".

Admittedly at the time of this conversation I was a little confused not to say miffed, how could he not recognise me?

This account would later confirm my understanding, that I was indeed "hijacked" too on that day, and those people actually saw an angel which presented to them whatever form they needed to see to elicit the response that calmed the situation.

If only they knew!

Chapter 8

~ A DEATH ~

"If you desire healing, let yourself fall ill, let yourself fall ill."

Rumi

I received the sad news that a friend Tish', was dying of inoperable liver cancer. You never expect it of a young and vital person.

Even recalling what I had once been told by the "lovely man", the angel known to me as Samael, in the hospital; I could not help but feel regret for the inevitable loss of this beautiful young woman.

Tish had always adopted a lively and irreverent approach to life; audacious, dynamic, flamboyant and colourful in everything she did, in her work as a designer and in her personal life. Tiny in stature, Tish wore outrageously high shoes, and microscopic shiny sequinned dresses even for regular day wear, her long curly black hair gave her the looks of a fairytale princess.

Now, in this cheerless hospice room, she lay there, as small as a child, pale as dawn, and swaddled in hospital sheets soaked in sweat and smelling bitterly of rank despair.

This was to be a horrific, messy and painful end for her.

Tish had been introduced to me by Athena a few years earlier, they went back a long way together as co-workers and as friends.

Now, between us, Athena and I made sure Tish had everything she needed keeping her spirits up with frivolous girly gifts, trashy magazine, gossip hot from the "fashion front" and whatever else made her happy in her end days.

It was clear she didn't have long.

One evening when I visited, I was asked by the nurse to wait outside her room as she was with a Healer, having some "healing".

I had never heard of healing, and I was intrigued.

What did a Healer do? What did they look like? What would I even say to one if they spoke to me?

The mystery was soon resolved when Richard, a young, attractive but otherwise unremarkable looking man emerged. He came beaming over and said hello, smiling warmly he shook my hand. I felt something like a bolt of lightning shoot up my arm leaving a residual tingling and warmth in my own hand.

WOW! Is that what they do? It felt very odd. It felt very good. Healing eh?

I popped in to see Tish just briefly.

She was by now drifting in and out of consciousness, she seemed very far away. Athena assured me that the healing session would have helped her feel better for a while. It could not cure her, but it could help relieve the pain and discomfort that the tumour within her liver was inflicting upon her tiny fragile frame.

When I left the hospice later, I found myself literally running home. It felt absolutely imperative that I got back to my workroom as soon as possible. Crashing through the front door, I ran straight upstairs to my studio and grabbed the nearest piece of paper and a pen.

Without hesitation, or pause for reflection, I wrote:

"*When you came to me and took me by the hand; you whispered to me of another land.*

You told me how my pain would be at ease; and how my mortal suffering would sudden cease.

You stroked my cheek and softly promised true; that if I simply said "I Will" to you, that you would take me from this fearful pain; and let me live as I once had again.

When I was strong and loud and full of love; and took my share of life without reprove.

I never thought that there would come a time, when health and strength would not be, by divine right, mine.

Oh, you tempt with your soft and velvet voice; seduce me without hinting I have choice!

But Death; I look you in the face and say, "I choose to do this my way!

I am not ready to take your hands, nor listen to your promises of other lands.

I still have things I want to do and say, and so I choose to go MY way.

YES, my pain is real and cuts me deep, And YES, the cancer grows and YES, I weep.

Save your pleasant whispers for another day; take your cool and tempting hands away.

For when I choose to take your hand, I do it willingly, NOT on demand"

I knew this was for Tish.

The feeling was overwhelming as I wrote it, the words just flowed through me and out of my pen. There was no struggle or correction of error, no scribbling out, no amendments. It just came as it was. This was not really the sort of thing I was used to writing. Although I knew assuredly it was for Tish, I felt uncomfortable to give it to her, I didn't know how she would take it.

Despite my reservations, I made myself a promise to leave it with Athena the next day and she could take it for her; that might be easier.

When Athena read it, she wept.

It was indeed for Tish; and she promised faithfully to take it to her.

When Athena got to the hospice, Tish was already leaving her mortal body. She never regained consciousness and her soul made its transition on 16.11.94.

♥ According to my angels: It was time for me to reacquaint with Death and Healing.

This was my first experience of a channelled message. I had no idea.

It was to be another six years before it would happen again.

Tish was ready to leave, and this was a death facilitated with love present.

It made it a "good" death, as far as it goes. It was her time.

This was my first experience of a Healer. I still didn't fully understand what they got up to, but I had felt the energy in that handshake.

It had touched me.

I am not sure whether the handshake from Richard facilitated the writing of the message or not. I do feel it opened something up. Maybe the two things were linked or perhaps it was just co-incidence!

NB: Even as I was writing this chapter, the angels conspired to reconnect me to the man I had met at the hospice, all those years ago. I had no idea of his name, and, unsupervised, I would never have recognised him.

The angels found a way.

We had been invited to a music recital in a local village hall. When we arrived the venue was already packed to the rafters, and we just about managed to find some seats at a corner table. A young, attractive woman came beaming over, all smiles and greeted me warmly, by name. I had no idea who she was, even when she gave me her name, Elaine, I was still covered in bafflement and embarrassment. She proffered further that we had once worked together, as designers, some 17 years ago, and she named the company and the circumstances. Slowly recognition dawned. Then she threw me completely. Surely, she suggested, I remembered her partner Richard?

Nope!

Further confusion and mild sweating ensued on my behalf, and then she joined the dots to remind me that her partner, Richard, had been the Healer at the Hospice for Tish! It felt to me like several lifetimes ago, and I could only stammer my apologies for my very poor memory. It then transpired that Richard is a very good friend of the friends we had arrived with, and they insisted I went over to say hello, to reintroduce myself. I was relieved that Richard didn't actually remember me either, but he did remember Tish, even after all this time.

I feel sure the angels wanted me to honour the part Richard played in my awakening, by brokering that re- connection and allowing me to know his name.

Thank you Richard, you had no idea the part you played on my journey!

Chapter 9

~ NEW BEGINNINGS ~

"The beginning is the most important part of the work"

~ Plato

The job in Birmingham had been kept open for me.

A whole new start.

One of those who now worked for me was of course Athena.

My new boss, Charlie, the Managing Director was a chatty Scot who liked to micro manage. This was an instant irritation to me as in my previous world, I had been used to calling the shots. I had felt that I could do this job with one hand tied behind my back. That was just as well because that is pretty much how it was. I was still physically weak and had been out of touch with the "fickle world of frocks" for over 12 months. I need to get back in the swing of things quickly.

My experience of this company was like entering time warp. Steeped in traditions going back to when the business had been first founded in the wake of the Second World War, they had funny little ways of doing things.

My wings were feeling well and truly clipped.

Charlie had priority on egotism! The design team all fussed and clucked, with increasing frustration, as our creative efforts were dismissed on various pre-texts by a man who simply did not want, like or welcome change. In effect, we were paid to design what had already been designed for the last 15 years.

Ultimately, after 2 years battling with new ways of designing a spotty frock without changing anything, the business was bought out by another company and we were all put out of our creative misery by redundancy. This time redundancy felt very different. It was a timely blessing and I saw it as such. Athena and I were in it together, and we accepted the situation with good grace and not much emotion. We drove home together and ate cakes to celebrate!

Despite my growing frustration and impatience, I had been given recovery time, physical and emotional, and had managed to re-connect with many of my original business contacts. One of my great strengths has always been my networking skills. I put them to good use.

Over the next few years I got myself well and truly back in fashion harness. I dusted off my shoulder pads, polished up my gold buttons, tottered on my highest heels and re-applied my bright red lips. My aim was to reclaim my fabulous career and to return to the dizzy heights I had once known. Executing a series of smart career moves within the industry and with a good professional reputation, I soon was poised to make that prospect a reality.

Oh, please do be careful what you wish for . . . as you may just get it!

Out of the blue, I was approached by a professional Head Hunter on behalf of a fashion retail company based in London. As it happens, this was a company I had assiduously avoided during my career because I did not like them much. Their reputation as an employer, was "hire and fire". I knew people who had gone to work there and lasted 5 minutes. They were Central London based and I lived in Nottingham, a journey of over 2 hours each way by train.

However, the job proposition they had in mind for me, was made to sound very appealing. They had a unique Executive position available and it would require someone of outstanding fabulousness to fill it. (Me!) They were able to offer a very attractive salary status related package. It felt like my prayers were to be answered, and my original loss, all those years ago, would be restored unto me.

The interviews were all arranged. I met with the MD and the HR Director and various other key personnel. They seemed very nice. It was however, by no means a simple process, I made several trips to London, over a period of weeks, to undergo a series of psychometric tests and practical demonstrations of my skill and judgement. The results of these tests would determine whether my personality and expertise was likely to be a good fit with the culture of the company.

When I was offered the position, I assumed my personality and skills were approved!

Wrong!!!

Within the first few days of my arrival I knew I had made a most dreadful mistake.

My now more extensive spiritual vocabulary would now allow me to say "The energy was all wrong" but in those days that was not my language. It just felt disappointingly crap.

It began with little things.

As the "new girl" if I needed something from another department I would take the trouble to go and find the person, introduce myself and ask the favour or query. Invariably, I would get a blank fish eyed stare and "Put it on e-mail. I'll deal with it later" Nobody seemed keen to communicate face to face.

More worryingly, the Managing Director who had originally appointed me, was inexplicably moved to another division, within days of my arrival. The HR Director, left the company without so much as a wave goodbye.

Apparently, this was normal, employees moved around a lot!

I was left in the less than tender care of a female Executive, a co-worker, who had not been part of my interview process and she made it her business to make my life a misery from the start. She was now, by default, my boss.

Systematically, I was cut off from my direct team and any decision making. Appointments with suppliers or colleagues were made on my behalf without consultation, dates were never put in my diary, making me look tardy and unreliable. Overseas travel was booked for me and never mentioned until the last minute when tickets were slapped down on my desk. I had no choice but to scrabble around making half-considered preparations with my team looking on in confusion and dismay. It played havoc with my home life too.

Even my choice of car was ridiculed and called into question. As I was travelling on the train every day from Nottingham to London, I opted for a small yellow Fiat Cinquecento rather than the big status vehicles my colleagues chose to drive. This economical choice made me the laughing stock of the board room.

A final insult was meted out when I handed in a presentation document to my default boss for approval, prior to a Board meeting. It was galling enough that I had to go through the charade of seeking approval, but what was to come knocked me sideways. The report was returned to me in an "Internal Mail" envelope. Scrawled in red pen, across and throughout the document were comments like "*No!*" "*Rubbish!*" "*What do you mean?*" The whole effort summarised by "*You cannot submit this, you obviously have no grasp of what is needed. I suggest you re-write in language we can understand*"

The key lay in that single word "language". We were obviously not speaking the same one.

At an Executive training session with my Board colleagues, we were asked to draw a vehicle which represented our journey with the company. Most people drew sleek, flash cars, or super yachts or sky rockets, but I drew a pair of wings. The feathers looked a bit ruffled and tatty but they were unmistakeably wings. When it came to my turn to share, I explained that my wings were my responsibility, it was my job to look after their condition and suitability for purpose, if I kept them preened and well maintained, they would carry me anywhere I wanted to go. I got quite excited about my wings . . . I liked the idea. My colleagues had a right good laugh at my expense, and we moved swiftly on to some other executive game.

At yet another team-building session, we were given a visualisation exercise of a swimming pool, with a shallow end and a deep end with a diving board. We then had to describe where we saw ourselves in that scenario; to fill in the rest of the picture. I described the feeling of being right in at the deep end, not knowing whether sharks were lurking beneath the surface ready to bite, and calling out for help but the lifeguards were just standing on the poolside ignoring or laughing at me.

After that session, despite it being "confidential", as in, what happens in the training room stays in the training room right? I was called into see my boss, to explain myself. How dare I say such negative things in front of my team? What kind of message was I trying to send out? A great big S.O.S sprang to mind.

My confidence was taking a severe battering, and there was no one for me to confide in . . .yet again.

As part of the recruitment package for Senior Executives (for that is indeed what I was !) an Employment Psychologist had been appointed, ostensibly to help me to integrate within the culture of the company and to develop my long term career plans within it.

These very private one-to-one sessions did not go too well as I was none keen to become part of the "culture" and I was not sure I wanted a long term career with this company. However, undaunted by my lack of co-operation and compliance, the meetings continued on a regular basis. I was becoming increasingly unhappy and beginning to bitterly regret my decision to join them.

It was not surprising I felt this way.

The alarm bells had been going off for a long time, ever since I got "the call" from the Head Hunter.

Ego had stepped in, big time, and brusquely elbowed common sense and intuition out of the way. If I had listened, and trusted, things would have never gone this far.

My next appointment with the psychologist was to be my last.

This time, the meeting was not at the regular venue. I was called to a very grand office, just off Oxford Street, it was rather like a gentleman's club, all overblown faded grandeur, with portraits of the long dead and long forgotten Captains of Industry peering in distain and scrutiny from the walls. Dark antique furniture and the smell of dust and beeswax polish permeated.

The meeting room was up some many flights of well worn stairs.

I was breathless by the time I got there.

Having knocked politely, and hearing no direct summons, I let myself in to the room. My heart was fluttering madly, I had no idea what to expect.

I was faced with three unfamiliar men, sitting at the long highly polished table.

Brusque introductions over, and we were ready for action.

I had never met any of them before, but I was assured they were all working for the same team, to "help" me.

They looked decidedly grey faced, grey suited and grey spirited. I didn't warm to them at all.

A few minutes into the conversation, and one of them held up his hand, as though stopping an oncoming bus and asked pointedly *"Alison: has it ever occurred to you that the way you talk is quite irritating?"*

Well no. . . frankly, it had not!

I defended myself by stating that a Northern accent was not a crime, and I was perfectly coherent.

"No. .no. . .it's all THIS with your hands" The grey suit was gesticulating dramatically and jumping up and down as he spoke.

I could not help it, I laughed warmly and reassured him *"I am a designer darling! I am creative! That's just the way I am . . expressive!"*

He eyed me dispassionately.

"No." he stated *"In your position, in this company, this is inappropriate behaviour. I cannot take you seriously with all this . . . gesticulation. In fact... for the rest of this interview I want you to sit on your hands! Do you understand?"*

What?

I was summarily instructed to sit on my hands, for the rest of the interview.

To my everlasting horror and shame, I did as instructed.

My heart had already left the building.

During that interview, I endured an experience not unlike torture. I felt totally shackled. For all the difference it made, I may as well have had irons locked around my ankles and ropes around my chest, tying me fast to that heavy wooden chair.

I could not speak.

I could not breathe.

I could not think.

Ashamed, I felt diminished and broken.

The conversation continued, limping, for another hour or so.

Is this what it had come to? Here I was fighting for my professional life, with my tools of expression denied to me. Worse yet, this was not something worth fighting for.

In what must have been a moment of pure revelation, I saw everything so clearly.

THIS IS HOW IT WOULD BE FOR ME, EVERMORE, IF I STAYED!

My future was now in my own hands.

Stay: and trade the material rewards for spiritual death.

Go: and risk my career for my integrity.

I left that meeting a hollow and broken woman.

There were no tears, just absolute numbness.

I was in shock.

♥ *According to my angels: It was time for me to WAKE UP, to break my addiction.*

Let's just pause for breath here!

Angels often have to resort to a "sharp smack" to bring us to our senses. This was them administering a sharp smack.

I was addicted to ego, and to the status and trappings of my job.

This was my path of learning and my route to enlightenment!

My "work" had always been my Achilles heel. This was the measure by which I defined myself, my self worth was in direct proportion to my status and salary. The angels saw this route in, as the most effective and obvious way to get me to pay attention.

They could reach me through my addiction.

I had just been tested again.

My ego had almost won.

The package I had been offered, although it was dressed up beautifully and presented as very shiny and desirable, was not what it seemed. The warning bells had gone off, all klaxons were blaring. I chose not to pay attention. Deaf and blind to the obvious. Often, these dire situations we get into are entirely of our own making. Of course we cast blame and look for excuses, but ultimately we make the choices.

We do well to remember this.

I know how easy it can be to stick with the "devil you know", when the prospect of change feels just too daunting.

We fear being judged by others, found wanting and lacking in commitment, feeling that we have failed. Sometimes, we become paralysed and like a rabbit in the headlights, we cannot move.

When help comes, we don't see or hear it. Maybe it is not that bad after all, maybe we should just stick with it a little longer. By the time you make your move, your soul will be crushed beyond recognition.

Mine was.

We all have two very powerful instruments of discernment available to us at any time.

The heart: this will shrivel and flutter like a trapped bird when we choose against our highest good. Conversely, it will soar, expand

and sing, seemingly out of all proportion to the circumstances you are facing, when the choice presented is to your highest good.

The belly: will run thin and cold and the collywobbles set in. You may find you are running to the loo and/or feeling nauseous, even vomiting. You have a "gut feeling" things are not right.

Even if you cannot explain why, TRUST THESE SIGNALS. It will save you a lot of heartache in the long run.

The grey looking men, were in fact, also angels.

Yes! I believe that absolutely. They had to bring me the message, to show me the choice; stay or go. In or out. Is your soul for sale or not? To risk the shame of being faithless in order to be faithful to myself.

True, they were not attractive, as angels go, but they were not meant to be. They were perfect for the job. They delivered exactly what I needed to hear and see. More importantly perhaps, what I needed to feel.

As humans, we are blessed with the gift of free will. No other being can coerce us into anything we are not willing, at some level, to undertake or engage in. The "bad" stuff has lessons for us and as long as we do learn from them, we should not have to repeat the lesson. Some of us learn faster than others.

The angels are only ever able to guide and support, not to undertake or to judge.

I had to take responsibility, make my own choice for my future now, or have it forced upon me.

Either way, it was going to be painful.

Breaking an addiction always is.

Chapter 10

~ THE SHAME ~

"Shame is the lie someone told you about yourself."

Anais Nin, attributed

The train journey home that evening to Nottingham was interminable.

I carried my shame with me.

I wondered how many people could see it.

Looking around the carriage at all those weary commuter faces, the dull tired eyes, slumped shoulders, I was half listening in to the interchangeable conversations between dispirited Executives returning from the commercial fray to head office, reporting the days successes and failures to other equally dispirited colleagues, I knew I didn't want to be part of that any more.

Was I really one of them?

My mind was racing and heart pounding.

What was I going to do?

What about the money?

What was I going to say to Martin?

I zoned out; and slept the sleep of the dead until we reached Nottingham; fortunately the end of the line or I could easily have ended up in Sheffield. (not for the first time.)

As it happened, I didn't have to say anything much to Martin. He took one look at me and bundled me into his car with a small suitcase and our over excited, yappy little dog Minnie and we headed off to the coast; to Whitby.

Whitby is a small fishing town, we love it up there. It boasts a rather famous fish and chip restaurant "The Magpie" and the town is the inspiration behind Bram Stoker's "Dracula". The North East coast had become a bit of a sanctuary for us over the recent years, favouring the rough edges of North Sea and the higgledy piggledy Robin Hood's Bay, Sandsend, Boggle Hole, and Runswick Bay with the occasional foray to Scarborough for a bit of proper sand.

So, for three days I walked on the beach.

Sometimes I might talk to the dog, but mostly I couldn't speak.

Martin was infinitely patient.

When I was finally able to tell him what had happened, he just held me tight and said "Thank God! You're back!" I saw him crinkle around his edges and I knew everything would be alright.

Just for a few days, we could behave like children again, no one to impress but the dog and the seagulls. We wore our wellies even if it wasn't raining, had chips for breakfast and ate ice cream for lunch! The sea was re-energising, calming and the silence welcome.

We could just be ourselves with each other.

I still had to face my future though, and I knew it would be necessary for me to go back into that place and call it a day.

The next time I walked into the office in London, it was to offer my resignation.

I had met with the newly appointed HR director. I told her simply, and unemotionally that I felt both parties had made a huge mistake. For all the psychometric testing, and employment psychology, we didn't "fit" together in any way, shape or form. She heard me out, and then equally unemotionally, agreed.

I was cut free.

I left immediately. There was nothing to go back for, no sad goodbyes, no round of jolly drinks at the pub at lunchtime with my colleagues.

The deal was negotiated, and I came out of it very well. To help me adjust to my new found unemployed status, I was given access to a local organisation of "outplacement counsellors" to help me get my career back on track again and to reassess what I wanted to do with my future. Although I had just a belly full of counselling and coaching, I felt it was a nice gesture, under the circumstances. I was paid 3 months salary in lieu and allowed to buy the little yellow Fiat car for a nominal price. I cashed in the balance of my rail season ticket and that was that.

A huge weight had been lifted off me.

Now, the shameful prospect of facing my friends and family loomed; to confess that I had just walked out of my "fabulous" new job.

The shame was as nothing compared to the liberation I felt.

When I lost the first "fabulous job" to redundancy, I could be all sorry for myself and feel hard done by. Poor me! Now, it was all my own doing.

There was also the little matter of the mortgage and the household bills to pay! The redundancy cheque would not last forever.

Now, I was going to have to take full responsibility for my own action of walking away. Of course, some hands were thrown in the air, eyebrows raised, questions asked, sharp breaths taken in, but actually that was all over with very quickly.

To my surprise, the overwhelming response to my news was "Hurrah". I had been so doggedly determined in my mission to bag that dream job, that I had not listened to either my own innate warning mechanisms or the well founded concerns of my friends and loved ones.

Within a matter of days, I was ready to tackle the future and made my first appointment with the outplacement counsellors. The process was very tough and made me take a long and hard look at myself, to identify my true strengths and weakness' and to really understand where my boundaries of integrity lay. With good help, I realised that I was perfectly positioned to work independently. I planned to offer my design experience and ability on a Consultancy basis, within the fashion industry. My reputation was still very good. My network of contacts hot! I knew if I could just secure an initial contract, I would be flying again.

The Universe is always listening and conspires to help us get what we ask for.

The phone rang.

It was Mike, an ex-boss from the job I had left to go down to London. He was thrilled to hear I had left and wanted me to re-join his team.

I said "No thanks" but my goodness, it would have been so easy to say "Yes please" right then.

I could run back to safe territory, a comfort zone where I knew I was well liked and respected and to people with whom I knew I could work well. I explained my future plans to Mike, and asked whether there was any prospect of the "job" being turned into a project? He promised he would get back to me.

The phone rang again.

It was Mike.

There was indeed the potential of a project which would take 6 months.

I took a deep breath and asked for what I needed financially to undertake the contract. I had carefully worked out the figures and what flexibility I would need regarding travelling etc and felt confident to go for it. My newly appointed outplacement councillor had advised that I should add an extra 0 to the figure I was asking as my rate. It felt audacious, but I took the advice. I could always apologise and take it off again if anyone noticed!

My proposal was accepted, with the extra 0, and I was able to begin the contract almost immediately.

♥ *According to my angels: I was learning the importance of responsibility and values.*

Sometimes the choices can be really hard, we don't know the "how" but we just recognise that we have to do it.

Shame can be borne and overcome.

How other people choose to react is their problem. How I choose to react to their reaction is mine!

By taking responsibility, I had now set a precedent for my own value. I would never take that 0 off again.

Once you begin to live your truth, or something that gets you closer to it, good stuff happens.

Chapter 11

~ NEW EXPERIENCES ~

"We know sunlight moves through us. Water moves through us. Everything moves. Everything comes back. Back from the darkness. And the Earth is green again."

Susan Griffin

With increased confidence, I undertook the new project in London.

It was amazing.

I felt reborn.

Things seemed to just fall perfectly into place, ideal solutions presented themselves and nothing seemed beyond me. I was in my element and in my flow.

As my working life settled into a new rhythm, I found my breath again, I was able to enjoy a different kind of existence. I was responsible for "me" and how I used my time. If I was not working for my client on their project, then the day was mine, to do with as I wanted.

A whole new vista of opportunities lay before me and I was drawn to use some of my available time to explore unfamiliar experiences.

I had increasingly felt the need to undertake some form of exercise. I was no gym bunny and so when my attention was caught by an article on Pilates in "Vogue" magazine, I resolved to find out more.

Pilates is a form of exercise which strengthens and lengthens the abdominal core muscles. It develops great posture, flexibility, firmness of limb, and gets you in touch with what it feels like to have a physical body that works well.

Through Pilates I met Rachel, a young practitioner working near Derby. Rachel could offer one to one tuition which felt good to me. Little did I realise just how important Rachel was to become in not only my recovery, but as a friend and as a vital key to my spiritual awakening.

As I had felt physically "crushed" for so long, this was ideal exercise for me. The slow gentle repetitions and focus on breathing correctly were just what I needed. I had no idea how to do slow. I had no idea how to breathe properly. What I was now doing, without realising it, was laying the foundation for what was to come later. A preparation for a more mindful life. In the meantime, I was gaining a flat stomach and posture to be proud of. I learned to stand tall and to stand within my own strength.

We had started my programme with regular weekly sessions and very quickly I warmed to Rachel and her down to earth, no nonsense approach, her strong North East accent and her cheeky sense of humour made the business of pelvic floor exercises so much more fun! There was always a lot of giggling involved. As we got to know each other a little better, Rachel would avail me of other marvellous techniques and practices that she was involved with. One such random conversation turned to the healing practice of Reiki.

Rachel described Reiki healing as a way of accessing a positive healing "life force energy" which is available to anyone if they are shown how to do it. I remembered the Healer, Richard, who I met when Tish was in the hospice. I recalled how the handshake had felt electric and I had been left with a really good warm feeling. Maybe that had been Reiki?

I was still very unschooled and rather closed to spiritual practices. Maybe I didn't quite understand her description of the process, so to be honest I couldn't imagine what possible good a bit of hand wafting over a cellular blanket would do. The lying down for 30 minutes bit sounded attractive though.

Although I put the conversation to the back of my mind, I didn't let it go.

A few days later I was window shopping outside my local health store, I spotted a notice board with a business card of a local therapist offering Reiki treatments. Despite having no pen or paper on me, I managed to write her number on the back of my hand using an eyebrow pencil. I then had to call her promptly when I got home, before the numbers wore off !

An appointment was made.

I was due to fly out to Hong Kong on business that week and so I felt a nice little lie down before hectic kicked in, would do me the world of good. I was anyway curious to find out more about Reiki.

The therapy room, for my appointment, was not quite the spiritual oasis I had imagined; merely a curtained off section of a busy beauty salon. The therapy bed was privy to all the gossip between the therapists and resounded with the ringing of various mobile phones.

I was singularly unimpressed.

I was a little nervous.

The Reiki Healer was a lovely lady, who bustled in all of a fluster, apologising profusely for her lateness. She was wearing a full nurses uniform, which seemed rather extreme for a little healing session. She must have seen the look of incredulity on my face as she explained she had just come straight from work, she was a nurse at the local hospital. It never occurred to me that Healers would have other, normal, day jobs too. I am not sure what I thought they got up to, I had only ever met the one bloke before at the hospice, and I didn't get chance to ask him. (It turned out he was a filmmaker for the BBC)

I was gently reassured, invited to relax and lie down on the therapy couch. A little pillow was popped under my head, another under my knees, and a soft blanket draped over my fully clothed body.

Calming New Age music drifted whale songs over the chatter of the manicurists, and some lovely scented oils were burned to fragrance the room.

At first, the therapist put her hands on my head and I felt a distinct heat emanating from them. As she worked down my body, I was not sure if her hands were on or off me, but I was aware that my body was very relaxed and tingling very pleasantly. I felt cocooned.

As the feeling of relaxation and general blissfulness increased, I started to experience an incredible sense of colour, unlike anything I had ever known before. It was as though these other worldly colour sensations, invaded, pervaded and vibrated within every single cell of my body! They were of size, dimension, fragrance, taste, sound and physicality. They went beyond pigment, these were colours as yet unseen by my own eyes. As I lay there, they drifted in and out of me, washing over and through me, my head space was flooded with them and my ears were ringing with them. I experienced a deep violet pulse within the centre of my forehead, and glimpsed a large eye peering at me from within my own skull. Occasionally, a strange squiggle, like a Chinese symbol would drift through my consciousness and drift out again, followed by another different one. These squiggles were more metallic in colour, like gold or silvery, very beautiful indeed.

This was totally outside of my sphere of experience. I had no words sufficient to describe what I had seen and felt. Everything felt lumpish, gross and heavy when the treatment was over and I "returned" to this normality.

I wanted more!

I was completely blown away by Reiki Healing.

The next time I saw Rachel, I related my experience to her. She asked if I could draw the squiggles I had seen. I put my best efforts on a piece of paper and she studied them intently. "Had you ever seen these before?" she asked. No, I had not. Rachel explained that what I had drawn were the Reiki symbols, they were recognisable things, not just squiggles.

She suggested, as I had such a profound experience, perhaps I should consider taking a first degree Reiki attunement. This would in effect be a transfer of the energetic imprint of the energy between a Reiki Master and me. She had already explained to me that anyone could do it; you just needed to be shown how.

She was now specifically suggesting that the "anyone" was me.

Rachel recommended her Usui Reiki Master, a guy named Chris.

It was all very well seeing marvellous colours and squiggly things but I wasn't at all sure about this. I was still rather suspicious of this strange world of Healing. What was it to do with me? Why would I want to be a Healer? I was a very happy and successful designer wasn't I?

Despite my deep resistance, Rachel very generously gave me Chris' number and I stuck it in my handbag and promptly forgot all about it.

Some weeks later, the paper with the number simply popped out of the bag onto the floor, just at a critical moment for me. Something in my schedule had been cancelled, and I was wondering how to use the free time. Perhaps this was the answer.

I dialled the number and promised myself, if there was a course running that weekend, and a place was available, and I could afford it, then I may as well do it.

Of course, there was, I could, so I did!

The day of the session loomed, 16th July 2000, and I was getting the collywobbles about it all. Not the gut wrenching warning bells, but the noisy discursive little head monkeys that like to chatter and distract when we are considering something new and possibly life changing. I told the monkeys to shut the f##k up.

The course was being held in Altrincham at the Reiki School (where else?!) the venue was a large, airy, private house.

It looked so normal.

I was greeted by Reiki Master Chris, a bright eyed, slightly built man, perhaps in his early 50's. He looked very normal too, wearing chino's and a nice shirt.

The student group was small and quite intimate and Chris quickly put us all at our ease with his bad jokes and proffered glasses of special water from the Chalice Well in Glastonbury. I would have liked a nice cup of builder's tea.

I had already decided; if I didn't like it, I would leave at lunchtime. No one would miss me; I could just scoot out the back door. I was already feeling like a fraud in the midst this lovely warm hearted group of potential Healers.

We were invited to share, among the group, our reasons for coming. It soon became clear to me that I was indeed a total fraud. All the others had deeply moving or profound reasons, a sick mother: an autistic child: someone recovering from spinal surgery: a deep and innate desire to be a healer. . . .oh the list of altruism went on and on until it came to me.

"What about you Alison, why are you here today?" asked Chris.

All eyes were on me!!!

I answered honestly *"Err. . I don't know"*

"That" said Chris *"is one of the best reasons for being here!"*

I thought he was trying to humour me, make me feel better about my lack of purpose. However, he was adamant; an open heart and mind were the perfect combination.

I would like to tell you what we got up to, but frankly I have no idea what happened.

We spent quite a lot of time sitting in a circle as Chris went around the group mumbling incantations and waving his hands over us. We had been asked to close our eyes, and so it was difficult to know exactly where he was. Sometimes it felt like he was standing right in front of me, so I would risk a little peek, and discover he was on the other side of the room. Then I would feel his reassuring hand on my back, and again, a little peek established that he was nowhere near me. By the time he did come to me, I don't think I bothered peeking again, it was just too confusing.

When we were all done, we got chance to discuss our experiences.

Some people had felt very emotional, and openly wept buckets, others felt elated, and one or two of us reported this odd experience of feeling hands, or a gentle brushing past us, or a ruffle of the hair when in fact no one had been near. This, we were assured is "normal" and is just spirit getting involved.

Nothing at all to worry about.

Chris assured us, that nothing, would ever be the same again.

That sounded a bit dramatic, but I paid attention.

Apparently, it was highly likely that our circle of friends would change, we would attract a different type of person into our lives now, our energy would be difficult for some to cope with, and so they would just drift off or fall out. No offence. We may find ourselves draw to different places and life experiences. Things we would have paid no attention to before suddenly would become very attractive. Things we may have once loved and felt strong attachments to, we would lose interest in. Our food tastes may change, we may find we have strange cravings or strong revulsions for certain things. We would need to drink a LOT of water.

We had a little go at "healing" each other, laying hands on, wafting hands over, and generally feeling lovely about our new skill. I still had no idea why I had done it although I could probably see the value for those who had sick or disabled folk to help.

I drove home thinking "That was nice".

Little did I realise what was to come.

The first level attunement to the Usui Reiki had some powerful and worrying health related side effects for me to deal with.

Within a few days, I was experiencing a fierce burning sensation, a heat that seemed to emanate from deep within my body, not unlike a volcano about to erupt. It manifested as a livid red raised rash across my chest and around my neck. It was as though I were wearing a breastplate of fire. At that time, I used to wear a lot of silver necklaces and the heavy chains had cut deeply into the swollen flesh around my neck. I had to pull them out one by one and the removal was so painful but I could not continue to wear them.

I became aware of a subtle but revolting smell, like putrefaction that seemed to follow me around. I felt disgusting and "unclean". It became embarrassing to go out in public, or even to go to work. Of course, I went to see my GP. I didn't mention the Reiki, because I didn't want the GP to think I was mad. I had convinced myself I was allergic to some herbal supplement skin tablets I was taking. The doctor prescribed anti- inflammatory drugs and a course of antibiotics. I was advised to stop taking the herbal tablets.

The prescription drugs never even touched my symptoms! I had already stopped taking the supplements.

The burning sensations continued unabated, and my skin now started peeling away in great horrible flakes. The palms of my hands became itchy and sore developing into tender raw patches which bled and oozed. I would understand much later that this was the palm chakras opening.

The long bones in my legs and arms and my spine felt as though red hot pokers had been driven into them. The very marrow was on fire.

I went back to my GP who looked rather disappointed that his previous prescription had failed so spectacularly. He prescribed some antihistamine instead.

That also made no difference.

In the meantime, I was keeping a diary, of sorts, to record my experiences and to fulfil the follow up work necessary for the Reiki certification. It occurred to me to phone Chris and ask his advice, he must have come across this before.

Chris suggested that I drink lots of water and sleep as much as possible. He explained that it was just old energies clearing out, nothing to be unduly concerned about.

Really? It sounded too simple.

I decided to ignore that bit of well meaning advice.

The burning and the peeling continued and I temporarily banished myself from the marital bed to sleep in the back bedroom as poor Martin could not bear the heat I was generating. I guess the sight was not too pretty to wake up to either!

When the worst of the ordeal was over, I felt a bit more "human", I went back to my Pilates class with Rachel and took the opportunity to fill her in on all my developments. She gave me some sound advice "Drink plenty of water and sleep as much as you can, it's just old energy transmuting". Where had I heard that before!!!?

At this point I decided to stop fighting it, and did exactly as I was recommended by Chris and by Rachel. By nature I am not much of a water drinker, (in fact I still drink shockingly little even to this day, knowing all I know about why I should!) but I was prepared to give it a go.

The water and sleep treatment obviously worked. Over a period of weeks, the strange symptoms subsided and things returned to "normal".

From time to time, I practised my Reiki healing on Martin, the pets and a few willing friends and they all seemed to survive the experience, if not exactly be cured of anything.

I was still puzzled as to why I had undertaken to do this. I couldn't see it going anywhere as a career option.

Imagine my surprise when six months later, on 14th January 2001, I found myself taking my Second Degree Usui Shiki Ryoho Reiki with Chris!

During this attunement, I was delivered of the symbols (those funny squiggles I had seen when I had my first experience of the healing treatment) which would allow me to work with the energy through time and distance. Each symbol has a different name, meaning and purpose.

It was all good fun. It was necessary to learn how to draw the symbols exactly and how to pronounce their names correctly. We were bound to honour the symbols and work with respect at all times. They are regarded as sacred.

Unlike the first experience, this was a breeze. The impact was much more subtle and there were no nasty side effects.

Over the next few weeks we were asked to keep up our diaries and to practice our new found skills on the group. This exercise involved telephoning each other, to arrange convenient "energy exchanges" and to share our experiences and understandings. We were able to develop our confidence with the Reiki symbols and assimilate the energy within ourselves.

At the end of the period, a full record was to be submitted to our Reiki Master, Chris, in order that we may receive our certification to level 2.

I qualified.

So far so good!

I would suggest that if you want to find out more detail about Usui Reiki you can contact Chris and Penny Parkes http://www.thereikischool.co.uk

NB: There are now many new forms of Reiki available, including Angelic Reiki, if you Google Reiki you will get a huge and potentially confusing list of options. My best advice is to find someone who has been personally recommended. Not everyone has the dramatic reaction that I had, and to be fair not everyone would want that! Go with what you are drawn to and trust how you feel about it. Recommendation is always the best way.

♥ *According to my angels : I was now in my first phase of spiritual awakening.*

I had begun to explore new experiences well outside my comfort zone.

Rachel had taught me how to listen to my own body; how to pay attention when it calls. I am forever grateful to her and she is now one of my greatest friends and best beloved teachers. We have been through a lot of growth together.

I had made time and space for myself, within a now very busy life as a Self Employed Consultant, this time with a proper business and clients in place. It felt good.

My shattered self esteem was being restored by my own efforts.

I was attracting, people, opportunities and resources which would bring me closer to my path, and ultimately my purpose.

By making changes to how I lived my life, I could accommodate this. If I need a snooze, then I could take a snooze. If I drank so much water I needed to pee every half hour, then so be it, who was to know, I was not office bound any more. As long as I delivered my contracted work on time and to plan, then I got my extra 0's.

The transition had begun in earnest. My adverse physical reaction to the newly integrated energy of the Reiki was, I believe, due to dispersal of old stagnant energy. This had to be cleared and released before anything new and better could begin operating. It was dense and yukky stuff so yes, it took a bit of shifting.

I learned to look after myself better, to feed the hunger that is within the soul and to respect myself. My reliance on others for sustenance and approval was diminishing and self-reliance was growing. My ego needed less stroking and stoking.

New and marvellous things were being shown to me, I was seeing them through newly awakened eyes.

Chapter 12

~ RUNNING ~

"If you are seeking creative ideas, go for a walk. Angels whisper to a man when he goes for a walk"

Raymond Inmon

Little did I know, the next big thing would happen on a run around the block!

It was early Autumn 2000, a chill was just starting to nip around the edges of the air, and garden bonfires began to fragrance the neighbourhood.

I am not naturally a sporty person, and so it came as a bit of a shock to feel an urge to go running.

It just came from nowhere.

There had been no thinking about it, toying with an idea of physical fitness, planning a programme of training, just an implicit desire to get out there pounding the streets.

From the recesses of the shoe cupboard, I dug out a rancid pair of old plimsolls, and from the nether regions of my wardrobe, dragged a dodgy old tracksuit bottoms and a mismatched hooded sweat shirt. Without more ado, I pulled my elite sports kit on and set off around the block.

Despite my total lack of fitness and unreliable kit, I initially managed a few blocks before returning home, breathless; gasping for a glass of wine and a lie down.

Incredibly, I continued my self imposed routine for several weeks, rain or shine, I was out there . . . running. By now I had started to actually enjoy it. There was something liberating in the freedom of movement, the repetitive thump, thump of one foot after another, the feel of the natural elements on my skin, knowing that my heart was alive and kicking within me, and having a little bit of clear space in my head.

I felt good.

By way of acknowledgement to my new found regime, I even invested in some proper trainers and upgraded the track suit and felt almost professional!

One evening, seemingly no different to any other, I set off as usual, quickly entering my "mindless" state. I had discovered that I could switch off when I was running, just adopt an "automatic pilot" mode and the mind would settle down for a nice nap whilst the body did all the work.

However, the mind was to be rudely interrupted by a thought of such profundity that it sent me reeling.

"Design a range of garments, for relaxation and exercise using the auric colour spectrum"

I staggered home, falling through the door into the arms of my bemused Beloved; demanding that pen and paper be brought forth immediately!

I wrote this "message" down and read it out to Martin.

"Ah," he stated deadpan, *"You'll need to find out what all that means, won't you?"*

At that moment, I would not have recognized an auric colour spectrum if it came and stared me in the face. The other bit was dead easy;

I could design a range of clothing for relaxation and exercise, no problem.

Somehow; I suspected, there might be a bit more to it.

Over the next few weeks I found myself engaging in some strange activities outside of my normal sphere of creative, technical expertise.

I had scanned into my computer an image of my right hand. The hand print was coloured blue and had a row of multi coloured dots running down from the middle finger tip to the wrist point. It was almost like a very fancy traffic light system. I had typed a name underneath: "CHAkRA". The strange use of upper and lower case letters intrigued me but I felt absolutely that this is how it must be. (*more about this phenomenon later!*)

What staggered me most, was my ability to use and manipulate a computer design system for which I had no training or knowledge. Somehow, my fingers found the right keys and applied the right applications. To this day I doubt I could replicate exactly how I did that. I must have had a little help.

Martin, scrutinised the little blue hand logo, he declared it "quite nice"; praise indeed from the guru of graphic design and corporate identity. Ever practical and professional, Martin suggested I get the name and icon registered as a trademark. Although I didn't know what I was going to be doing with it, the suggestion felt right and I promised myself that I would do that, very soon.

The next phase of creation brought forth a series of printed discs, each one subtly shaded within tones of a particular colour, they were related to the human chakra system.

Chakras are subtle energy centres within the body, they have colour and to those who have the gift to see them, are like swirling circles or sometimes rather like opening petals of a lotus flower. If your chakras are blocked or out of alignment it can effect your energy and well being on many levels. It's not exactly something you can pop to your GP for, but increasingly there is mainstream recognition that well balanced chakras are part of a healthy living plan. You can find practitioners in almost any Alternative Practice Centre these days, but again, use discernment before you allow anyone to work on you, if it doesn't feel right, don't let them do it.

If you mess with your energy centres, you can leave yourself unwittingly open and vulnerable to stuff you don't want. You will need to learn to close them down properly as well as open them up.

The main 7 chakras are as follows:

- Crown ~ top of the head, usually depicted as silvery, white or a pale violet. This is the centre of divine connection.
- 3rd Eye ~ between the physical eyes on the brow. Depicted as deep violet or indigo. This is the centre of wisdom and insight.
- Throat ~ throat area. Depicted as blue. This is the centre of communication and truth.
- Heart ~ heart centre. Depicted as pink or sometimes very pale green. Connection to Universal and Self love.
- Solar Plexus ~ under the ribs. Depicted as golden yellow. Connection to emotions and feeling.
- Sacral ~ in the belly . Depicted as orange. Connection to creativity and reproduction.
- Base or Root ~ base of the spine. Depicted as red. Connection to sexual power, grounding, passion, vital energy.

If you are interested in Chakras you can Google it and find out more.

I ploughed my way through reams of books on the subject but none of them felt exactly like the information I needed. I decided not to worry about what I did, and did not know or understand, but to trust what I was being given, and simply write it down.

Eventually, I had a series of 13 images which I felt should be printed onto T shirts. I also knew that each "chakra" was linked to a crystal, but how?

Something was really bothering me, it didn't feel quite "there" . . . like some vital element was still missing.

I was temporarily stumped.

Maybe I needed to go for another run!

My 41st birthday was at the end of January 2001, and I had invited a new friend over for dinner to celebrate.

Ray had come into my life in the Summer of 2000 through Rachel, my fabulous Pilates teacher.

Rachel had suggested that I might like to attend a "Bodytalk" workshop run by her good friend Ray. I was assured, it would be nothing too heavy, just about relaxation, mindfulness and basic self awareness. Ray was apparently, a "good bloke", lots of fun and very knowledgeable. That sounded okay to me and so I signed up for a forthcoming workshop in Derby.

I liked Ray immediately, he was warm and funny and reassuringly very "normal". I do so appreciate normalness! I remember he wore a really nice jumper which made him seem cuddly and approachable. The workshop was indeed good fun and much of the exercises taught to us, have stayed with me even now, in fact, I still have his workshop booklet for reference, lest I forget his words of wisdom!

Looking back at that "Bodytalk" workshop booklet, I can see that my main concern was my inability to control rogue thoughts and "heebie jeebeies". I am smiling to myself because even now, knowing all I know, the "heebie jeebies" still come knocking on my door and ask if I am coming out to play.

These days, I am more confident to tell them "No!"

One of my favourite exercises I recall involved jigsaws.

We were divided into groups of 3 or 4; each group was given a jigsaw puzzle. The task was to put it together. We quickly established that the pieces did not match, and there was more than one puzzle in the box.

Maybe other people had our puzzle parts?

Were we allowed to ask? we wondered.

Of course we could ask, said Ray.

So we did.

Before long we all had our correct bits to work with.

We also realised that we had no picture to work to, the box lids were all missing.

Could we have our lids please?

Of course we could, but we had to discern for ourselves which picture we were working with.

Did we have the basket of kittens, the steam train, the ballet dancer, or the alpine meadow? Once we knew the overall picture putting the puzzle together was easy, even if a few bits were missing. The point of the lesson being, that if you ask for the bigger picture, get a sense of what you are working towards, then ask others for help to make sure you have all the right pieces. .. then the puzzle usually works out beautifully.

I often think of that little exercise as I am yet again confounded by some oblique and unformed information. The angels can at times be infuriatingly vague with their messages and requests.

More of that later . . .

Over the coming months, Ray and I had became good friends and I valued his wise and common sense approach to the more spiritual side of life. He knew his stuff.

Ray had travelled the world in the course of his professional work as a business coach and trainer to the Hospitality Industry, and in the course of his personal spiritual development.

Ray always seemed so composed and comfortable with this strange world, readily balancing it with "normal" whilst injecting a whole lot of fun and laughter. There is a saying "Angels can fly because they take themselves lightly". I never saw Ray fly, but he had a lightness of heart and spirit that belied his greatness.

I nicknamed him "Ray of Light".

Despite my spiritual naivety, I was never made to feel foolish or embarrassed with Ray, and so I had felt I could trust him with my strange CHAkRA message.

Although Ray was not able to decipher the exact meaning, he helped me to understand the more subtle references and I began to learn about the energetic fields within the physical body and the aura around it. Much of the information led me back to the feelings I had experienced with the first Reiki treatment, the incredible colour and light which had its own life and dimension, this seemed inherently linked to what I was now trying to understand.

So, we were to have a celebratory 41st birthday dinner together, the 3 of us.

As Martin and Ray had never met, I was very nervous, worried that Martin might not like Ray and that Ray might not like Martin. Fingers were crossed and the table was laid. Dinner was served up.

Ha, I need not have worried,. . . it turned out that Martin and Ray were like old pals. I felt like a gooseberry at my own birthday dinner!

Ray had brought me a gift, a book, "Healing with Colour" by Lori Taylor.

Within its pages, lay my missing link!

When I picked up the book, a chart fell out, a large, full colour printed poster folded into 4.

I opened it up, and gasped in amazement.

What I saw; was row upon row of T-shirts with two-tone coloured squares printed on them. I had to do a double take!

Second shock; I had been mistaken, they were not T shirts at all but glass bottles, filled with a coloured oil and water which formed a healing system called Aura~ Soma. I was breathless with excitement because actually this was not the first time Aura-Soma had been shown to me.

Some months before, I had been for a crystal healing session with a wonderful couple named Mick and Michaela. Mick, is one of the foremost teachers of crystal healing in the UK and happened to live on the corner of our road. During the session, he spoke to me about the importance of "communication" as a really important part of my work. He felt this was something I needed to acknowledge within myself.

Just as I was about to leave, both he and his partner shared a glance at each other, and I stopped in my tracks. Was there something else they needed to tell me? They both felt I needed to have a reading using a system called "Aura Soma" and recommended a practitioner named Julie who could help me.

A few weeks after my appointment with Mick and Michaela I found myself ensconced in the kitchen of a delightful little cottage, somewhere in Lincolnshire, and in the gentle company of Julie.

I was invited to choose 4 Aura~Soma bottles from a huge selection presented in a little backlit cabinet, and to do it without thinking too much about the process. From these bottles, Julie could give me a reading which would help to unscramble some of the mysterious issues I was dealing with.

Why was I running?

Why had I been given this message about T shirts?

What was the significance of all this colour?

Was I just going quietly bonkers?

With patience, Julie explained that I was simply in a process of awakening to my Truth.

It still all sounded a bit strange and unlikely.

The running was a way of getting me into an altered state of consciousness. The rhythmic, repetitive action of putting one foot in front of another was helping me to leave my "mind" for a while and allow my unconscious to open up a little. This allowed the angels to speak to me, and to deliver their cryptic message.

Perhaps angels do whisper to a man when he walks, but they seem to shout at a woman when she runs.

The most specific and significant part of the reading related to one particular bottle number 37, called "Guardian Angel comes to Earth", it was a gorgeous blue/violet colour.

In times to come, I would realise the importance of these two colours in my work.

The message was simple "communication on a big scale". Julie was not able to be specific about what this meant, but it echoed exactly what Mick and Michaela had said. There was also a warning about "protection". The need for practicing discernment showing up yet again.

We further discussed "silent voices" which deliver the instructions and guidance that is so very different from the usual chatter and clamour that goes on inside my head. I described it as a "implicit knowing" which was suddenly there; as opposed to, not there, only seconds before.

Julie was rather embarrassed that her reading had been quite short and to the point. Usually there was a lot more to be said, but she was honest, there was no point waffling and making up things to fill the gaps.

I felt very comfortable with what she had said, although I didn't understand it, it felt right.

Time would reveal the true meaning. As I left, Julie gave me some Aura~Soma leaflets which she thought I might find interesting. I put them in my bag and promptly forgot about them.

When I called Julie, to let her know how much I appreciated the time she had spent with me (I do believe a "Thank you" goes a long way) she gave me a little challenge. Could I help her out, by thinking of a phrase or word that she could use to describe what she did?

After I put the phone down, I casually picked up my "Guardian Angel" Aura~Soma bottle and just asked for a bit of help. There was no great ceremony or hoo-ha, I had no specific agenda as to what or how that help might be delivered.

Within moments the "silent voices" had delivered a word - ENERGESSENCE.

Wow!

The fusion of "**energy**" and "**essence**" seemed perfect for Julie.

When I phoned her back a few minutes later she was delighted and astounded with the speed of delivery.

It had been that simple.

I have not been in touch with Julie for a long while, but as far as know she still uses this word.

♥ *According to my angels: The Silent Voices could finally speak and be heard.*

Running was a way of getting me out of my own head space, and allowing my unconscious to have its moment.

Out of my normal routine and environment, closer to the elements and nature, the angels could get a word in edgeways.

By taking responsibility for myself again, I found a new freedom in running that allowed me to be more "me".

Finding and working with Ray was very much a" getting to know me" process, because I was not sure who I was, and whether I would even like "me" when I found her!

By relaxing more, and going with the flow, I found life so much easier.

The prospect of undertaking new things was not as daunting as I had first imagined.

I was doing what I was good at, and having a great time simultaneously,

The angels had begun their whispering, and they still use my "mindless" time when I am out walking to have a good old chat.

The title of this book, was delivered to me just recently in exactly these circumstances. An ordinary walk with the dogs, in a wild and windy weather. Suddenly, kerplunk, the title was there. A Silent Voice had delivered. I don't hear audibly with my ears, it is much more a feeling that resounds throughout my whole body, cell by cell, like a tidal wave ripple effect. I cannot ignore or dismiss it.

My new found computer skills astounded me. Where had they come from? Who was showing me the keys to press? Again, this was an innate knowing that required no prevarication.

People were being placed in my life, Rachel, Ray, Julie, Mick, Michaela, these were to become my jigsaw pieces, people who had some of the answers to the bigger picture on the box lid, if only I was prepared to ask the right questions.

Martin, my husband, was quietly revealing himself to be a powerful ally and anchor point in all this. People often ask about my husband. How does he cope with all this? He copes very well. I appreciate I am not an easy option as a wife and life partner. I never was, even before angels. He is in his own right a very spiritually aware being. I will share something amazing about Martin with you in a later chapter! I promise.

I now understand, it is not good practice to put all the answers with one person. It is safer to spread them around, like the jigsaw pieces in different boxes. This makes things more secure until the information is ready to be pieced together. Such information would be at risk if only one person had access to it.

Although these people had answers, they did not always know that they carried them for me. They also did not know that other people had the other missing parts.

It was up to me to find them.

It was up to me to ask questions.

It was up to me to listen for the answers.

Chapter 13

~ A MAGIC INGREDIENT~

"Most of the fundamental ideas of science are essentially simple, and may, as a rule, be expressed in a language comprehensible to everyone."

— Albert Einstein

A new project I was working on required that I undertook some High Street research and I was planning to take the train down to London. It made sense to buy a train ticket the night before, to save rushing in the morning, and so I hopped into my car to drive to the station. As I slammed the door ready to set off, I got a very strong feeling that I should not go to London, but should go to Manchester instead. It was such a strong feeling that I paid heed and abandoned my trip to the station.

For all the difference it made to my project, Manchester would do just as well. I decided I would drive up in the morning.

As I set off the next day, I unaccountably kept thinking about a guy I had met whilst working for one of my Consultancy clients. His name was James but I always called him "The Twinkle Man" because he worked with a specialist product that was highly reflective, such as is used in safety clothing.

Whenever he was in the Head Office, he would create a kind of twinkly grotto in one of the windowless showrooms, with all his products displayed around the walls and with the lights turned off.

The magic happened when you wore a special pair of goggles with small lamps on either side of the eyes. The light beam would hit the reflective material and you would be bedazzled by the illuminated clothing.

Why was I thinking of him so strongly right now?

I was driving northwards on the M1 and had just stopped at a service station for a break when my mobile phone rang.

It was not a number I recognised.

"*Hello! Is that you Alison?!*" asked an unfamiliar voice.

"*Yes. . . .who is that?*" I queried?

"*Ah,. . . . it's James. . . . the Twinkle Man! Do you remember me?*" he replied.

Without knowing why, he had just decided to call me for a catch up.

Well, we had a lovely chat and I established that he was still working with the magical material and I felt inclined to press further and asked where he was based these days.

"*Manchester!*" he proffered.

We made an arrangement to meet that very day straight after work.

I just beamed with serendipitous happiness as I continued my drive up the motorway.

When we finally met up, we talked about all sorts of stuff, I was particularly excited to share what I had recently learned about how it is possible to programme crystals.

I love the combination of pure science and spiritual "magic".

We had learned that all crystals have a vibrational resonance.

Quartz is particularly reliable, and is used commonly in high-tech instruments such as cars, computers, watches and radios, TV's, GPS, in fact almost all modern electrical goods have a circuit board with a silicone chip. These chips are programmed. There is a multi-billion dollar industry in creating these chips, and a by product, is the beautiful crystal singing bowls used for healing and meditation.

We discussed this information in relation to my T-shirts puzzle, I had felt there was a connection somehow to the energy of crystals.

Without missing a beat, "Twinkle Man" James suggested that I find a way to pulverise the crystals to a fine powder, down to around 40 microns, and mix it with printing ink. He felt sure that would achieve the desired effect.

Crystals, like hologram fractals, hold the whole programme no matter how big or small the piece. Powder or lump, it could work! I had no idea how, but it felt right.

With much hugs and thanks shared between us, we said our goodbyes, and just as I was leaving "Twinkle Man" offered to send me a pot of the reflective material he was using, just for me to have a play around with.

Within days, as good as his word, a litre pot of a Reflec 40 microns aluminised silica powder duly arrived in the post.

I was so excited!

This was the missing ingredient, but what was I supposed to do with it?

It didn't take me long to work out that silica is crystalline and so would, by its nature, be able to hold any programming I chose to put into it. All I had to do was incorporate a small amount of this silica based material into my prints and not only would they have the most amazing energy, they would have an incredible ability to reflect light.

At this stage, I had no idea just how significant this material was to become in my work with the angels.

In the meantime, I was on a roll with the concept of CHAkRA.

I had already applied to trademark the concept and on 30th August 2001, I received final notification that my trade mark application had been approved.

Because I had been in the fashion industry, and knew my way around, it was no problem to find a company who could print some T shirts for me.

It was possibly quite a different challenge to find a company who could print these particular T shirts though, because they would have to be made rather differently.

I knew that the thing that would make these t shirts special would be that each coloured disc would be energised according to the particular chakra.

I now knew exactly how to do it.

Whilst watching the TV news one evening, I saw a priest bless a whole truckload of goods being shipped by a charity organisation to Croatia. The priest was asked why he didn't have to bless each item. He said it was not necessary, the blessing would "take" on everything if he simply willed (prayed?) that it should. Apparently he had a whole fleet of trucks to bless so it was rather convenient he could do it that way.

I had also since learned, through the leaflets that Julie left with me, that the Aura~Soma bottles were energised on a kind of production line so the liquids within were activated according to the specific meaning and purpose of the particular colour. In a similar way, it was a mass blessing.

When I saw the chart fall out of my birthday book, I registered the pictures of the bottles as T shirts. It was a subtle way of letting me make the connection.

So, all I had to do, was bless the printing inks with the appropriate colour energy using my new skills taught by Chris in the Reiki class.

It seemed very straightforward.

I knew of a local printing company, and they were willing to make an experimental batch of t shirts for me. They seemed quite excited at the prospect.

Suffice to say, it worked.

I got my first T shirts, they looked fantastic, and I got a few of my new found spiritually awakened friends to try them out. They loved them! They got a definite good feeling from them and they liked the concept.

I got Mick to advise on the best crystals to correspond to the various chakras, and I invested in a quantity of appropriate tumble stones. Each T shirt was then packaged with a small crystal and a lovely message presented in a tiny canvas pouch.

But I am getting way ahead of myself here. There was still a lot of other stuff happening before I could get my CHAkRA t shirts out there in public domain.

This was just a start. . . toe in the water time!

♥ *According to my angels ~ There is no such thing as co-incidence only perfect timing.*

Sometimes, we just have to trust the guidance we are given.

Sometimes, it all seems crazy amazing; beyond belief.

Synchronicity loves to help us out when we are open to receive it.

We cannot possibly know the nuts and bolts of the process and our wildest imaginations cannot come up with the reality that will be delivered to us.

If I had ignored the "directive" to go to Manchester and continued with my original plan to go to London I may never have found the missing link, this vital element?

I do believe the angels try all the tricks in the book to get us to pay attention, because whatever it is we are meant to be doing, we will end up doing it at some point or other whether we know it or not. In this case everything conspired to get me to find the special "magical ingredient" which I still use in my artwork today.

After this encounter, I never kept up the connection with "Twinkle Man", I guess our business was concluded together and we could go on our way.

Chapter 14

~ A BELOVED MASTER TEACHER ~

*"I would have the strength to handle this
as The Master would handle it"*

White Eagle

As my work with the CHAkRA concept evolved, there was so much more I need to learn and to access.

I needed help from the highest source.

At this critical spiritual growth point, I was introduced to a Master Teacher, by Ray of Light.

Mrs G was a Master of Tera Mai Reiki and Seichem, a form of energy which works with all five healing elements of earth, fire, water, air and ether, unlike the Usui Reiki which just accesses the healing of the earth element.

Also, Mrs G was a Master of The Violet Flame and The Order of Melchizedek.

Ray felt her energy and wisdom would suit my needs and help me to find my way forward through to the next stage of things. It was not just a question of giving me her number, he would have to call her himself and ask permission for me to speak with her.

Permission was granted.

I was forewarned. Mrs G didn't always agree to see people, even if she did speak with me, it might just amount to the telephone conversation.

The call was odd to say the least. I was asked a series of complex questions relating to my spiritual understanding, my expectations, and my intentions. I felt rather like Neo in the Matrix when he goes to meet with The Oracle. (If you haven't seen this cult film, you really should, as it will help you understand how my life felt at this stage!)

However, I was not to be disappointed. After my first call to Mrs G she suggested I come for an appointment, as a matter of urgency.

On 22nd Feb 2001, I had my first audience with her at her home in Yorkshire. I was rather nervous to say the least. I had no idea what to expect. I bought her a bowl of flowering daffodil bulbs as a gift, I deliberately chose living flowers because I sensed she might not approve of cut blooms.

I was greeted warmly by a small, round, softly blonde lady of indeterminate age, beaming from ear to ear and literally radiating loveliness and positive energy.

She accepted the daffs eagerly, declaring them to be "her favourite" and welcomed me into her immaculate little cottage, urging me to sit and make myself comfortable.

My impressions of Mrs G were immediately very positive. I knew I would like her. She bustled away to put the kettle on. We quickly established that I had much work to do.

I had come into this lifetime with great purpose, apparently. Just like Mick and Michaela, and then Julie, had foretold. She confirmed her intuition that I was to be "communicating on a massive scale". She also reminded me of the importance of protection, for myself and my work.

To be honest, I have no idea what we did that day. We just talked, but I am aware she geared her questions to ensure she got as full and honest a picture from me as possible.

I was able to share the story of my experiences of the first Usui Reiki attunement with Chris, and subsequent "messages" regarding the "auric colour spectrum".

I do recall that Mrs G opened and rebalanced my chakras; using a slim silver bangle which she held in her hand and shook about a bit.

There appeared to be a problem with my throat chakra which was tight snapped shut, like a clam. This was not good news for a person supposed to be on a mission of communication.

A series of exercises with sound vibration helped shift things a bit and free me to "speak my truth". It involved quite a lot of giggling on my behalf.

I was also shown how to protect myself. To close my eyes, and visualise a protective bubble of white light; this could be drawn down over, and around me. If I did this on a regular basis, I would be protected from any negative energies or entities. This is an easy and powerful exercise when undertaken in the right way, in trust and belief.

During the healing session, I was aware of a great tingling heat from Mrs G's hands as she moved around my body. It was similar to that first experienced with the healer Richard at the hospice, and again with the Reiki.

Although her touch was gentle and light, the connection was powerful and direct. It was the difference between savouring a fine vintage wine and glugging a glass of plonk. I was aware of a "downloading" of some kind. Again, it was not unlike the experience of Neo in the film "The Matrix"; my head was filled with impossibly fast reams of numbers and letters all written in bright white or high vibration violet light.

Reprogramming or rebooting a computer would no doubt have a similar effect if you could see it. I was almost pinned to the chair whilst this was happening and felt blissfully incapable of any movement.

My crown chakra felt as though it had blown off, leaving the top of my head feeling wide open like a neatly sliced, boiled egg.

It was surprisingly in no way frightening, just very tangible.

When the downloading had finished, I was pleasantly exhausted and Mrs G closed all the energy centres again and encouraged me to take a drink of water, then to sleep a while.

Through half open eyes, I saw a group of beautiful, strange, beings standing around the treatment bed. Tall, thin, shimmering, white, they bent over me and peered at the strange little human lump struggling so hard to understand what was going on. I must have drifted off.

When I awoke, I asked Mrs G about them. I thought that they might have been angels, but she enlightened me that they were in fact Light Beings, or Illumined Ones. These are other dimensional beings who are part of our ascension process. They have our Highest Good at the forefront of their purpose.

Mrs G had given me the best part of her day, and now it was time to pay her consultation fee, and go home and let all this assimilate.

Some months later, I had been back to Mrs G for a Secheim attunement. This was a kind of upgrade on my original Reiki, and would help me with the colour aspects of my work.

We had together discovered some interesting things about my spiritual development.

The old throat chakra block was in fact a kind of energetic safety valve, which can lock tight if I am not meant to speak. This was a "gift" rather than a gag. It could be frustrating when my head was full of stuff it wanted to share or to ask, but my throat clamped tight and not a peep was uttered. This would explain some things that would come later.

A session of past life regression work, helped me to understand my seemingly irrational fear of water in this lifetime. Past life regression is a form of hypnotherapy where the subject is put into a deeply relaxed state and guided through a series of questions which facilitates access into other lifetimes. It is possible to retrieve information which may be helpful to understand why we have certain fears, behaviours, addictions, or traits in this lifetime which may have no apparent cause or logical explanation. It is not necessary for the subject to even believe in past lives, just to have a willingness to go through the process with a qualified Practitioner.

At this stage, I didn't understand the whole process of "how" but I did have an innate feeling that I had been around the block a bit, and have been here before.

Over time, Mrs G became my greatest mentor, teacher and ally; a no nonsense Yorkshire lass who called a spade a spade. I grew to love and trust her implicitly, as a spiritual mother.

Under her tutelage I grew into myself, blossomed, unfurled, and opened up to the magic of the Universe. I developed my own skills.

Initially I had been greatly in awe of Mrs G. Despite her seeming ordinariness; the simple stretchy slacks, jolly printed tunics, little white slippers and freshly scrubbed fragrance; her skills and Mastery belied her modest appearance.

She was a divorcee, had two grown up daughters and a delightful little grandchild. Her best friend, a Swedish woman who was skilled reflexologist, was often at the house when we visited, and we got to know her well too.

This "ordinariness" was very important. Sometimes the greatest work is done in the quietest of ways. Mrs G never advertised, nor did she ever attend the circuit of Mind Body Spirit events. Her clients "found" her and she always had time for those who were committed to their journey.

In due course, I was re-attuned by Mrs G to the Tera-Mai Reiki system, and also to the "Violet Flame" and the "Order of Melchizedek". These further attunements refined my own skills and energy to a higher level. There were no adverse reactions as far as I can remember; my physical body had started to learn how to assimilate energy safely without causing pain or suffering. I must have been getting used to it all.

Mrs G was always my spiritual rock. She was invariably the first person to call with news, crisis, celebration, or questions.

I must have driven the poor woman mad with my over excited telephone calls of the "You will never guess what has happened now" variety.

Mrs G was blessed with the patience of a Saint!

Although it was rare for Mrs G to venture out, she did actually come and visit us here in Nottingham on more than one occasion. The excitement in the Knox household, anticipating seeing her little battered Fiat pulling up outside the house was palpable.

At this time, Martin had also begun to explore his own spiritual path and had turned to Mrs G for guidance. So, it was always a delight and an honour for both of us when she came to stay with us.

We felt like family.

On the May Bank Holiday weekend in 2001, heralded by great, joyful anticipation, we had shared a very wonderful few days together.

I had been getting creative, making wall hangings from bits of driftwood and "treasure" collected at the beach at Whitby and Mrs G had been watching me at work.

My creation process had always seemed to me to be rather pleasurable, if somewhat mindless, activity; however it intrigued her. She recognised an energy pattern imprinted within my movements and the specific selections of the pieces I used. I was following old blueprints of some kind, shamanic storytelling through shells and bits and bobs.

One particular piece was being created for a friend of hers. I had never met this mysterious woman, the daughter of Mrs G's best friend, but I knew she was held in great esteem by Mrs G and referred to in hushed, almost deferential tones as "The Master". It would seem that the pieces I was intuitively selecting for this particular gift were very appropriate to this woman.

The final day of the visit had ebbed and flowed into early evening and I was concerned that Mrs G would get caught up in the rush of Bank Holiday traffic heading home. I knew she liked to get to the "dry land" of home or destination as soon as possible. However, this day, she seemed unconcerned and took her time getting her things together to leave.

When she was almost ready, Martin brought her up to my studio to say "goodbye".

The window of my workroom looks out over the street and a wide vista, the houses opposite appear to have endless open sky behind them and as the aspect is west facing; we enjoy some wonderful sunsets from time to time. This was one such moment.

All three of us, plus Minnie, our little Wire Haired Fox Terrier, looked out onto a sky of flame, scarlet red and indigo violet tinged with deep gold and burning amber.

The whole scene seemed to vibrate, throb and grow in intensity and colour, and as we stood there . . . agog. . . we felt an almost seismic shift as an energy wave of tsunami proportions hit the house.

Instinctively we each grabbed a grounding crystal from the abundant selection on the window sill. Then, we grabbed for each other.

Manifesting before us was a scene that could only be described as "heavenly". Angels were everywhere, sitting on the roofs of the houses opposite and coming right up to the window in shimmering, vibrant, multidimensional light. Wave after wave hit us. We felt almost intoxicated. I have no idea how long all this magnificence lasted, but when it was over we were all exhausted.

There was no way Mrs G was going home that night. She felt she had been "detained" so she could experience that exquisite moment with us.

The only thing to do after such a seismic experience, was to go outside and walk barefoot in the garden eating a large bag of potato crisps each. Did you know that potato products are very good for grounding? It's because they are of the earth! Chips, crisps, baked potato, mash . . .all good stuff! I always keep a bag of "Kettle Chips" in; just as a precaution, you understand!

We all felt blessed and honoured that we had been permitted to experience such a profound and beautiful moment of Grace together.

As my greatest and most beloved teacher; ultimately, Mrs G was to prove my greatest challenge.

One day, I would have to make a choice between my relationship with her, and my own burgeoning Truth .

♥ *According to my angels; When the student is ready, the teacher appears.*

I feel Mrs G needs this introductory chapter all to herself as she formed such an important, formative, part of my spiritual awakening and life.

As a modest woman, who never sought attention, you will appreciate that I have been deliberately circumspect regarding her private details. For the purposes of this book, it is not necessary that you know any more than this.

The White Eagle quote, at the beginning of this chapter, was given to me by her, as a small printed card, for inspiration and guidance. I don't know whatever happened to the actual card, but the words have lived within my heart ever since.

Oh my goodness, there have been many times when I nearly wept with frustration because I didn't know HOW the Master WOULD handle it.

In those moments, I just did my best.

Although Mrs G was by no means my only teacher, without her, assuredly I would not be who I am today. I love her and I wholeheartedly, thank her, for everything she did for me.

Over time, and when it felt appropriate, I was able to recommend others to go to her. I have always worked on the basis of advocacy ever since, it is a far more powerful tool than advertising.

When somebody comes into our lives with great wisdom, knowledge and presence, it is natural to feel somewhat awed and overwhelmed.

Mrs G taught me that this is not necessary.

We honour and respect our teachers, but we in turn, are to be honoured and respected for what we bring to them. The greatest teachers have much to learn from the humblest pupil. Mrs G was always generous and open with her love and support. Martin and I, were like fledgling chicks in the nest, waiting with ever open mouths to be fed the next feast of information. Like the mother bird, her purpose was to fledge us and let us go.

Because we are human we form attachments and ties, we develop reliance and dependencies.

This is not what was meant for any of us.

When the time came to cut the ties, to fly the nest, a challenge was set for me that would change everything. I will share that with you later; it forms part of another chapter of this book, and of my life.

In the meantime, as far as I know, Mrs G is still very much alive and well ; continuing with her wonderful work.

I hear news of her indirectly these days, from others who know of her.

I still love her dearly.

Chapter 15

~ FINDHORN ~

*"Perhaps it is better to wake up after all, even to suffer,
rather than to remain a dupe to illusions all one's life."*

Kate Chopin ~ The Awakening and Selected Stories

Martin and I were invited to join a rather spiritually and personally challenging couple, Mrs and Mrs M on a trip to Findhorn in Scotland. This is an well established centre of Spiritual Community, a place of unity, love and personal growth a self sustaining Community, growing their own food, making all sorts of useful things, and printing their own books and materials on spiritual practice and teachings. http://www.findhorn.org/

Mrs M was a Healer and closely worked with one of the Saints. She made it clear she had no time for "Reiki dabblers". Her manner was often very brusque, strident, lacking in warmth or humor. She was always very interested in what I was up to, but shared very little of her own information other than to show off her testimonials in a way that felt crass and egotistical. I found it intriguing that she drove a high performance sports car with blatantly personalised plates. (Remember, I was now used to working with a Master Teacher who was modest, down to earth and subtle.) On recommendation, Mrs M had done some necessary "energy clearing" work for Martin a few years earlier at his workplace. She had apparently, made a huge and positive difference. It was through this previous connection with Martin that I had eventually met her.

Her husband, Mr M, by contrast was a warm, softly spoken, gentle and downtrodden soul. He and I discovered we were originally from the same part of the world, Liverpool, and that he had at one time worked for a company that Martin had dealings with through his own work. That was our commonality.

The idea of the trip to Findhorn all sounded very lovely, but I didn't feel I wanted to go.

Martin thought I was being ungrateful, and so with great reluctance, I yielded.

We were to travel up to Scotland together by car. Mrs M insisted on driving us in her Porsche 911. A bit of a squeeze for four adults.

Pretty much as soon as we got into the car, Martin zoned out. He fell into a deep and heavy headed sleep that would render him almost incoherent for the rest of the trip. That didn't bode well.

The drive up to Findhorn was not much fun.

I felt anxious and slightly out of control of my own destiny.

Mrs M was driving the whole way, and it was she who called the shots, deciding when and where we should stop. Mr M said very little, and only spoke when he was spoken to. I learned Mrs M had some very controlling traits. I didn't yet feel confident enough to challenge her.

We arrived at the little hotel just before midnight.

I was shattered with exhaustion and just wanted to go to my bed.

Cheerfully, Mr M suggested that we go straight down to the beach and open a bottle of champagne to celebrate, as it was their wedding anniversary! He had suddenly perked up and was a "man with a plan".

We all trooped, rather solemnly, down to the seashore, clutching the travel weary bottle of fizz and some plastic beakers.

A light but steady mizzle had settled in, and the unseen beach was a hazardous challenge of driftwood, slippery rock pools and large stones amongst which there were random seals trying to sleep.

Undaunted, Mrs M struggled to open a large golf umbrella, and huddling beneath it, the M's guided us to the perfect spot.

There was some fumbling with the champagne cork, and plastic beakers were dropped onto the shingle, curses were uttered, and a mild domestic ensued between the celebratory marrieds.

I picked my moment, and whilst they were distracted, I distanced myself, heading off across the beach and down to the water's edge.

There; I stood in silence and wonderment.

The vista in front of me had no structure. In the absolute darkness, there was no horizon, no differentiation between water and sky, just a very bright star hanging like a living jewel directly above me.

I focussed my attention on that star.

In a nanosecond, it felt as though I was blasted into a billion pieces and put back together again in the same moment. I was everywhere and nowhere . . . it was, the most exquisite feeling.

Somewhere in the distance, I heard my name being called. I wanted to ignore it. The call became louder and more strident, angry even, I had to come back, to pay attention.

It was Mrs M, berating me for my foolishness, what was I thinking of wandering off?

She demanded I come back and enjoy the champagne celebration.

Reluctantly, I left my star struck reverie, and slowly scrunched my way back across the soggy beach to the weary little huddle under the brolly.

Martin didn't even seem to notice I had been gone.

Celebrations duly celebrated, we retired to the hotel, and for the first time in hours, it was just us.

We both wanted to go home, but we were tied into the plans of Mr and Mrs M.

We slept.

The next few days were fairly meaningless, in as much as I have no recollection of anything significant happening. We visited a whiskey distillery, tramped across endless pebbly beaches, admired the sleeping seals, ate in some nice cafés, and paid a very fleeting visit to the Findhorn centre.

Having travelled all that way, we spent about half an hour in the gift shop, and that was that.

Mrs M had decided she didn't feel comfortable there.

So we left.

To be fair, I didn't feel all that comfortable either, but it was harder for me to attribute where that discomfort came from. Was it Findhorn, or was it the company we were keeping? I didn't feel too disappointed that we didn't stay very long.

Mission somehow accomplished, whatever that may have been, the M's bundled us back into the car and we travelled at warp speed back home.

It took Martin and I days to get over that trip.

We both felt disorientated, ungrounded and very out of sorts. We ached a lot and we slept a lot.

The M's called us intermittently to see how we were, but I didn't really want to discuss anything with them. Every conversation drained me dry. I would become diminished and weak, angry and confused.

The trip to Findhorn had been a way of disorientating me a little, putting me on my back foot, weakening my energy and resolve. I felt there was something unspoken that Mrs M wanted from me, and she was working hard to get at it.

Mrs M had not reckoned on the powerful back up team of angels, guides, Light Beings, Masters, Elementals etc that I now had on standby. The Forces of Light would be protecting me, whether I knew what I was doing or not.

A few days after our return, I was eating dinner in front of the TV, when I had a most unusual urge come over me.

Abandoning my half eaten meal, I dashed upstairs to get a sketch pad and some wax crayons. Returning to my place in front of the TV, I hurriedly opened the pad and the crayons and began scribbling frantically across the page. It was a wild and joyful scribbling, an expression of something that had been trapped like a bird within me; something I had no words for. I grabbed a tea spoon and used the edge of it to score marks in the thick build up of wax.

Martin understandably quite astounded, asked me what on earth I was doing.

I replied honestly, I had no idea.

What I had in fact created was an impression of the experience of standing on the edge of the sea up at Findhorn. There was a dark, brooding horizon, a wild and choppy sea, a low and heavy sky, a lone figure standing in the middle, and above the figure a distinct single bright star. The star was not drawn in, but quite the reverse, the result of not having scribbled on that particular spot. I was amazed at the powerful feeling this picture engendered, the sense of reconnection to that moment. It was so simple, so beautiful, so real.

I had never created anything quite like it before.

♥ *According to my angels: Beware the angels of darkness posing as angels of light.*

Our strange and discordant relationship with the M's was important, as part of my growth and understanding.

It served to teach discernment.

Are you familiar with the saying "putting your hooks into someone"? This is what Mrs M specialised in. Once the hooks were established it was very hard to extricate them.

After our dismal Findhorn trip, Martin and I went up to seek the solace and counsel of Mrs G. She spent some considerable time extricating the energy hooks from us. It felt literally like barbs were being pulled, excruciatingly painful, tender, and with a necessary period of recovery needed.

During this recovery period we were advised to keep out of that energy, not to call or take calls from the M's to take the Bach Rescue Remedy, and to bathe in salt water which is cleansing and purifying.

Our connection with Mr and Mrs M quickly dwindled down to nothing as the lesson had been learned, not without cost, but learned never the less.

I can only be grateful for the part this couple played in my journey, and the gift that they gave me in terms of the lessons.

Discernment. . . discernment. . . discernment!

Please be aware, that there will be times when the sky looks less blue, the bunnies less fluffy, and the path a little more arduous and thorny.

There are those, who despite appearances and all the "right" words are not what or who they purport to be.

They have their own agendas.

Give them a wide berth, and send them only Love.

The value of a"Dark Angel" experience depends on what you choose to take away from it.

Chapter 16

~ UNCHAINED ~

"The truth will set you free, but first it will piss you off."

Gloria Steinhem

For many years I wore an ever multiplying "armour" of silver chains and bracelets.

I loved them, they made me feel safe and strong, and grounded, if a bit clanky!

Each piece had great meaning and significance to me. I had perfected a sure fire way of getting something exactly suitable for my birthday or Christmas from Martin, as all he had to do was follow my pointing finger to a certain display cabinet in my favourite store. I would treat myself to special pieces too, to celebrate my good days, and to ease the pain of my bad ones, I didn't need much excuse.

Since I started my spiritual journey, I had become increasingly frustrated that these silver chains kept breaking, with increasing frequency, usually at night ending up in pieces, lost in the bedding.

It was costing me fortunes in repairs at the silversmiths.

One afternoon I was at the Pilates studio, meeting my teacher, Rachel, for lunch.

We sat at a refectory style table, already occupied by a few students and another Pilates trainer named Dai. We chose to share the table.

Over lunch, I bewailed my broken silver story with Rachel, unaware that Dai had been listening and paying attention too.

Eventually, Dai leaned over towards me and made a simple suggestion "*You don't need to wear those chains any more. . .why don't you take them off. Why are you hiding behind them?*"

WHAT????? I was outraged!!!!

Who asked you???

I took great umbrage at the unsolicited advice and I drew my remaining chains ever closer to my chest.

I don't really remember what I said in response, but I suspect it was ungracious.

On the drive home, I was having a little rant to myself, involving much under breath mutterings and harrumphings but somehow, in the midst of all that, I came to a point of reconciliation that perhaps indeed the silver had to be taken off. . . just for a while. . . not a permanent thing you understand.

That very day, I removed each piece with respectful care and consideration and placed them all in a beautiful oriental box, with a promise of reinstatement in due course.

I almost immediately felt "the wobble"; a strange light headedness and mild disorientation without my ballast in place. I then resorted to wearing a heavy knitted jumper and a pair of stout boots to help keep me grounded.

Athena dropped by and declared I somehow looked "lighter"

A few days after I had divested myself of the silver, I called my mum for a bit of a chat.

I was just recounting the strange story of the silver, when mum interjected, wanting to tell me about a news item she had heard recently.

However, first, she insisted, she needed to hear me out.

Once I had finished my story, mum told me hers.

She had been listening to a news report by the famous war correspondent Kate Adie, who had described how towards the end of the 2nd World War a group of refugees had been ousted from their hiding place by the military forces, and as a punishment the children had been chained, taken in a boat to the middle of a lake, overturned and drowned. Mum saw me, in that moment, as a child in chains, drowning, and wished with all her heart that I would take off all the silver that I wore.

Now, here I was, telling her that I had done just exactly that.

She was almost tearful with relief and asked me to promise I would not put those chains back on.

I never have.

I did manage to gather sufficient gratitude to thank Dai for his insight and wisdom which was delivered via Rachel who could not resist giving me one of her famous "I told you so" looks.

♥ According to my angels: It was time to come out of hiding.

I had been hiding behind my silverware for years.

It often proved to be a handy distraction, people would ask me about the spectacular jewellery rather than ask me about me.

It gave me a sense of physicality when often I had felt so diminished that I doubted my own presence.

It was a distraction.

It was another addiction.

I found comfort in the metal and some hunger in me was sated in the purchasing of the pieces.

My mums reaction to the news item helped me to see the energetic impact of the silver shackles.

I never put it back on.

My energy field is far happier without it.

Chapter 17

~ BLUE EGGS ~

The moment one gets into the "expert" state of mind a great number of things become impossible.

~Henry Ford, Sr.

One Saturday afternoon, whilst shopping in Nottingham, something made me stop outside a Chinese antiquities emporium. It was one of those places full of stuff and things, knick-knacks and objets d'art .

Curious, I ventured in.

There was a little jangly bell which burst into life as I entered the shop, but no one seemed to be around. The shop was much bigger than I anticipated, with several distinct rooms, and a flight of stairs leading to a lower floor. It smelled exactly as I remembered certain places in Hong Kong, a mixture of incense and hot soup!

I spotted a large wicker basket, casually placed on the floor right at the front of the shop. It was filled with rather splendid decorative marble eggs, all shiny and glossy.

I stooped down to take a better peek.

Nestled amongst the magnificent marble were some tiny, waxy, whitish looking eggs, about the size of a bantams' egg, certainly smaller than a hens.

As I picked them up, and gently turned them in my hand, something amazing happened . . . they seemed to "pop" and turned a very lively pale blue colour! They seemed to somehow switch themselves on, if a little blue chick had hopped out I would not have been at all surprised.

Staring at the magical little things they began to radiate a golden yellow glow, from deep within themselves, onto my outstretched palm. I thought there must be a trick to it . . . maybe they were battery operated or have a fancy silicone chip inside them?

I picked up a few more and each one did the same thing, a little popping, then a subtle glow. Holding them up to the light revealed that some had small bubbles within them which seemed to light up like oxygen under water.

I am certainly no expert on crystals, but I felt they were the most beautiful things I had ever seen!

I selected four eggs out of the basket and went to the till to pay for them.

The shopkeeper had now appeared from somewhere at the back of the shop, he was a smiley faced Chinese, quite young and very amused at my delight with these eggs.

He was unable to tell me anything about them other than that they had come in a consignment from Northern China. He had not ordered them and had assumed they were used for ballast, to make up the weight of the container or something. As they had cost him nothing; he was prepared to try and sell them.

He laughed, "You are the only person who has ever noticed them!".

How could that be? They were such delightful, magical little things.

They were also very cheap, costing only £1.50 each.

When I got them home, Martin was as intrigued as I.

We "Ooohed" and "Aaaahed" over them together.

I felt an increasing bond with them, almost like my response to small animals, a puppy or kitten. They felt very precious and vulnerable and I became fiercely protective and mindful of how they might be "feeling".

Instinctively, I poured a bottle of sparkling mineral water into a glass bowl and put the four eggs in. The bubbles effervesced and tickled the eggs, I could almost hear them giggling. When the bubbles had subsided, I went and found a small bottle of a very special oil which had jasmine and rose in it. The oil was named "Love" it seemed appropriate. Carefully, I dabbed a small spot of oil onto each egg in turn, and rubbed it in. This seemed to awaken them even more, they were now glowing ever brighter, with an added aura of a deeper violet blue and the inner golden light, vibrant and strong.

Martin and I sat mesmerised and simply watched, hardly daring to touch them.

We chose one each. Martins had a large bubble inside it and mine was perfectly solid, with no bubbles what so ever. They felt like a pair.

It was extraordinary how these unidentifiable crystals affected me. They delivered a kind of euphoria; a lightness of spirit and playful giddiness when I held them. They made my heart palpitate and "grow" . . . not an unpleasant feeling, but certainly very unusual. I didn't want to put them down. I loved them!

My emotional attachment to them was growing by the minute and I was aware that I had to find "good homes" for the other two.

I intuitively knew who had to have them.

A good friend of ours, Julie, was celebrating her 40th birthday, it felt appropriate to give her an egg. As a very harassed mother of 3 young children and a rather demanding husband, Julie rarely had time or energy for herself, and was always thinking of others needs first. She was delighted with her egg, and didn't even ask what it was. She appreciated it as a thing of delicate beauty and simplicity.

It was housed in an egg cup on a shelf in her busy kitchen. She felt she wanted it near her, but not to be obtrusive and draw attention to it, otherwise one of the kids would claim it, then lose it somewhere. Incredibly, Julie later reported that since the installation of the egg, mealtimes in the kitchen had become much calmer, chaos had been reduced and tempers less frayed. She could not explain it, but that was the fact of it. In months to come, Julie and her young daughter would go to Mick for crystal healing and for Reiki attunement. The egg seemed to "open" them to the first steps of spiritual acceptance.

At that time, we had a "gardening angel" Erick.

At first sight, Erick looked nothing less than a thug.

Muscular, scarred, his arms and hands covered in home tattoos, a thick Scouse accent and a "number 1" crew cut, you would not want to meet him in a dark alley that's for sure. However, looks are often deceiving, and beneath that fearsome exterior beat a gentle heart of pure gold.

Erick had magically transformed our garden from a pristine "civic" rectangle, to a naturalised wilderness where nature, animals and fairies and elementals could live in safety and comfort undisturbed. A sensitive an intuitive man, he well deserved an egg.

He held this small throbbing crystal in a big muddy paw and grinned openly, whilst wiping a tear from his eye. He knew exactly where it was going to go, he had a special place for it on his window ledge where the sun comes streaming in.

I knew it would be in safe hands.

What were these magical things?

The following week, I went back to the shop with my younger sister Gaynor in tow, and I bought 4 more eggs. Gaynor bought 3.

Gaynor was very intrigued, she likes a bit of wonderment as much as I do.

Gaynor is also incredibly creative, an artist with an eye for minutia and detail.

By her own admission she is a micro manager, which is handy as she also runs a farm.

Her artwork requires infinite patience and painstaking labour and the results are always so breathtaking.

I see her connection to the elementals as she is always drawn to nature and animals, even as a small child she was just the same. She has a very "pixie" look about her. So, when I gave her the story of the strange Oriental curiosity shop and the mystery consignment from China. Ooooohs were oooohed and aaaaahs were aaaaahed. She had insisted on coming with me to investigate further.

When we got home with the new batch, my Brother in Law Eric (no, not the gardening angel, this is a very practical German man without a "k" on the end) took a more clinical approach to the mystery. Eric suggested he had seen similar things in Switzerland when he worked there, they were quite common and found on the mountain roadside. If I wanted, I could choose the least attractive of my eggs and he would smash it with a hammer and show me that they were just some sort of glassy stone.

My heart nearly stopped with the horror of it!

I cannot express the range of emotions that ran through me at that innocently barbaric yet entirely practical suggestion. I grabbed my poor eggs and whipped them away to a place of safety, I found myself apologising to them, for allowing them to even hear of such an ordeal.

My sister had to promise me not to let her husband loose with heavy tools near her eggs!

After Gaynor and Eric had left; I began twitching with anxiety because I knew that my only mission in life (at that moment!) was to acquire the remaining eggs from the Chinese shop, the very minute it opened the next day.

I had a very sleepless night.

9 a.m. saw me on the doorstep of the Emporium, peering through the window for signs of life. When the shop finally opened, I fell through the door like a sack of spuds and then stopped in my tracks . . . the basket was gone!!!!

Like a demented thing, I demanded to know where it was, who would have moved it?! Despite my obvious derangement, the proprietor calmly pulled the basket out from underneath a large ornate wooden day bed, and explained that he always tucked it away at night "for safety". There were just 16 eggs left; I bought them all. He laughed, openly, at my enthusiasm for them, I was the only person who had ever bought them, well, apart from my sister I suppose.

Clutching my precious cargo, I made my way up the road to the shop where Mick and Michaela often worked with the crystals. I was fully hoping that Mick might be in, to identify what they were. I assumed they must be some sort of crystal.

Mick was not in, but the assistant Debi was.

Debi was training with Mick as a crystal therapist, she was also intuitively knowledgeable about crystals so I opened my bag of eggs and handed one to her.

Immediately, she felt a surge of energy rush up her right arm. She told me this often happened when she held a powerful crystal. After much peering and scrutiny, Debi declared she had no idea what it was, but it felt amazing and had a really beautiful energy. She seemed to have bonded with her egg, so I suggested she might like to keep it, after all it had only cost me a few pence.

There was another girl sitting quietly and looking a little forlorn in the corner of the shop, a client who was awaiting her appointment with another therapist. Her eyes had lit up when she saw the little egg, and as she had looked so sad and dejected, I offered to let her hold one too.

The transformation was immediate and incredible, her face lit up, shining! Her eyes became bright and clear. Her whole demeanour changed from dejected and slumped, to vigorous and alive. She declared that holding the egg made her feel *". . . as though I have taken a whole bottle of Bach Rescue Remedy!"* She told us she was a nurse and that she had been having a really hard time of things, she had been feeling so depressed and worthless, this little thing had really cheered her up, lifted her spirits somehow.

I heard myself offering her the egg to keep.

Well so far, I had bought sixteen "magic eggs" and already given away two, to people I barely knew, in the space of half an hour. At this rate I would have none left! I scrunched the brown paper bag shut and shoved it deep into my handbag. I was going to make my way home whilst I still had them!

Despite my unseemly adoration of my eggs, I knew eventually they would all be given away. I sort of "felt" that I would know who was to have them. I was just the custodian, to enjoy them whilst I could.

The next few weeks saw all the eggs re-homed and I took great care to "feel" my way to getting them to the right people. I just did my best.

I learned very quickly the likes and dislikes of the eggs.

They adored being in the sun and seemed to soak up the rays and energy like sleepy cats. They also enjoyed a good thunderstorm and buzzed and glowed as the air crackled and the rain fell. The harder the better! This seemed to energise them too. Of course they enjoyed a tickly bath in the effervescent water, but not a bubble bath with soapy water. Soft sweet oils, lavender, rose, ylang ylang, magnolia and my special "Love" perfume oil, rubbed gently into the surface made them almost purr with delight, but anything harsh like tea-tree or rosemary made them shudder and switch their lights off.

Once, I took our two to the seaside at Whitby. I put them into one of those mesh bags used for washing machine tablets and swished them safely around in the briny. Oooooh, they really perked up with that!

Sometimes, a curious but uninvited hand would snatch at an egg, wanting to grab and hold them, and the egg would turn whitish, go cold and "turn off".

They are very good barometers of discerning intention and energy. Often I would sleep with our eggs under my pillow, on those occasions I would dream very vividly and wake up feeling as though I had been travelling the Cosmos.

Sometimes, they would "merge" and render themselves invisible. I amused myself on a very boring train journey one day, letting them disappear and reappear in the palm of my hand.

The "getting to know you" period was lots of fun, but very much trial and error. They didn't come with a manual.

The next recipient of an egg was my Mum. When I handed it over to her, she simply put it in her pocket, and didn't make too much fuss of it. I had expected her to show it to my little nephews and nieces who were foregathered for a family lunch, but no, it was squirrelled away. She later confessed she could not bear the thought of one of them dropping it or losing it.

Mum isn't "openly" spiritual, she is inherently spiritual.

She found a safe haven for her little egg in a bowl of pot pourri on the dressing table, away from prying eyes and curious fingers. Even Dad was forbidden to mess with it.

One day, some months later, Mum phoned me in a tearful panic. Her voice was muffled as she was actually scrabbling around in the outside bin, searching for something. Her egg had gone Walkabout!

I asked all the usual questions "Had Dad or anyone moved it?" "Where had she last seen it?" "When had she last seen it?" She wailed some more before confessing she knew what had happened "*You see, it's just like the cat, if I ignore him, he takes the hump and disappears for a while to teach me a lesson. The egg has done the same thing!.*"

According to Mum, she had not paid her egg much attention recently, just the odd tickle when she thought about it. She believed the egg had taken itself off as punishment for her ignoring it.

I suggested she call on St Anthony, who is very good at finding lost things, and ask him where the egg was. More wailing ensued, before a reluctant agreement to do it.

Twenty minutes later, she rang again.

The egg was found!!!

She had made herself a cup of coffee and gone up to have a lie down on the bed.

Halfway up the stairs with her brew, she remembered to call on St Anthony.

"*Saint Anthony, Saint Anthony, Saint Anthony, bring back to me, that which is lost which is mine*" goes the prayer.

She then lay down on the bed, and turned over at a funny angle, which provided her with a perfect view of the egg, sitting smugly in the far corner, under a chair. She was so relieved she brought it out and made many promises to chat to it every day, and pay more attention to it. So far, it has never run off again.

My dear friend Athena had a similar experience. She could not find her egg for love nor money. She had looked everywhere to no avail. In despair she called on good old St Anthony. As a distraction from her anguish, she went into the back bedroom and started folding some freshly ironed clothes which were lying on the bed. There, in amongst the ironing, lay the egg!!! To this day she has no idea how it ever got there.

Of course there was one for my mentor Mrs G.

The next time I visited, it was delivered as a gift.

Mrs G looked upon her egg as a "baby". She saw its innocence and purity and showed me the tiny sparkles that danced upon its surface. In her inimitable, humble way, Mrs G declared she had no experience of crystals, but embraced this unidentifiable, strange "crystal" as an important tool, returned.

Some days later, I had a rather extraordinary phone call from Mrs G, who was clearly struggling to tell me something and almost didn't dare.

Eventually she spit it out.

She had given the egg away to a friend of hers. I was puzzled. Why had she found that so hard to tell me? This friend, was only ever known to us as an unseen "Master" and we accepted that without question. We had benefited from the energetic connection with "The Master" even though we had never seen her physically. So, if the egg needed to move on to her, then it needed to move on. I had no issue with that. In fact, I felt rather delighted.

Mrs G had explained to me that the reason no one else had seen the eggs in the shop, was that they made themselves invisible, or at least dull and uninteresting because they had to wait for me to find them.

It was always just a matter of timing.

As ever.

Of course, I made sure Mrs G got another one to keep for herself.

My relationship with my eggs deepened and evolved over time. My sense of responsibility towards them was at times overwhelming. I had never experienced anything like it. I have always had pets; cats and dogs mostly but even that love felt diminished in the face of my love for the little blue eggs.

Often, I would take them with me on my travels because I felt they needed to "experience" stuff, like they were learning about life on Earth and I was their teacher. One time, I took them to Los Angeles on a business trip. The hotel was so chic, everything was minimal and perfect and oversized. The bed was so HUGE, you could sleep a family of four plus a dog comfortably, but there was just me, and a little blue egg.

I fell asleep virtually hanging off the edge of the bed, unused to such luxurious space, I kept my little egg in my hand.

At some godforsaken hour of the morning, I awoke with a start, an increasing awareness told me that my egg had . . . gone!

Bolt upright, I scoured the sheets and floor, but it was nowhere to be seen. All the lights were put on, the bed pulled out away from the wall, in my sleepy state of mind, I looked in every possible hiding place.

I had just resigned myself to making an emergency call to Housekeeping to ask them to help look for it. As I leaned across the bed to find the telephone, I felt a small familiar lump under tightly tucked in sheets. There it was; the other side of the vast wasteland that was my bed, uncharted territory for me, but not for the "happy wanderer".

My relief and joy was palpable. We were re-united. I swear I could hear muffled laughter.

Remember Debi, she got one of the first eggs, although I barely knew her at the time. Well, we had not seen each other for quite a while but one day she turned up at an event I was at, and we took the opportunity to catch up.

As a Mature Student, in order to make ends meet, Debi had taken in a lodger, the same nurse who had been in the shop the day the eggs arrived. Apparently, the nurse just packed her things one night and disappeared, leaving a note of apology and a small sad blue egg on the kitchen table.

My eyes lit up and my heart went "bang!" . . . did Debi still have the returned egg?

Well yes, she did, somewhere.

This was another little miracle because someone had just come into my life who desperately needed an egg and at the time I had no idea where to acquire one for them.

This was the perfect answer.

Debi came to see me the next day with a tired little egg in her pocket and I welcomed it home with deep joy. It responded immediately to a bit of TLC and was soon winging its way to a loving new home.

Many times I asked crystal experts for an opinion on them, and mostly they were regarded with disinterest or blank looks.

No one seemed to know. . . or care.

I had long reached the end of my supply from the Chinese shop and he never did get another batch. I felt I had no hope of finding any more.

One weekend I was at a local Mind Body Spirit event. (I'll come back to this in the next chapter, as the person for responsible for introducing me to the events, has not been introduced to you yet!)

I needed a comfort break, so I picked a quiet moment, and headed for the ladies. En route, I was distracted by a young guy selling crystals from a rather unprepossessing stall. His half unpacked boxes lay in a haphazard fashion and nothing looked particularly fabulous. . . yet. . . I found myself drawn to his table.

My hand hovered . . .then found its way into a box, bringing out a very pale, travel weary egg. My heart skipped a few beats, and the egg smiled wanly at me. There were a few more in the box, so I retrieved them and handed them over to the stallholder.

He looked me up and down, then asked "Do you know what these are then?"

I was very circumspect in my reply, "Yeah . . . I know what they are."

I felt a huge surge of protectiveness, as though I didn't want to discuss the nature of these things with this man. "Ah well" he replied, equally circumspectly, "You don't need me to tell you then."

I paid up (rather more than the Chinese shop) and he popped them in a bag. He proffered the fact that he found these things from time to time at the suppliers' warehouse. There was not much call for them, but if I was interested, he would ring me next time he found some and let me know.

So that was the arrangement, and good as his word, that is what he did.

We left it at that.

When I took my new batch home they were a sorry looking sight. These particular eggs were much bigger than my petite originals, more like extra large hens eggs. Many of them bore scars and wounds, I felt I was looking at a battalion, returned from war. I attended to them, gave them the "perky pick you ups" that had worked so well on my first batch, but it was hard work.

ontrol

Some of them were barely alive. I administered Reiki healing and Rescue Remedy and hoped for the best.

Eventually they all recovered and went on to fulfil their destiny with the people who needed them.

In more recent times, I have been able to collaborate with another amazing guy, Paul, a designer and maker of metaphysical tools, who works directly with crystal suppliers in China.

Paul is able to acquire the small blue eggs for me, as well as overseeing the production of a very special "Angel of Light" pendant which we devised between us; and a special "Divine Trinity" pendant which was shown to me as a Sacred channelled device.

Today, there are very many beautiful carved opalite products on the market. They all have to a greater or lesser degree this same visual beauty, the blue with the golden inner light. Usually, the crystal is highly polished, although my original eggs have a more distinctly waxy look, a quality which makes them feel softer than the highly polished finish.

However, we don't get all sniffy. Just because something is manmade, does not mean it cannot be a Divine tool. Ask yourself how did the original recipe or formulation of Opalite even come into being?

We humans are only Divine tools after all.

The people who make these crystals probably have little or no idea of their potential.

Spirit, creates the magic and the connection when it is right to do so.

More important than what it is . . is what they are. . . what they carry, and what they are capable of.

♥ According to my angels : some things simply cannot be explained; they just are.

How could such innocuous little things have such a huge impact?

My belief is, that these particular eggs were sent as tools of Divine connection.

The opalite material has been chosen as a vehicle of convenience because of its ability to carry this extremely high, fine and very new energy. Nowadays it is comparatively cheap and readily available, which means it is hidden in plain view, for those who have the eyes to see and the heart to feel it.

Each egg seems to have its own distinct personality, no two are the same.

They work at a very high vibration, and at a deep soul connection level.

Like a birds egg, they contain everything that is needed, they are whole and complete.

When they come to me, they are in a dormant state, just ticking over like an animal in hibernation, waiting to be energised and brought into the next phase of "life". When I hold the eggs, I am able to activate and awaken this energy and bring them into being. For as long as they are with me, they are nurtured and cared for on a regular basis, although I do not form attachments to any of them except the original two which I Martin and I chose. My job is to facilitate them, to set them free, to work with the right people.

The final phase of activation happens when the egg meets its new custodian, the person with whom it will work. At that point something incredibly subtle yet powerful is shared, and a bond is made that will never be broken.

It has been really important to trust my intuition as to where these eggs should go.

They are embryonic angels, connectors to Source and the Divine, healers, counsellors, sanctuary, meditation tools, wise ones, and so much more.

At times I have been able to enter the energy field of my eggs and be within that space. It is like going back to the womb (but without all the mess!) a feeling of complete bliss and euphoric joy, freedom and expansion. I see them as angelic energies made manifest and tangible for our earthly human delight and edification. They are the embodiment of joy, beauty, magic, optimism and innocence; they bring peace, courage, strength and wisdom.

When I first found these eggs, I knew nothing much about anything.

Certainly, I knew nothing much about crystals.

I knew even less about angels.

Was this another test?

Of course it was!

I had to prove that I could handle the responsibility of what was yet to come. The angels monitored my responses and reactions, checked me out for final approval before they took their leap of faith, and came knocking on my door.

Around this same time, I was travelling on business to Hong Kong. At the airport, I realised I had not packed a book to read on the flight. I nipped into a book shop at the airport and at random chose a book which was to prove to be yet another test.

Against commonly held advice; I judged a book very much by its cover.

The novel, The Vintner's Luck written by Elizabeth Knox was chosen primarily because of the "Knox" connection, and because it had a rather lovely golden cover.

I read it, totally consumed it, on the flight.

Within the story lay the test for me.

It is an account of a passionate and often harrowing relationship formed over a period of a lifetime between a human peasant, a Vintner, and a fallen angel. It is at once exquisitely beautiful and grotesque.

There is a part of the story where the wings of the angel, Xas, are forcibly removed with a chicken boning knife, to keep the angel earthbound, in the name of human LOVE!

When I read that account, my stomach churned and my heart froze! How could anyone treat an angel so?! It was a kind of gelding. What would be gained from entrapment of such a being? In that moment, reading that fictional scenario, my anguish, revulsion and disgust was approved of, by the angelic realms, and I was deemed to be pretty much ready for this forthcoming challenge.

Even now, I cannot read that book without feeling the same pain. Sometimes, I read a relevant passage to my workshop delegates, to illustrate the feeling that needs to be felt.

So, why did I feel such a responsibility for these small strange things, and have to show such discernment in placing them in their new homes?

My ability to accept and honour these most magical of things was, I believe, the herald of the arrival of the first angels.

They had needed to test my attitude.

They needed to know how I was likely to behave towards them and how I might treat them.

Had I kept the eggs all to myself, or given them away thoughtlessly, or worse, enslaved them or sold them to the highest bidder on the basis of their magic, then things may not have turned out quite as they have.

What if I had let my Brother in Law smash one in the name of curiosity?

Even the ones I may have given to the "wrong" people; they had their job to do with them for a time.

They always made their way home if they needed to and when the time was right.

I continue to look at mine with wide eyed wonder and joy. Even after all this time, they still bring their magic and beauty and they always help me through each stage of my own spiritual evolution.

Chapter 18

~ GABRIELLE ~

"Come to the edge" he said. "We are afraid", they said. "Come to the edge" he said. They came. He pushed them. They flew."

Guillaume Apollinaire

My life was by now positively drawing people into it with gifts and skills that would help and enable me along my path.

Often they would come in *"through the side door"*.

I would be engaged in something somewhere which seemed a little disconnected from my usual pattern or habit and in the process, a special "someone" would breeze in and that would be that!

So it was with Gabrielle.

I had been browsing the shelves in Waterstones bookstore, and noticed a small crowd gathered around a young woman who seemed to be tying another woman in knots. I was intrigued so I went over to investigate. I had just missed a demonstration of Thai Yoga massage. Absent-mindedly, I picked up the practitioners card and slipped it into my bag.

Some days later, out it popped (this does seem to be a habit!) and I decided to treat myself to a session.

The appointment was at a small holistic shop called "Alternatives" just on the outskirts of the city centre.

I soon found myself lying on a squidgy mat with one leg behind my ear and the other being pulled by a small but determined woman. This was my introduction to Thai yoga massage!

Between sharp intakes of breath, and long gasps of "release", I made polite conversation.

Once my session was ended. I unknotted myself and prepared to leave the shop. On my way out, I was accosted by a strawberry blonde whirlwind, wondering if I had enjoyed my session and whether I would like to book for another. Well, the truth was. . it had been an interesting experience,. . but not one I would be rushing to repeat. So, thanks, but no thanks on that one!

After a bit of chit chat, she introduced herself as the owner of the shop, her name, Gabrielle.

Over the next few months, I visited the shop regularly and got to know Gabrielle quite well. Irish Catholic through and through, she had lived life in the fast and dangerous lane for many years. Now Gabrielle was married to a man many years older than she, with two gorgeous little girls. Some years earlier, Gabrielle had experience a near death experience, resulting in a personal and spiritual epiphany. She knew she must turn her life around or, lose it. (. .but that is her story, and not mine to tell!)

As well as running her holistic shop, Gabrielle worked as a counsellor.

Never was so much energy and dynamism contained in such a tiny frame!

This woman was a "doer", capable of a hundred ideas a minute, and she wanted them all finished by teatime.

It is no accident that her name Gabrielle is related to the Archangel Gabriel and means "Bringer of the Gift and Life". No obstacle was ever too great, no adventure ever too risky and no uncharted water too deep. . . Gabrielle was always there, out front leading the charge. A born enabler and facilitator. . if a little bossy!

As my journey unfolded, and our friendship developed, Gabrielle would always be there with her "kick up the backside" approach; encouraging and chivvying when I started to flail around or get stuck.

She was the one who invited me to take a small corner of her table at a local Mind Body Spirit fair when I first started painting angels (we *will* get to that bit very soon. . . I promise you!).

She was the one who persuaded me to jump in the deep end and take a table at the Spiritual haven that was the Manchester G-MEX event. My goodness, how I stalled and spluttered at the suggestion; it was too soon, I was too small and unknown, it was too expensive . . . my list of "cant's" was endless.

Gabrielle sat at my kitchen table, surveying me through half closed eyes of ice blue, head in hands, and when my protestations got too much she slammed a piece of paper and a pen down in front of me and demanded that I write down all my objections to the prospect.

Duly chastened, I scribbled away, aware of her hard stare boring into me.

When I was done, I showed her the paper with an "*I told you so*" flourish.

"*Hmmmmmm,. . what a load of bollocks!*" she stated flatly "*Get your cheque book out and write me a deposit now! You are going to G-MEX*"

That was me told then!

Of course Gabrielle was absolutely right, we went to G-MEX and had a hoot of a time. Apart from a most successful sales and marketing opportunity we met some truly wonderful people and had some great adventures.

Incredibly, only mere months before this event, Gabrielle had been diagnosed with breast cancer.

It had required major surgery plus chemo therapy.

During this time she lost such a lot of weight and all her beautiful strawberry blond locks fell out. Undiminished, she took to wearing an outrageous "Dolly Parton" style wig, chosen especially for her by her young daughters who thought it was fabulous.

It was typically a child's vision of "beautiful hair"; long, outrageously curly, devastatingly blonde and obviously fake. She wore it with audacious panache, because that is how her young daughters saw her, a woman worthy of such beautiful hair. Once her own meagre curls started to poke through again, she let the girls have the wig to play "princesses", she resorted to a trendy headscarf. I will always see her as a woman worthy of magnificent tresses.

Whilst in hospital, Gabrielle had an incredible experience.

Here is what I recall happened.

Concerned about my friend, having been through such an ordeal, I breezed into the hospital ward the day after her surgery, to be confronted with a grotesque sight. My dynamic Gabrielle was sitting there, swollen and bloated, wrapped in a kind of tin foil, unable to move and barely able to speak.

She smiled weakly as she saw me and just about managed to beckon me over indicating for me to sit near her.

As a gift, I had brought her one of my angel paintings. It was obviously one of my very early pieces, a small watercolour. I felt it would protect and support her through the recovery process. She asked that I put it beside her bed where she could see it.

I stayed only an hour or so, as she was very weak and needed her rest.

A nurse was quite shocked when she walked into the ward and saw me, as Gabrielle was to have no visitors for 48 hours, and even then only immediate family.

How had I got into the ward? demanded the outraged nurse.

Well, I just walked in. . . no one challenged or stopped me. I had no idea she was in isolation. I guess the angels must have sorted that one out! I had perhaps been rendered invisible.

The next few hours were not good for Gabrielle.

She had developed a very high temperature and a nasty blood clot, which was moving dangerously close to her heart. The Consultant surgeon wanted to operate again immediately, but she felt too weak to withstand it. She begged for more time; insisting that her Catholic faith, and praying to the Saints would sort it out. Despite the fact he was not of the Catholic faith, the Consultant could see that Gabrielle absolutely was, and so with due respect he reluctantly agreed that she could have one more night. If things had not improved by morning, she would find herself on a gurney heading back to theatre . . . no arguments!

Apparently, a lot of praying was done.

Before she was finally settled down for the night, a nurse popped in. She picked up the small painting of the angel, and very deliberately and without discussion, moved the angel from the bedside cabinet, to a pinboard, positioned on the wall opposite where it could be clearly seen from the bed.

During that long night of prayer, Gabrielle was dimly aware of unusual activity around her.

At some point, she woke up to see what appeared to be a group of "beings" gathered around her bed "working" on her. As Gabrielle related it to me, they were tall, shimmering and light, young looking, androgynous and featureless. There were no wings, halos or golden trumpets. As they worked they spoke a language she didn't understand, yet she felt safe with them and was able to drift back into sleep.

By morning, Gabrielle felt decidedly more chirpy.

Her temperature was back to normal and the life threatening blood clot had diminished and moved well away from the danger zone. The medical team were amazed and asked her what she had been doing to make such a miraculous recovery. "Praying," she replied matter of factly. "Well, whatever you are doing, you keep doing it," encouraged her Consultant. Apparently, as one Medic shared; they had experienced Faith at work many times before, and could not deny its efficacy, it is an amazingly powerful thing.

Gabrielle's recovery was indeed spectacular and swift. There were one or two little scares along the way, usually to pull her back into line when she had gone off at a tangent, but broadly speaking, she had made a miraculous recovery.

Before long she was back at work, and bossing us all around, clients, employees, customers and friends alike. Hurrah!

Gabrielle had given me the confidence, and permission, to step out of the twilight zone and go public with my angel work.

Her boundless energy and enthusiasm booted me straight through the pain barriers of my experience and her no nonsense approach kept me with my feet firmly on the ground. I am ever grateful for her practical attitude to everything, her willingness to take a risk, and her sense of outrageous fun and ready laughter.

When the time was right for her, Gabrielle moved away from the holistic practice and into other areas of professional interest.

Her shop, was sold lock stock and crystals to Mick.

For my part, I had always relied on Gabrielle to book and organise the increasing round of Mind Body Spirit events. I always saw myself as a "tag on" and when the inevitable happened and Gabrielle moved on into other things, I had to take responsibility for booking my own events.

It was in fact a subtle process.

Initially, we went 50/50 on costs and space. Then, as Gabrielle got more involved with the shop and had her health issues to consider, I booked the tables and leased her the space. She would bring her shop stock along on the day and set it all up.

Eventually, I would take the stock from her shop and sell it for her when she could no longer find the time, or energy, to join me.

Eventually: in the recuperation period, even this arrangement became unmanageable for her; the idea of stripping the shop of stock for 2 days proved too much, and so then I simply booked the table space for my own requirements.

Now I was flying free and loving it.

Thanks to Gabrielle for pushing me off the edge.

♥ *According to my angels : I needed a push to take the plunge.*

There is no doubt that we are sent the people who can help us on our way.

All we have to do is recognise and embrace them.

Sometimes, at first encounter, we wonder what we could possibly have in common.

I was challenged, constantly.

It would be fair to say that at times, my dynamic little Catholic friend scared me with her forthright passion, religious fervour and faith!

Of course, this was all my "stuff" and I would be dealt that lesson later on the journey. My greatest lessons have always been dealt from my greatest fears and prejudices.

Gabrielle showed me how to "see" my gift and how to honour it in a practical way.

The relationship was by no means all one sided.

In turn, I was able to help her with many of her lessons and to support her through her many dramas and crisis. We enjoyed each other's company immensely and laughed pretty much all the way there and back. We are still in occasional touch and although we don't see each other as regularly as we would like, we can always pick up exactly where we left off. We still laugh uproariously at life and its vagaries. Her girls have grown into beautiful, talented young women, and I am proud to know them.

From time to time that original, ridiculous list of my excuses "why not" shows up in a pile of paperwork, or from under some books, and I read it through again and laugh at my own fears.

Here's my original list of WHY NOTs (feel free to laugh too!)

Premises ~no studio (I now have a perfect studio right in my own home)
Contact with printers~ none (I print all my own materials)
Advertising/editorial MBS mags ~ can't afford (I have never had to advertise)
Website/sales ~ don't know how to do (My nephew Craig set it all up for me)
Space/time to keep creative (My whole life is dedicated to this work)
Must be able to "gift" what I feel I need to (of course I can and I do!)
Getting paid ???~ what if people don't pay me for my work (They always do)

So, knowing what I now know, I look back on that list with affectionate recognition and compassion for the woman who had just been catapulted into an unknown world without precedent.

I was so very good at putting blocks in my own path, creating brick walls and limitations where none existed.

It is a wonder that the angels ever got through.

~ SINCE ANGELS ~

Chapter 19

~ THE FIRST ANGEL ~

"Difficult things take a long time, impossible things a little longer."

Oriah Mountain Dreamer ~The Invitation

I promised you we would get to this bit!

You must appreciate, that without the previous chapters, this point would never have been reached, so thank you for bearing with me.

By now, my life had been re-arranged in many ways, and space created for me to breathe again.

My design consultancy work was going well, the spiritual path was unfolding in a mysterious and wonderful way, and my health was now good. I was even out there running, as the T shirt experience would testify!

I had become more accepting of the weirdness that was becoming the norm' in my day to day existence; I was working with a wonderful spiritual mentor to help guide me, listening to messages from my plimsolls, tracking down hi-tech magical powders, hatching mysterious blue eggs, visiting healers with multi-coloured bottles, consulting crystals and exploring the excitements of Gabrielle's shop.

On a day much like any other; a dullish, winterish, pre-Christmasy kind of day, my life changed, irrevocably.

It was Thursday 22nd November 2001.

You may remember that 10 years previously, to the day, I had been awaiting surgery, in conversation with a certain angel who asked me "Do you trust?".

So, here I was, writing a letter to Mrs G. Just a bit of a chatty thing, a catch up before the momentum of Christmas took over.

As I was writing; I felt an overwhelming compulsion to stop what I was doing and to paint!

This was not a whimsical fancy, a mere distracting idea, nor was it something I had been pre-planning in any way.

I had to temporarily abandon the letter writing, and start pulling my papers and watercolour paints together. This was not such a difficult prospect as I always have my art stuff around in my workroom, although it had been quite some time since I had been inspired to use any of it. The last time being, when I used my wax crayons to create the image from Findhorn.

I was very aware that my actions seemed direct and purposeful, although I had no idea what I was going to do, nor indeed had I any idea what subject I was going to paint.

I do know how to compose a painting. I went to art school and I was actually rather good at it.

My formal art school training would require me to have a concept, or a subject in mind, to plan it out as a rough in terms of perspective and composition and to experiment a little with paints and colour levels.

This was totally different.

I was conscious that my hands were active, busy, that a painting was taking place on the paper in front of me. I could not seem to focus on the work with my eyes as it was emerging from beneath the brushes. My vision was somehow slippery, I could not hold it. There was no blindness or darkness involved, it just felt as though I was trying to read small print without reading glasses. My vision couldn't latch on to anything.

As I worked, I had become aware of a sensation; unlike anything I had ever experienced before.

It was as though something HUGE, from the outside, had entered my very being.

A warm, flowing, liquid sensation with a fizzy electrical, metallic quality filled my whole body, entering through my ears and then swiftly flooding down my body into my feet.

It took a millisecond.

It hit the inner walls of my toes; exploding back upwards like an uncorked bottle of champagne, blowing me into a billion microscopic pieces, then pulling me back together again in the blink of an eye!

I was left in a very euphoric, blissful state; warm, fuzzy, slightly disconnected from my own body somehow, but in no way frightened.

This was similar to my experience at Findhorn, but a far more powerful feeling and sense of connection.

I would now use the term *"At One with All"*

Bliss.

In that state of being, I created a painting.

As the blissful sensations eventually subsided, slowly, I began to regain my grip on reality, and normal service was soon restored.

As the final approach to earth orbit began, I heard myself say, "*I call on the Divine Light to bless and empower this angel*" three times I said it, and I was aware that my hands were held in a very distinctive position over the paper. I had created a powerful symbol, but it was unlike any of the Reiki symbols which I had been taught.

My thumb tips met, and my first finger tips met, to form a triangle, through which the energy was now directed.

I was a little bit stunned.

What angel?

What Divine Light?"

The questions were running riot through my head. The painting now before me was indeed, if I had to name it, a depiction of a rather scrappy angel.

Up to that point, I really had no thoughts about angels one way or another. I certainly had never considered what they might look like. However, this, was undeniably, to all intents and purposes an angel.

Actually, my ego jumped in to declare it looked a load of rubbish; as though a child had painted it. I was disappointed in myself and my efforts, and felt I should have been capable of something far more competent. I had been to galleries and seen what angel paintings looked like. If I put my mind to it, I could do a far better job than this.

The painting was almost destined for the bin.

Sometimes ego does strange things, it easily gets in the way of Truth.

This time, it got very short shrift as the Heart waded in and demanded that the painting be reprieved; in fact it absolutely insisted that I should send the painting to Mrs G, along with my yet to be finished, chatty letter.

This was not a question of putting my mind to it; but of giving my heart to it.

It seemed a very good idea. Mrs G had a lovely healing room, and it might make a nice bit of original art for her wall. Yes. . . I felt sure she would appreciate it.

The postman could hardly have left her doorstep, when she phoned me in a state of great excitement.

"How did you create this painting?" she asked.

I gave her the low-down.

"Do you understand what actually happened?" she continued.

Well, truth be told . . . no. . . I had absolutely no idea. Order had been swiftly restored to mind, body and spirit with a nice cup of tea and a packet of digestives. I had felt no inclination to provoke a repeat performance by nit picking over the experience.

With infinite patience, Mrs G gave me her take on events.

In that moment, a moment of Grace, when all the Cosmic energies were in absolute alignment and my soul was receptive and ready to receive, an angel merged with me. I had been imprinted at a cellular level with all the information I would ever need to undertake my life purpose.

This was to be my work.

I was incredulous, and possibly not a little ungracious.

"What work? What are you talking about?" I demanded.

Calmly; and with infinite patience, Mrs G explained to me that part of my souls undertaking had been to do this work. To bring the angelic energies to Earth, creating a Bridge of Light between the earthly and angelic realms and my paintings were to be their vehicle of choice. I would in effect be in Service, painting angels in perpetuity!

Mrs G gave me this deep insight, **"Through your work, the Light of Humanity and the Light of the Divine are unified"**

At the time, I had no idea what those words meant, but my Soul recognised them and they were seeded deep within me, to germinate, sprout, and eventually blossom and deliver their fruit. Over the years to come, my work would nurture and sustain these seeds, and I would come to understand the meaning of this prophesy.

At the time; I demanded a reality check and a recount.

Mrs G was adamant.

This was my calling, and the work had already begun.

♥ *According to my angels: A bridge of Trust had been upheld between Human and the Divine.*

It was exactly 10 years, to the day, between my cancer operation and this first angel arriving.

During the intervening years there had been much preparation, many tests, and my life had transformed dramatically to accommodate this gift.

I feel that in some ways I had indeed "died" and been reborn, whilst still in my physical living body.

The ten-year interval had delivered me a new way of being, a new way of seeing and a whole new world of friends and teachers.

I had been brought back full circle to my first love of painting and "scribbling" and, I was able to earn a good living from my Design Consultancy whilst allowing the connection with the angels to develop. This was my Gift.

In the hospital, ten years earlier, the angel Samael had asked if I could TRUST. I had committed to my "YES!". With all my heart I believe this question related not only to that particular moment and circumstance, but to all that was to come. That "YES" determined my future.

You may well wonder why, having such an extraordinary experience, with such profound feelings, didn't frighten me.

Firstly; it felt so good!

Secondly; I had already been prepared, unwittingly been given little tasters of this experience so it wasn't as shockingly unfamiliar as it may have first seemed.

Thirdly; the angels do not seek to frighten or harm us.

From that moment, henceforth, nothing would ever be the same again.

Chapter 20

~ AFTERMATH ~

"It's not easy to have your reality stretched to the boundaries of the Cosmos and then be squeezed back into your physical body"

Caroline Myss: Entering The Castle

Phew, how would I follow that?

Despite my protestations, and the enormity of the experience, I must have had some tiny microcosm of acceptance.

The seed had indeed been sown and the Light was now feeding and nurturing it within me. Over the next few weeks, on the build up to Christmas, painting after painting, angel after angel came through me. No prizes for guessing what friends and family got as Christmas gifts that year!

Each time, the experience was similar, if not as profoundly startling, as the first.

An early painting went to my mum. She keeps it framed in the spare bedroom. Whenever I go to stay it is a joy to reconnect to that angel.

I am not sure what happened to the rest of them, there were so many.

I do still have one myself, retrieved from Gabrielle's shop when she decided to sell up to Mick. Unbelievably, I had never kept one of the first ones for myself.

I grew to enjoy my times of Divine Connection and tried to embrace the whole thing with an open mind and heart. I had no inkling of where this would eventually lead. I was still working very much in the thick of the fashion industry.

Still, to me, fashion was my world; my life; my comfort zone.

These mystical experiences happened to other "special" people, not to ordinary folk like me.

In a letter to Mrs G, dated 22.1.02, I was recounting an experience with Ray. He had been over for dinner and we had inevitably discussed the angels. I had asked Ray if he would like to watch me create one, as to date, only Martin and our dog Minnie had been witness to the proceedings.

". . . as I applied the first process, we could feel the energy come in. Ray did not even have to put his hand over the picture, as I do, to feel it. The second part of the process which involves applying colour was intriguing because Ray thought I would labour long and hard over it to get the colours in place. NOT SO! I can only take credit for the basic application, then I have to let the "energy" develop the colours and the angel reveals itself through the paint. When the twinkly greyish dust is added, that sort of seals it all in and the light begins to reflect most fabulously. It is very clear when the picture is "done" and all I have to do is add some power symbols. . . . and ask for the Light to join the picture to help it to do its work.

Simple.

Ray showed me how to "feel" the different energy levels by raising my hand a few inches up over the picture to access the mental, then the spiritual energy. I had only been feeling the first level, the physical which gives the heat and the tingles"

I was learning about all this "on the hoof".

Many times I tried to buy books by well known angel "experts" and each time I was thwarted as something got in the way of the book ever being read. I would leave my purchase in the shop, or on a bus or train, or have to give it away immediately to someone else. It was so frustrating. I felt so ignorant.

There was one exception to this. Whilst browsing at "Alternatives" one day, a tiny little book caught my attention by falling off a shelf. "The Allure of Angels" by Mary Grace Rodarte is all of 7cm square!

Delighted, I picked it up and opened the pages at random.

I read *"Be not forgetful to entertain strangers for thereby have some entertained angels unawares"* it was a quote from the Christian bible ~ *Hebrews 13:2.*

I liked it!

Gabrielle had been watching, and from beneath a quizzically raised eyebrow she told me to put the book back. Puzzled, I insisted I wanted to buy it. Adamant, she refused to sell it to me, reminding me that I wasn't "allowed" books. Anyway, she demanded, what was it that I had read that tickled me so much? I recited the words. Well, she declared, if you can remember the words, you won't need the book.

It would have been nice to have had the book though.

A couple or so weeks later, we were setting up for a Mind Body Spirit event and one of the boxes fell open, the little book fell out and shot across the floor, in the process scuffing a corner of the cover.

Gabrielle picked it up, surveyed the damage and asked. . . what was that quote you liked again?

I recited it back to her.

Casually, she lobbed the book over to me, and declared it to be mine. I could now have it, on the basis I didn't need it.

I was overjoyed!

That little book has been such a blessing to me over the years, and serves to illustrate in simple terms the importance of paying attention, and the simplicity of how the angels communicate.

It lives in my "toolbox".

I do understand now, that I had to be taught first hand, by the angels themselves, in order to understand the value of my own story.

At this stage, too much reading and "head stuff" would have got in the way of the heart stuff, and proven a distraction.

As I grew more familiar with the work and more comfortable with the energy, the angels started to deliver their written messages as well as their visual energy imprints through my art.

Each time, the experience was different, yet familiar, I never quite knew what was going to emerge from my brushes, only that it would be beautiful and pure. The words too were delivered "blind" with no corrections, or amendments.

I lost count of the times I would type something onto my computer screen, then make a few tweaks to please my logical self, only to find the computer screen would crash. All my amendments would be lost, leaving only the original unaltered message. I learned quickly, don't mess with their words! They know better than I, what they want to say.

Up to that point, I was never given names for the angels.

I never thought to ask, as they were not for me and therefore it was probably none of my business. Their names were unpronounceable anyway, more like a resonation, like the sound of a crystal singing bowl overlaid with dolphin song; high, thin, undulating and carrying a powerful vibration which enters the very soul rather than the ears. How could I begin to translate that?

Perhaps out of politeness, and knowing how we humans like to identify with our experiences, they chose to give names "by which they may be known".These amounted to familiar names that perhaps didn't sound very angelic.

My mums angel is called Hazel.

Sometimes the angelic clamour would be overwhelming. I often felt like I had entered a Conference Centre full of noisy chatty delegates, all wanting to have their say at once. Putting my hands over my ears was a waste of time, because the sound was not inside my head, but in and throughout me.

I would get extremely frustrated and cross and insist that they be quiet, especially if I was in the car. More than once, whilst driving, I had pulled into a layby and rant at the top of my voice "ENOUGH!!! Get out all of you and make your own way home!!" I must have looked like a mad woman to any passers by. It usually did the trick though.

From time to time, whilst out shopping at a local supermarket, I would get the "call". I would be happily browsing the aisles when the unmistakeable buzz would begin to sing in my ear and quickly spread to the whole of my being. It is impossible to make wise food choices under such conditions, so the only recourse would be to abandon my half filled trolley and stalk, muttering furiously under my breath, out of the supermarket and back home to my studio. There the angels would be waiting with eagerness to begin work, and I would once again pick up my brushes on their behalf.

I am sure I got a reputation at the Supermarket as "that woman who never finishes her shopping" I bet their CCTV cameras had some amusing footage! One time, I even drove off from the fuel station forecourt without paying, such was the distraction. Fortunately no harm was done.

I often felt physically propelled from behind, as through unseen hands were on my shoulders, marching me smartly back to my studio and my paints. The angels were (and still are) hard taskmasters.

Remember, I was fitting all this around an already very full life. Admittedly, certain arrangements had been made to allow that I had more flexibility, more support, and more time, but frankly it was little enough when I look at what was being asked of me.

One afternoon I was at my wits end.

I had delivered an important presentation to a Fashion client, late, because of my distractions.

I had forgotten an appointment with Rachel for a pilates class. . . unheard of!

Martin had been snapped at when starvation had forced him to ask when his lunch might be ready.

The dog had been sitting with crossed legs whilst I studious ignored her baleful eyes asking for walkies.

I was probably still in my pyjamas at midday!

The angels, fabulous as they were, constantly distracted me with their chatter and activity, I swear they were almost hanging off my skirts! I began to feel out of control of my own life, overwhelmed, a little resentful, and nostalgic for "normal".

This was starting to feel like a decidedly unbalanced relationship.

If I was to stay sane, balanced, and continue to earn a living then I MUST be able to have time to myself, undisturbed.

I decided to tackle it as plainly as possible.

I put the kettle on and got the digestives out.

Sitting at the kitchen table, I poured myself a good strong cuppa, and called the angels in.

"Right you lot. . . we need to talk" I declared. There was no ceremony, no incense, candles or lala music laid on for the occasion.

I poured out my feelings to them.

I needed balance.

I needed time to myself.

There was no question that I would undertake the work for them, but it had to be an equal partnership.

I was not on 24 hour call.

This was all new to me and I was having to get used to a very different way of working. Could they please cut me some slack and back off a bit. I would be no used to them if I was constantly exhausted, stressed about fulfilling my Consultancy contracts and frankly feeling a bit, . . well. . .manipulated.

After my outburst, silence prevailed.

I had a sense of angelic conference, mutterings and discussions.

I sipped my tea and munched a digestive.

More angelic mutterings.

We finally reached an accordance.

We would work together at times when it suited both parties. .

They admitted they had got overexcited at the prospect of a real live physical being who could communicate with them and undertake their work. They had forgotten all about human time-scales and linear existence, they had forgotten all about the practical considerations of "earning a living", having dinner, and the domestic stuff we humans have to do.

Apologies were offered, and accepted.

Together we would be able to move forward as co-creators and equal partners.

In Accord. In Unity. In Collaboration.

There ... that felt a lot better.

♥ *According to my angels: My "Service" was going to require some getting used to.*

This was an unprecedented experience.

The fact is, you cannot take on this kind of work without having to make some adjustments. There is no way you can just carry on regardless; there is no "normal" any more.

To this day, people come to me seeking guidance on how to fulfil their own destiny, how to connect with their souls purpose and wanting what they perceive I have. They often want it without disruption to their existing lives. They fear what making changes may mean, what will they have to sacrifice, what will they lose? Conversely, they may feel they want to give up everything they know; their relationships, their homes, their jobs, to move away "somewhere" more appropriate.

I am here to tell you, you are kidding yourselves. It is not necessary. You can fulfil your souls purpose exactly where you are, around what you do, with the people you love still in your life. It is not the external stuff that really matters, but what is happening within you, within your own heart centre. If you are prepared to walk and work in your own Truth, then you can be anywhere, with anyone, and you will still do it.

OK, that sounds a bit simplistic, and I underwent a process which facilitated certain changes in me, but we each have our own process, it is not a one size fits all experience.

Find your path, feel your way, stay open and aware.

Do your best.

If you have a yearning, a calling, a pull . . . please follow it.

Don't try and second guess what the purpose might be.

Don't judge your own competence either. Whatever it is, find a way to follow through.

Take a class, join a group, take a trip, make the leap of faith.

You may find the "thing" is just a stepping stone to something bigger, as Reiki was for me.

Nothing is ever wasted if you learn something from it.

With awareness our whole life becomes our practice.

PS: I just want to share a final thought, it made me giggle when popped into my head . . so on that basis here it is.

As we may go on workshops, or meditate to connect with angels and the spiritual realms, I have a vision of all these angels on a workshop hoping to make connection with a physical human being. As we get excited when we manage to connect, and then assuredly make the most of that connection, I am sure the angels feel the same when they find one of us who is able to communicate with them. Do you think they ask each other "Do you believe in humans?" Maybe on their side of the Light, there is an inspired Angel painting images of us, and there are a few "humans" pinned on a celestial wall?

Chapter 21

~ EVERYDAY ANGELS ~

"For of those to whom much is given, much is required."

~ *John F. Kennedy*

I had been given rather a lot.

I was being expected to deliver rather a lot too.

As well as juggling my professional work as a Design Consultant, my domestic life as a wife, and my spiritual work as an artist to the angels, I was being directed to keep my physical body fit and healthy.

So, not only had I started going out running, I had also joined a local gym.

My usual training routine included a 30 minute stint on a cross country ski machine which counted the calories and gave a very comprehensive readout of effort expended.

Starting the session always involved a certain amount of moaning and groaning and reluctance as I counted down the minutes "Oh God, 29 minutes to go!" then "Oh no. . . . still twenty minutes to go!" It was mind numbingly boring and I could not wait until the ordeal was over.

This is when the angels like me best. . . when I am occupied in mind numbingly dull stuff! This; is when they seize their opportunity to move in and tell me things.

I had barely started my dull routine, when I was "downloaded" a whole concept of what my work with the angels was to be called.

The name "EVeRYDaY ANGeLS" appeared large in my mind, rather like a Cinemascope screen, and their words followed in a torrent.

"EVeRYDaY ANGeLS *have been sent to us to help us deal with the trials and tribulations that get in the way of everyday happiness and well being. Created as individual artworks- each angel carries its own healing energy. Practical, willing and joyful workers, they demand nothing more than to be welcomed into your life and allowed to carry out their loving, healing work.*"

I was brought back to the moment by a loud pinging noise, the timer had just rung for thirty minutes. I stared in disbelief at the screen in front of me. The reading registered over 4,000 calories . . . for 30 minutes work! This was a confirmation for me that the information I had just been given was indeed from the angels, the machine had read the powerful energy as "calories burned" and had given a most spectacular readout.

In my wildest dreams I could not expect to burn more than around 300 calories on that particular exercise, even on a good day. 4000 genuine calories would have left me in a melted heap.

I felt I had probably done enough exercise for one day.

I decided to use the name, and to produce some stickers and leaflets using the words and logo which would appear on my artwork.

The name entirely suits the work. We are practical, workaday, grafters, we do indeed work together every day (no high days and holidays off) . The angels have become so totally integrated into everything I do, they are ubiquitous and omnipresent. We are unified.

I had begun selling a modest amount of my work through the Mind Body Spirit fairs facilitated by the generous kick up the backside meted out by Gabrielle. The new name seemed to resonate, people liked it and I felt comfortable using it. It became our working title and "flag of convenience"

In deference to the angels, and as a matter of common sense, I had the name registered as my Trade Mark.

The unusual use of upper and lower case was an important part of the process. Somehow, this undulation created a visual "key" and created an energetic connection at a very subtle level. Initially I found it hard to remember to change the script every time I wrote it, and eventually the computer seemed to "get it" and write in that style whenever I was working with the name.

Take a look.

Experience how different it feels if it is simply written in more traditional font and regular use of upper and lower case.

Everyday Angels

or

EVeRYDaY ANGeLS

Around this time I also registered my website domain, but found I was not allowed the simple www.everydayangels (already registered to a community care group) so I had to go for www.everydayangelsart. com which forced me to acknowledge the "art" part of my work.

Flying under the now well recognised auspices of EVeRYDaY ANGeLS, I am not only able to offer my artwork, original paintings, cards and prints, but written channelled words which when delivered in public domain at my workshops and talks, undoubtedly touch hearts and souls at the deepest level. I am always delighted when I am invited to work with a group of spiritual adventurers, to deliver a workshop experience or to contribute to a special event. I spent many years behind my trestle table at the Mind Body Spirit events around the country, which introduced me and my work to a receptive and wide audience. I and my angels remain accessible, it is important that we do so, or otherwise there is no point to what we do. I am so grateful that we found each other.

♥ **According to my angels: I am the custodian of their Word and their Light**.

As a very capable designer, I have often had struggled with concepts especially around names. Often, the devising and anchoring of a Brand name (for that is what EVeRYDaY ANGeLS have become) has been a job for committee and consensus.

I must also acknowledge that my husband Martin works with this kind of Branding in his own business. It was mildly confounding to him how I just "got" stuff, when in his world there was a process to follow and certain rules to be applied.

My way with a font often left his hair standing on end!

However, my directive, be it words or images was so clear and perfect it required no alteration or amendment.

The simple visual style of my angels belies the complexity behind them. They are "devices" and are as identifiable in the world of angel art, as the Nike tick is to sportswear.

At this point. I still struggled with the concept of being recognised as an "artist".

It felt a bit fraudulent and I still found it easier to refer to myself as a "designer".

Old habits die hard even on the path of Light! By registering the website domain, including the word "art" forced me to acknowledge that part of the deal.

Those of you who are sharp of eye and mind, will also spot that the word "art" also means "is" or "to be", as in "Our Father who art in Heaven. . ."

So, EVeRYDAY ANGeLS art!

Indeed they are!

There was always a misplaced coyness within me when asked "Are you the artist?". I would reply "No, I just paint the angels" which confused quite a few people,. . . sorry if you were one of them.

It took a long time, working with the angels and selling my paintings and cards before I finally accepted, with good grace, that I was absolutely "the artist".

I am often asked why I do not sign my name on the artworks. The reason is that even as the artist, I am merely the channel and I have no right to claim the work as mine in that way. Also, I find it so distracting when looking a piece of art which I would regard as meditative, to find my focus distracted by a scrawled name across a corner. The "signature" on my work is more subtle, it is the device of the angel itself, or sometimes and more recently a small coloured feather may be worked into the paint in the final stages of completion. Sometimes, not always, as I have to listen and follow the guidance of the angels not my own ego.

I am the artist.

The difference is these days, this is not how I define myself.

These days; I am indefinable but immediately identifiable!

Chapter 22

~ THE ANGEL T-SHIRTS ~

"The main thing you will tell people, is that they are ready for what is about to happen. Many will be fooled by the simplicity of the message; but remember – the deepest truths are always clothed in the humblest garments. . ."

James Twyman – The Secret of The Beloved Disciple

If you ever bought one of these T shirts from me, you will probably remember it with great affection.

Is there anything more humble and simple than a T-shirt? Everybody wears them, everybody loves them. They are Universal garments, honest, classless, timeless, and uncomplicated.

My experience with creating the concept of the CHAkRA T shirts had well prepared me for doing the same with the angels.

It took no time at all before the angels were nagging me for their own T-shirts.

So, they channelled through me a series of seven very specific angels, each relating to the physical chakras which were to be used as the graphic image.

It was never going to be enough just to have a pretty picture and some clever slogans printed onto the garments. The purpose was much more than to simply wear an image, the purpose was, to wear a vibration. Using the same technique that I now used for channelling my angels, I could energise each t-shirt with my own touch!

When I say my work is channelled; I mean it comes to me without my own consciousness getting in the way. I work in a state of freeflow, without a fixed idea of the outcome or any fear of whether I may be able to "do it" or not. This is fantastic, because everything I have been called upon to create for the angels, or indeed any of the Divine Realms has been beyond my experience.

If I had relied on what I know, I would never have done any of this.

I knew it would work, it was exactly the same principle as before.

The guys at the printers were ready for me. Once the T-shirts were printed they were returned to me, unpacked, so I could put the finishing touches to the whole thing. I selected the crystals, wrapped them in a small scroll of channelled words and popped them into a tiny canvas bag, this was attached with a pin to the back neck label. Each T-shirt was then pressed, blessed, folded and packed into a neat cello bag and sealed with a special sticky label.

Perfect!

I was even guided to a brilliant selling fixture which comprised a collapsible metal frame with a canvas shelving system, each compartment the exact size to fit a folded t-shirt pack. This meant I could easily take the garments to the Mind Body Spirit events with my angel paintings. They looked very professional and very fabulous!

Now here's a funny thing!

The printers related a very strange story to me which they believe was directly connected to the angel T-shirts.

One night, the factory was broken into. The burglars got in through a window which opened directly onto the printing table where the angel T-shirts lay drying. Ignoring all the new state of the art, hi-tech equipment that had just been installed, they helped themselves, with some considerable difficulty, to some old defunct kit which was due for disposal.

Nothing else was touched although there was quite a lot of personal stuff lying around and much of their finished stock was highly desirable designer brands. From time to time in the past, whole collections of designer goods had been stolen from the factory premises. The printers believed the angels saved them by attracting the thieves to the unimportant stuff. You see, the angels cannot intervene and stop events happening, what they can do is damage limitation.

Everybody loved the angel T shirts, they sold really well and I could not get enough of them.

As a habitué of the fashion world, it astounded me to experience the response to these garments. They were touching people at a very deep level, far beyond the remit of a basic T-shirt. I kept the whole thing very simple, one background colour (white) and two fits, "fashion fitted" and "baggy". The quality of the T-shirts was excellent and meant they could be machine washed at 30 degrees. This was very important as the garments quickly became favourites and were worn time and time again. The angelic energy never left them, even after washing.

I repeated my orders several times over a period of a couple of years and then suddenly, despite continued interest and sales, I was guided to stop making them.

It just felt like their time was done. All my retailing instincts were champing at the bit, you never drop a "hot" product. My inner guidance was quietly reassuring me that this was OK, time to let go. Something else would be waiting for me.

So, I simply sold out what I had left and that was that.

They live on fondly in my memory, and I know that is true for a lot of my clients who had them.

Right now, I have no plans to re-introduce those t-shirts, but then again it is not my plan is it?

♥ *According to my angels: I work with intention and it is enough.*

This had been another massive learning curve for me.

The exercise was to understand the practical magic of putting a positive vibration into a simple everyday product, by intention alone. .

Without complication or protocol, the angelic energy was made available to everyone and could be worn next to the skin to provide a very direct contact. The energy was programmed in, wearing or washing in no way diminished the efficacy.

The process of "empowering" was nothing more than the time it took me to fold and pack the garments, running my hands carefully over the fabric, just so, and working with LOVE. This was not a task to be delegated or undertaken by me half heartedly or begrudgingly.

I now understand, absolutely, that all I need to do this work is already within me.

It requires no fancy machines or special gizmos, just pure intention and absolute unconditional love.

If I listen, then I hear.

When I hear, I can act.

When I act, I create.

When I create, I am expressing my TRUTH.

All things have their time, their season and their reason, and that was part of the lesson too.

To let go when letting go is required.

Alison Knox

♥PS: *Very recently, a friend returned a brand new unopened angel T shirt to me, saying she just felt I would like it back. What a perfect and timely reminder. It was still 100% zingy after all these years.*

Chapter 23

~ GETTING TO KNOW YOU ~

"Employ your time improving your self by other men's writings so that you shall come easily by what others have laboured hard for"

Socrates

Great advice, Socrates; but there was to be no easy route for me, everything had to be learned from my own experience.

No books, however well known and esteemed the author, were permitted on the subject of angels. I have to assume the angels who worked with me wanted me to learn directly from them rather than gleaning from the experiences of others. I am anyway not a particularly academic learner, I am far more experiential. If I fancied and bought a book on the subject of angels, I would invariably lose it, leave it in the shop or anyway never get to enjoy reading it.

For a long time, the only reference I had was a cheap paperback "A Dictionary of Angels", by Gustav Edmundson. I had bought it many years before all this happened and pretty much shoved on a shelf and forgotten about.

It was to prove a Godsend as I got to know who's who!

There were times when I became frustrated at my own ignorance, and ended up having tantrums.

However, I understand now that the angels were hard taskmasters for a reason.

I had to understand this experience in my own way. They would show me all I needed, and explain everything in ways that could be shared with others, in simple words and by example.

Initially, I had no idea who was who.

Sometimes it just felt like one big noisy clamour of "voices" all demanding attention at once. I struggled to hear what was said and to understand what was asked of me.

So here are a few of my favourites.

ATHENA'S CHIPPENDALE ~

One afternoon, Athena turned up with a large canvas under her arm. It was plonked down on the kitchen table and made available for inspection. There was no actual picture as such, just a subtle merging of colours, not unlike a sky-scape.

Athena asked that I should paint some angels onto it.

I balked.

I didn't do canvas', only watercolours at that time.

Athena was adamant; she needed to see angels on it.

I went up to my studio and got my twinkly glue stuff and my twinkles. Taking a deep breath, I applied three angels to the surface, just where it felt right. It was as though I could see where they need to be positioned, even though there was no obvious markers.

Whilst the angels were drying and settling in to their new canvas space, we had a cup of coffee and a gossip and when it was time to go, Athena took the still damp angels home with her.

A couple of days later I had a rather excitable 'phone call from Athena. She needed me to go over to her house around tea time; she had something important to show me.

As requested, I pulled up outside Athena's house just as it became dusk.

With great excitement, Athena invited me into the house, and insisted that before I went any further than the porch, I take a look at the painting.

She switched off the lights, all except the porch light.

From where I stood, the painting could be seen resting on the back of a sofa against the wall at the far end of the lounge. It was illuminated in the most inexplicable and bedazzling manner, the angels were almost leaping off the canvas and the whole spectacle was quite breathtaking. WOW!

Athena explained that when she had returned home with the painting, she just pretty much plonked it down on the sofa for want of anywhere better to put it.

She then had to hurry straight out to an evening appointment and so had decided to deal with the positioning of the painting when she returned. When she arrived home some hours later, the house was in darkness except for the porch light. As she entered the house, she saw this gloriously illuminated sight of three angels dancing across the back of her sofa.

After a few moments of "Ooohing" and "Aaahing", we went inside to have a cuppa.

The doorbell rang and it was Anne one of Athena's colleagues from work, dropping off a big bag of low fat sausages.

Anne came in to join us and was quickly captivated by the three angels on the sofa. We all got up to peer at them more closely and

173

we all experienced the same distinct impression that the smallest one, kept flitting in and out of the painting. Sometimes it was there, and then not! It amused us for a good hour or so. Eventually, Anne had to drag herself away from the angelic entertainment, and bid us good night.

We both saw her to the door and waved goodbye at the porch.

Like a pair of giggly schoolgirls we could not resist putting the lights out and having one more look at the magical angelic display.

This time, we got more than we bargained for!

Written in light, as clear as day, was a perfectly defined head and torso of a very handsome male figure; not unlike the Michelangelo statue of David. The head was turned slightly at an angle and the body was well defined with a magnificent six pack of muscle. Disappointingly, the vision only manifested to the navel. We looked at each other in delighted amazement, then grabbed each other by the arm to take some tentative steps towards this vision of beauty, for a better look.

It required many peeks and giddy squeals before we felt we had probably seen enough.

Athena insisted I take the painting home to show Martin this magnificent being. I most certainly had not physically painted it in, so it was definitely "other worldly".

Martin was quite tickled at the idea of an angelic "Chippendale" and waited with great anticipation to see him. However, despite my attempts at recreating the lighting conditions prevalent at Athenas, we were to be disappointed. The "body beautiful" never showed itself again.

Discussing the incident with Athena, we both believe that this was sent to us as a little perky "thank you". Athena had prepared and delivered the canvas. I had placed the angels into it.

Things had just moved on to yet another level and my work was about to change quite dramatically.

ARCHANGEL MICHAEL ~

A few days after this delightful interlude, I was drawn to buy some canvas'.

It was another "deep breath" moment for me, it had been a long time since I faced a large, blank white canvas, and I felt a little nervous.

My initial purchase was quite modest, but included several different sizes which would give me a bit of scope to play around, see what happened.

The process of painting the canvas was quite different to creating the watercolour.

It was great fun experimenting.

In no time at all I was sent back to the art suppliers to get more materials. They had a special offer on the canvas', a very large one of about 100cm x100cm caught my attention and ended up in the back of my car.

I sensed this was going to be something or someone important, but I had no indication who or what was going to manifest. There was a vital urgency to begin work, and I had a distinct hankering for a cup of espresso coffee with a small piece of very dark chocolate on the side. This craving was hard to shake off and it seemed to increase in intensity as I worked, as a coffee guzzler, I had to give in regularly.

Most bizarre!

The angel that came was a magnificent being of great and powerful bearing.

The energy, most definitely male, and the shape formed on the canvas was most assuredly "handsome" (despite having no discernible features). The colours carried in the painting were gold, fiery oranges and reds and a high fine vibration of blue/ violet. The final effect was an explosion of heat, flame and fire, white hot and intense.

The name I "got" was Archangel Michael.

At first I was rather suspicious of whether this might have been my own wild fancifulness coming to the fore. I was kind of happy and pleased that it was Michael, despite his fiery presentation I somehow felt comfortable with him and rather liked his energy. He introduced himself as "Warrior of Light" (initially I misheard him and thought he gave me WORRIER of Light! That gave me pause for thought until he corrected me) He told me that he was the angel of the Central Sun, his mission; to cut us free from all that holds us back from fulfilling our life's purpose.

No mean feat!

Michael claimed that he carried a large and impressive sword which he used with great enthusiasm in the cutting free process. I challenged him on this as there was no sign of a "mighty sword" in the painting. Was I supposed to paint one in for him? I could hear the deep throaty angelic chuckle as he amused himself with my ignorance before explaining that it was simply a form of energy which was already imprinted into the painting. He was the sword; the sword was within him. I didn't need to take everything so literally. When he needed it, he would manifest the sword from within his own self.

Well . . . excuse me, how was I supposed to know that?

The reason I doubted my own perception was due to the fact that several months earlier I had watched a soppy film that became one of my all time favourites. "MICHAEL" was a rom-com road movie with John Travolta in the main lead as Archangel Michael. It was a silly, heart warming comedy with some wonderful moments. I particularly enjoyed the sequence when Archangel Michael makes his first appearance, walking down a flight of stairs wearing only his boxer shorts, with a beer can in his one hand and scratching his bottom with the other, a trail of feathers falling behind him as he made his way to the breakfast table where he proceeded to eat a bowl of sugar with a few cornflakes on top. The warm hearted, but embarrassing, image stayed with me . . . as you can tell.

It would have been all too easy to fancy the idea of it being Archangel Michael, especially when I envisaged him in his John Travolta guise.

This painting was truly beautiful and powerful

My concerns over his identity were quickly dispelled as I introduced him to the public at my Mind Body Spirit events.

He was instantly recognisable to those who were open to his energy. Many fell in love with him, and made generous offers to buy him from me, but the answer was always the same "*This angel is not for sale, he has come to share his light with all*"

Often, I would take him into a public talk with me and would invariably get someone from the audience who had been "zapped" by him. Once, at the end of an event I was approached by a healer who worked with crystal sounding bowls. Apparently, Michael had stepped in to work with her during a particularly difficult healing session. She had witnessed this huge, radiant being holding the energy for her whilst she worked. Although the therapist had not been into the main hall where I was situated, she had felt that was where he had come from and so followed her instincts until she found him, on a very large canvas.

Over time, there were several "upgrades" as my energy evolved, so it was possible for Michael to upgrade his energy through fresh applications of paint, as called for.

Ray had introduced me to a wonderful Shaman, named Lynne, who lived and worked in Hawaii and was experienced in the Kahuna traditions, working with the Ancient Ones. Lynne was one of those who helped me to hone my spiritual skills and knowledge further, and although we never met in person, only ever speaking on the telephone, we developed a powerful and spiritually intimate friendship.

Lynne and I shared a very funny moment with Archangel Michael.

One day, we were in the middle of a conversation and Lynne said "*Oooh, one of your angels has just turned up! He has something he wants you to know*" Intrigued, I asked her to tell me more. She declared it to be none other than Archangel Michael, and his message for me was, that he didn't mind how I saw him.

I was puzzled.

How do I see him?

Lynne laughed out loud and spluttered "*John Travolta in his boxer shorts!*" I was beside myself with laughter, how could she have possibly known that? It was a rather embarrassing secret and not one I chose to share publicly. The only one who knew was Michael . . .so it had to be him there in Hawaii. Perhaps he was wearing his beach shorts this time!

I understand that this way of seeing him had been a "softener" so that when I met his energy, I wouldn't be too overwhelmed. If I had that silly little vision to hold onto it would make it easier for me. He does have a great sense of humour . . . very entertaining.

ARCHANGEL MICHAEL'S CRYSTAL ~

Gabrielle had arranged an event at a local bookstore and I had taken Michael along as "star turn" with the selection of smaller more humble angels who were indeed available for sale.

As I unpacked my things, I was aware of a couple on the table opposite who were preparing a display of beautiful crystals. It became hard to pay attention to my own business and I found myself wandering over to their table and poking about in the boxes and packaging. My hand alighted on a large lump, carefully bubble wrapped, my heart started racing. I asked permission to unpack the crystal, and could hardly wait to get the wrapping off. Inside was the most staggeringly beautiful piece of quartz, about the size of a large grapefruit with an outer layer that looked like golden sugar and a highly polished sliced face revealing fathomless depths of light. Within the crystal there were splashes of bright red, almost like drops of blood and multitudinous facets of rainbow colour dancing and vibrating with life.

As I held it, my attention was demanded by Michael, I looked over my shoulder to him, and in that moment I knew,. . . this was his crystal and I had to acquire it.

I knew very little about crystals, per se, but enough to know that this was no trinket piece. The stallholder told me the technical term for the crystal was "dragons egg" due to the rounded shape formed as the rock bounced and rolled around the riverbed of its home in India. The orange and red were due to the iron content, and would balance the high vibration of the quartz with an element of grounding.

The price was not unaffordable, but more than I had available to me at that moment.

Again, I felt Michael prompting me, "Ask them to keep it for you. You will earn enough today to buy it."

Once I had set my intention, the crystal was reserved for me and I could relax a little.

We did indeed make enough to buy the piece, and a little more besides. The acquisition was another step to upgrading the energy for this very amiable but very demanding angel.

Alison Knox

Michael and I developed a very tangible relationship, although I never "saw" him with my eyes, I was always very much aware of his presence and energy. He has a bluish violet light which I often perceived around me as I worked. He also had this funny habit of getting me to take dark coffee and chocolate together. When that craving came, it meant he was not far away.

The painting of Michael had chosen a rather unsuitable roosting spot when he wasn't out and about working with me. In our bedroom, there was a very small bedside table which could barely accommodate the huge angel, but he insisted that was where he wanted to be. It made me laugh. . he looked like a great big parrot sitting on a tiny budgie perch. At night, as we slept, Michael would go about his nocturnal business. It was quite palpable when he was "in" or "out" and we were often awakened around three o clock in the morning by huge shifts of energy in the room. Martin referred to the "celestial catflap" clanging.

I suspect he must have spread the word to the other Archangels that I was an accommodating artist, because in due course, I was given other "calling cards" for each of them.

Michael stayed with me for a few years, earning his keep by being the "star turn" at many of the Mind Body Spirit events which I was now attending regularly as a stall holder.

MICHAEL LEAVES THE NEST ~

There was one particular Mind Body Spirit event weekend, when I was feeling very sorry for myself. My husband was working away, and our dog Minnie had recently died, I was feeling a bit bereft.

I had just set up my table and parked Michael in the most prominent position available. One of the other stall holders came by, and we got chatting.

180

I kind of knew Trish, she worked with the energies of Archangel Michael. In fact, in June 2003 I had gifted her a small Michael canvas in gratitude for her company and good humour;the message scribbled on the back says" *For Patricia. . . who made Lincoln worth it x*" .This became her "*working Michael*" who travelled around with her as Trish visited her clients and hosted her spiritual development groups. He was small enough to be discreet, but powerful enough to deliver the healing when called upon to do so.

Trish and I shared a bit of chit chat, and she was telling me that she had recently invested in a "Sanctuary" at her home. This amounted to one of those very well appointed sheds, squeezed into what she described as a pocket handkerchief garden. I knew Trish lived rather cheek by jowl with her very extended family, including an elderly mother, a husband, a school age granddaughter, and various adult children who seemed to drift in and out depending on what was going on in their own lives. In amongst this family chaos, Trish offered healing, spiritual development and ran a meditation group, hence the need for the Sanctuary.

As we were chatting, I felt Michael perk up. He had been listening in.

He made it clear that he was fully intending to go home with Trish and live in her Sanctuary.

I was quite taken aback.

He insisted.

This was potentially embarrassing.

I gave him the morning to change his mind, but he was having none of it. I had to go and find Trish and ask if she could possibly accommodate a rather large and demanding angel in return for his help and support with her meditation and healing sessions.

Trish looked at me as though I was a little mad.

She told me she didn't have the money to pay for such an angel, she had only just paid for the Sanctuary. I persevered; I was not asking for money, the angel was not for sale, I just wanted to know if she could accommodate him.

She, of course, said YES!

It was interesting getting him into her little hatchback car. You see, I now had to use an MPV for transporting my angels around, and he was the biggest of them all. I swear he "breathed in" to make himself fit into that little car, otherwise he would have missed out on going to his new home.

I gained two really important things from that experience.

The first gift being, Trish and I became firm friends, brokered by Michael.

The second gift was to be delivered later that evening.

THE LIGHT OF THE WORLD ~

Still feeling sorry for myself, with husband still away, and dog still dead, and now abandoned by my favourite angel who had flown off to a new home, I faced the drive back home to Nottingham from the event venue with a heavy heart.

There is a particular bit of road, which I always enjoy driving, and on this evening, as I turned onto it, I was aware of a brilliant, milky white light, pearlescent and bedazzling ebbing and flooding over the road. It was so bright and luminous, I felt I needed to pop my sunglasses on. However, they were just out of reach, so I had to keep my eyes open and pray that I could keep the car on the road as I could see nothing but this light. As I drove, the light infused the car, and once again I experienced that sense of pure blissfulness that comes with the presence of angels. It was beautiful, if a little dangerous.

I drove back home with a feeling of certainty that I must get started on a new painting as soon as I got in. I had no idea what or who it would be.

As luck would have it, I had a large blank canvas just waiting in my Studio for me to work on it. It was bigger even than the Michael canvas.

I started straight away.

No need to worry about making dinner, my husband was away, there was no dog to need walkies, the cats could entertain themselves, so the evening was all mine.

I applied myself to the work, and didn't stop until it was finished. The last thing I was guided to do was to apply a pearlescent glass heart to the chest of the angel. I have no idea where it came from, it was just there, on my work top, seemingly waiting for me to find it.

The painting was the exact embodiment of the experience I had felt on the road driving home, a vibrant, pale, shimmering pearlescent, beautiful Light.

That night I fell into a deep sleep and yet somehow managed to get myself up and ready for day two of the event.

I had hoped the angel would be ready to accompany me, as I now had a huge gap on my display which it would have filled very nicely. However, no, it was not to be.

When I saw Trish that day, I told her of my beautiful experience. She suggested that I had to let Michael go, in order for me to receive whoever this new one was. I also remembered that story of "The Vintners Luck" and my revulsion at the idea of entrapping an angel. I would never have done that to Michael.

This new angel soon revealed itself, bearing a most beautiful message.

> *"I am the Light of The World.*
> *Look into my heart and there you will find your true love.*
> *Is it not the most beautiful thing?*
> *Look into my heart and know; you*
> *have been there all the time.*
> *I within you; you within me. Perfect and Divine."*

The whole timing of the manifestation had been perfectly orchestrated to coincide with a Celestial event of "Harmonic Convergence ", where the Illumined Beings of Light presented themselves to Humanity, over the Teton mountains in the USA.

How did I know this?

Well, coincidentally I had just been sent an e-mail from an American Lightworker, Patricia Cota Robles, and it had been printed off, unread, left for "later". The information contained within that message resonated with my own experience and the descriptions of this "Light" matched mine perfectly.

Patricia Cota-Robles named the angelic presence "Immaculata"

If you take the last two words on my own angels message; "perfect and divine" that would neatly translate into a single word "immaculate".

I never had permission from my own angel to refer to it as "Immaculata", so it remains fully titled "*The Light of The World*".

I do appreciate that Nottingham is rather a distance from the Teton mountains, but I know angels are capable of omnipotence, so I do not doubt they seized their moment, especially as there was now a free space in my angelic line up.

When I shared this information with Trish, she was astounded as in her Sanctuary, she had a small print by the artist Holman Hunt, entitled "Light of The World".

A few weeks later I had a profound experience with this new painting.

SPEECHLESS ~

As a very regular exhibitor at a local Mind Body Spirit event I had been invited to give a public talk, on the subject of angels of course. Actually, I had pretty much cut my public speaking teeth at this particular venue, and was regarded as a popular and entertaining Speaker. I could usually pull a "full house" crowd of up to 100 people.

This particular weekend saw me slightly disadvantaged, I had lost my voice.

It was not a sore throat or a cold, just a loss of voice. I was barely able to rustle up a whisper which was OK, for more intimate over the table conversations but rather more challenging to deliver a whole one hour talk.

However, undaunted, I refused to cancel my engagement, and soldiered on through Saturday and into Sunday. Well meaning friends,healers and therapists, hearing of my plight, generously came over and gave me their best efforts, to help heal the throat, with crystals, sound, Om chanting, Rescue Remedy and even some very nice boiled sweeties.

Nothing made any difference.

Time was marching on, and I was due on any moment. The queue had snaked around the block, and people were now making their way into the lecture room.

The organiser came over and asked if I wanted to cancel.

I refused.

Originally, I had planned to take in a bevy of my finest Archangels, they are always excellent back up at a public talk. However, something made me take only the new painting "The Light of The World".

As I walked into the lecture room, bearing my huge angel canvas aloft, I could feel a frisson of excitement rippling through the crowd. I wondered if half of them hadn't come just to see the spectacle of how I would manage this with no voice.

I surveyed the room, taking in the beaming faces and the bright eyed anticipation.

I did a little reality check, my throat was still not co-operating. With dismay, I realised that I would have to declare myself unfit, apologise, and withdraw.

Pulling myself up to full height, and with as much bravado as I could muster I spoke *"Hello, everyone. .. I must apologise . . ."* but there was no apology needed, my voice was fully restored and vibrant. I coughed a little just to make sure I wasn't kidding myself, and started again, "Hello, . ."

Yes, I was back in business, fully voiced. I delivered my talk, an account of the coming of this amazing angel, and when my time was up, and the talk over, the voice left me again.

I was confounded.

People were already asking me; how had I pulled that one off? So many had heard me try to speak, whilst behind my table, and had offered sympathy and advice. They knew I had not improved sufficiently to deliver a one hour talk without pause or splutter. This voice had resonance, power and volume behind it.

This experience had been a perfect a way of testing my fortitude, and of showing me, demonstrably, that there are times when my physical being is "hired out" to the angels and simply provides a handy and safe vehicle for them to deliver their messages directly.

It is absolutely what I understand to be a Channel.

Although I have never had quite this same profoundly challenging experience again, I do have moments when the voice I know as mine, changes somewhat and the angels take over.

It still feels very strange.

ARCHANGEL RAPHAEL ~

As his "calling card", Archangel Raphael, the Healer, delivered me the sensation of chocolate mint chip ice cream just as it is about to slip down the throat. Actually, I am not very fond of chocolate chip mint ice cream, so I knew I had no ulterior motive for getting the taste of it.

Raphael always struck me as rather quiet and shy. Often, as "The Healer" he has to mop up after Michael has been out and about, wielding his mighty sword and doing a bit of cutting free. With the best will in the world, sometimes freedom causes pain and abrupt release from long imprinted patterns of behaviour and belief require rather radical surgery.

Raphael always appeared to me in a vibration of dark green, gold and blue, almost oily and iridescent and not unlike the plumage of a peacocks tail feathers.

His touch is cool and breezy, his fragrance is very clean yet earthy, like petrichor after a summer storm.

Often people call on Raphael for healing.

He would wish to point out however, that he can only provide the tools and facilitate the process, he cannot "do" the healing.

The healing must come from Self.

One afternoon, I received a phone call from a lady who wanted to buy a selection of my printed angel cards. She wanted several of the

Archangel Raphael . Curious, I asked why she needed so many. She told me that she often worked with Raphael in her healing circle and she wanted the cards to share with her group. She also had a real problem with her back, which had given her some considerable pain recently, she could do with the ministering touch of Raphael herself.

That sounded fair enough, not that it was any of my business, and so I promised her that I would get them in the post as soon as possible.

Barely had I put the phone down, when I was aware of Archangel Raphael's presence, that distinct breeziness and the fragrance of damp rich earth enveloped me gently.

He asked me to phone the lady straight back.

Why?

He asked me again, just phone her back.

I did as I was bidden, although I admit I felt rather foolish with no agenda.

"Ahem, it's me again" I ventured when she answered.

Before I could say another word, Raphael had taken over, and I just allowed him to take this lady through a simple visualisation, healing process. It was one I had learned myself, and used very successfully, but delivered directly by Raphael, its simplicity belied its power.

This is what Raphael asked for: ~

"Identify the source of your pain or discomfort as a shape.

Take that shape and soften it to something more bearable."

(for example, if the pain was a sharp spiky ball, then the visualisation process would take it to a soft squidgy ball with no spikes).

"How big is it?

Make it small enough to bear."

"Identify the colour. . . . soften it to something more bearable. . . then render it to pure white light."

(for example, if the pain was a deep fiery red, then softening to pale pink and then to white would bring relief).

"Give the pain a sound. . . and soften it to something more bearable."

(for example, if the pain sounds like thrash metal, soften it to some gentle harp music or birdsong).

"Give the pain a fragrance . . . soften it to something bearable."

(So, if the pain smells like rotting fish in a Wellington boot, then soften it to something beautiful like roses).

What I found so interesting was that at all stages he only ever invited this lady to "make it bearable for yourself", he didn't actually offer to take it away.

Sometimes, we need to feel stuff, to know it is real, and to accept that as humans we may from time to time have to feel what is uncomfortable. We are amazingly resourceful and resilient beings, and we can manage our own pain and grief, if we just allow ourselves to.

This simple exercise in Self healing required no special skills or training, just a belief and trust in its efficacy.

When Raphael was finished, he asked the lady to sleep. He suggested she sleep for as long as she could, to help the process of healing.

I said a polite goodbye, and put the phone down.

DASKOLOS ~

Raphael left, as he had arrived in a breeze of earthy sweetness.

I turned my attention to a small canvas, propped on my easel. I had already prepared the base, with a fresh coat of white paint, and now it was calling to me to begin work.

My brushes were at the ready, so we jumped in and made a start.

This was another experience altogether.

The portrait that manifested on my canvas was a beautiful depiction of a gentle, calm featured youngish man, with flowing locks of deep violet and blue hair tumbling around his face. Around the head was a multi-coloured aura, swirling and sparkling in a rainbow of soft hues.

The face was at once familiar, yet I was sure I had never seen it before.

When I finished the painting, I added the finishing touch, some special crystals of a type called "aurora borealis" they contain all colours and none, which give the eyes light and life, They suited this countenance perfectly.

The name I was given to use in reference to this beautiful being was "*Daskolos*". It is a Greek word, and can be used as a familiar yet reverential name for a "great teacher". Skolos means scholar.

I also knew that the face I had painted was in fact a depiction of the being we know better as the Master Christ or Jesus.

I felt a little uncomfortable with this knowledge, although by now, despite my non religious background, I had become more familiar with the Christ Consciousness.

In my understanding, the Being we know as Jesus or Christ, did indeed live amongst us as a great Master Teacher and left a great

ACCoRDiNG to my ANGeLS

legacy of teachings and wisdom, to help us as humans, make sense of our place and purpose within creation. Many of His teachings were deceptively simple, and are now referenced within that which we know as the Bible. He came to Earth with great purpose, and imprinted His energy upon the Earth plane through his day to day connection with it. What I recognise as Christ Consciousness has nothing to do with the bible or religion, but everything to do with what it truly means to love, consciously and creatively. Christ Consciousness exists within the most humble of tasks and circumstances if they are undertaken with that prerequisite of love.

I shared my thoughts, as stated above, with Serhat, a highly spiritually evolved friend we met whilst on holiday in Turkey. This is what he offered, and I really like his analogy.

"To my experience, one can only plant seeds of greater consciousness in another person, not a fully grown tree. And if the receiving person has the kind of soil and water to nurture the seed, then the seeds will sprout and grow, at the appropriate time"~ Serhat 22.09. 12

This particular depiction, with the dark violet hair, crystal eyes, and the rainbow aura of light and colour, takes ethnicity and racial ownership out of the equation and makes him accessible to all, as "Daskolos" the Master Teacher.

The next day, my lady phoned me back to thank me for the Raphaelic healing. She shared that she had not slept very well for days, due to the pain, but this conversation and process had permitted her a sound and wonderful sleep.

There was a slightly embarrassed cough, and she asked if she could share something else, something a little . . . well, odd.

Whilst she slept, she had a vivid dream.

She was visited by a beautiful man, wrapped in rainbows and light. She recognised the man as Jesus. Her staunch Catholic upbringing had never shown her quite this image of him, but in her heart, she just knew that is who had come to her. She felt very blessed.

I had to thank her profusely for sharing that with me, as of course it helped to verify my own experience.

Of course, I had to tell her about the painting, which must have been created at the same time as she was dreaming.

I took a photo of the painting and sent her the image. Yes, this was the man who came to her. The angels are not just facilitators for us humans, but for other Light Beings too.

They can pave the way for moments of Divine Grace .

In this instance; Raphael, created that moment for Daskolos.

ARCHANGEL GABRIEL ~

Archangel Gabriel chose another ice cream related experience, as his "calling card", except this time it was the smell of the ice on the outer packaging of a tub of raspberry ripple as it is taken from the freezer. (honestly . . . I don't make this stuff up!).

I perceive Gabriel as a light silvery pinkish violet energy, and he carries a bright orb or crystal which is set within his heart centre. It pulsates and rotates like a vortex. When the recipient is ready to receive the gift, this orb or disc can be made microscopic and is set as a tiny seed within the blessed one. It is in effect a "seed of potential" because although it has been set, it is up to us to nurture that seed into fullness and fruition.

As the bringer of the Gift, Gabriel is often the herald of news from the Divine Realms. I perceived him as a gentle presence and not given to unnecessary chat. I suppose when your job is to deliver messages of great importance to Humankind, you don't waste your words. I occasionally sense his frustration with us mortals as we can be very limited in our vision and expectations.

There was a time when I was hosting a workshop for a group working with Archangel Gabriel. The group were asking to be shown their "gift" and expectations were of course running very high.

At the tea break I went to put the kettle on and was rather abruptly pulled to one side by Gabriel, in all his pink and silvery light, he insisted I write a message down for the group.

I had to abandon the tea making task and go and find a pen and paper, pronto!

I detected a slight sigh of irritation in his voice as he delivered these words:

"Beloved; how was my gift to your Heart?

Do you feel a little short changed?

Do you wonder I could not have made more effort?

I smile at your disappointment.

The simplicity is familiar is it not?

You have seen this before and turned away wondering that it could all be so simple.

I am simple. . . . . I work in a simple way. It is you who choose complication as you feel it justifies you. You do not need justification.

The fact you are is all you need to know.

My gift to you is perfect, as you are perfect.

Consider your place in my Heart; and ask; would I offer you anything other?

Beloved; accept my gift of Self and know; it IS that simple.

Worth ALL. . . . as YOU are worth all."

Gabriel then challenged me to read the words out to the group.

There were more than a few tears shed as those words hit home, straight to the heart centre.

More recently, I had another experience with Gabriel which I would like to share with you here, as it is important, but it does require a bit of a jump forward in the whole time scale of events.

I had invited an interesting young man, Mark, to come to the place in Nottingham where I keep some of my most powerful paintings, and where I now run many of my workshops.

From time to time, I meet such people who hold a particularly bright light, and whom I recognise as a "soul connection". It is not necessary that I invade their lives, but simply to offer what I can to facilitate the journey. When my part is played out, we may never see each other again, or maybe we do . . . there are no hard and fast rules with this.

So, this young man was in the company of my angels, six of my special canvas's each 6ft x 2ft, holding the energies of a particular Archangelic presence.

I also now have a very special CD which has a sound experience imprinted, related specifically to each of these paintings. (The CD was created by a man named Ian Richmond, but more of him later.)

We sat in meditation before the angels, with the CD playing, and allowed whatever was to come, to come.

We had no agenda.

At some point, the disc started jerking and playing strangely. I knew it wasn't playing the actual track on the disc, but I didn't feel inclined to get up and try to fix it.

The sound now being played was very different, and strangely compelling. I hoped that my guest wouldn't get up and try and fix it either.

The tracked played its self out, and then the final track came on, playing perfectly normally. Phew!

Afterwards, we compared experiences, and we both laughed out loud about the wobbly track, as we both had hoped the other would not interfere.

I went to check the track, and discovered it was that related to Gabriel.

It had triggered a memory, it broke a dream I had the night before.

In the dream, Gabriel had given me a wad of long thin papers. They looked like the paper chains we used to use to make festive decorations at Christmas. Each paper was 8" long and about 1" wide. I was asked to hold them in my hand, with each paper layered on to the next in 1" intervals. There came a point of course where the layer of papers lay thickest, this is the point where Gabriel asked me to hold them, between thumb and forefinger.

I asked him, "*What is this?*"

"*You need to create the sound*" he said, nodding towards the papers in my hand.

I had no idea what he meant, and he was obviously not in the mood for explaining, so I woke up with a sense of having been shown something important, but no idea what!

This meditation had brought it all back to me.

Now the picture became clearer.

I had recently asked Ian Richmond to re master a track of sound which he had created for me called "Angel Heart", it had to be made exactly 8 minutes long. In the context of the dream, it was this particular track that I had held, layered over itself 8 times.

I just knew it to be so.

8 times 8 minutes in a roundelay.

As I shared the experience, Mark suggested that I needed to get Ian to re- engineer the track exactly as I had been shown it.

I am no musician nor am I familiar with the workings of a Digital Sound Deck, but Ian is.

The obvious thing would to be to ask him if it was possible.

I asked.

Ian declared that of course it would be possible.

A day or so later, I received an MP3 sound file with a cheeky little disclaimer "*Hee heee*" from Ian.

The track is known as "8x8" and it is indeed a gift from the angels, delivered by Gabriel.

I believe this "Soundscape" has the ability to open the human heart to its greatest potential, that the Seed of Light may be planted and stand chance of nurture and growth. The sound is created in such a way that within its repetition the heart is opened fully and wholly.

I feel truly blessed to have been gifted this amazing tool, and I love sharing it with others at my workshops, or when public demonstration allows it.

I urge you not to dismiss your dreams, even if you do not fully understand what they mean.

Time holds the keys and we can be assured that when the time is perfect we will know.

Sometimes, it takes another person to turn the key, to "break" the dream.

Gabriel is rather like a Celestial delivery driver, he often has to take the Gift back to the depot and reschedule delivery for when we are" at home" in a more receptive state!

ARCHANGEL URIEL ~

My experience of Archangel Uriel is quite subtle.

He kind of infiltrates my day and brings a gentleness and peace to the most frantic of moments. I feel held, and enfolded and stilled in warmth and sparkles.

Uriel brings Beloved Peace and seeks to show us harmonious ways to live our lives, in acceptance, without conflict or struggle.

He chose a non-food related taste, but one that was very familiar to me from childhood, the licked end of a graphite pencil.

My perception of Uriel is of crystalline lightness and beauty dressed in softest pinks, dove grey and a pearlescent silvery white that vibrates and radiates from beneath the colour.

It took me a while to get used to these familiar energies.

They showed infinite patience and grace as I stumbled my way through the "getting to know you" process.

At times, it is fair to say I got completely confused.

THE ANGEL of SOURCE ~

A beautiful, gentle angel had come to me dressed in pales gold and yellow with shards of apricot and soft peach, like a sunset on an early summers evening. The energy was feminine and the stance graceful and open. I had no name for "her" but knew that in time the name would be revealed if it was appropriate to do so. She didn't seem to hold her form for long, sometimes seeming to disappear from the canvas, as though she had to pop back to her own dimension from time to time to recharge her energy.

I took a phone call from a journalist who worked on a locally based spiritual magazine called "Source". He had been made aware of my work and wondered if he could come and interview me for the next publication. I saw no problem with that and so invited him over for a chat. After he had left, he called me again to ask if it would be possible to send him a photograph of one of the pieces of work for him to use as a front cover shot for the magazine.

With great enthusiasm, I gathered my angel paintings around me and asked *"Is there an angel for Source?"* Without hesitation, the beautiful golden angel vibrated resoundingly in response to my question and I understood she had put herself forward.

I took some nice photos of her and forwarded them on.

I was not quite prepared for the response of the journalist who declared that he absolutely must acquire the painting, he had fallen in love with it. I wasn't expecting to have to let her go, and not to that particular individual, but it is not for me to judge these things. I suggested that I take the painting to my next exhibition which I knew he would also be attending. Subsequently, I received several phone calls to ascertain that I would definitely be taking the painting, he seemed most anxious about the arrangement.

The beautiful angel was given pride of place on my table, and she attracted many admiring glances. When the journalist turned up, he walked straight past the table, then realising what he had done, he retraced his steps and stood in front of my work, hands on hips. "I thought you were bringing that angel with you?" he stated.

I pointed out the large, prominent position piece. The reaction was quite profound. He backed off, and became almost incoherent. I noticed he could not look directly at the painting. Words spewed forth, and I understood that the angel was not what he was expecting, he thought it was too expensive, and he would have to go away and think about it.

I was mildly annoyed, but in a way, I was relieved the angel had not gone to him. I was puzzled by the contrasting responses from "love at first sight" to almost; repulsion.

The beautiful angel came home with me again.

Eventually, I understood what had happened.

We had a misunderstanding, she and I.

When I asked for *"The Angel for Source",* she replied, because that was her name.

She was known as *"The Angel of Source"* or "Source" for short!

Source, was never intended for that individual and so she had to do some fancy footwork to make sure she did not go to the wrong place with the wrong person.

I was getting used to angels with well known names, this was a new energy, a being who felt as yet so very unformed and unfamiliar with this dimension and had only recently been given permission to come through. That was why she found it so hard to remain manifested and stabilise her energy.

Within a very short time I knew where she had to go.

Hawaii.

The wonderful Shaman, Lynne was the one who was waiting for Source, and it seems Source had been waiting for her too! They had much work to do together.

When the moment was perfect, I was able to post the painting off to Lynne.

Source came twice again.

On both occasions she moved on very quickly and knew exactly where she needed to be.

♥ *According to my angels: I will know them, as they wish to be known*

It was always very tempting to want to find out about the angels, but it was made very clear to me that reference books and other peoples experiences would not be very helpful, merely distractions, as the angels wished to educate me themselves, directly.

I had to TRUST and practice patience.

Chapter 24

~ ENTERTAINING ANGELS~

*Just fragments seen in the murky mirror of mortality; when bright
Beings shine momentarily in the brief dream of living."*

Ben Okri ~ Starbook

Many of the angels that come through to me now are of such a high
vibration that their names do not translate into human language.

Nevertheless, I am called to entertain them, even as they are
strangers to me . . . and they can of course be very amusing!

They often make their introduction rather like a hazy whispered
breath, drifting in and out of my awareness until their confidence
increases sufficiently to allow me to glimpse them. Even so, it is
rather like catching a brief glimpse of someone familiar in a mirror,
or a shop window; yet as you turn they are gone.

Here is how it feels sometimes.

Imagine, you have arrived as the honoured guest at a party or a
conference, and the room is crammed full of people. You look around
you; and there are those you recognise instantly, you know their
names and something of their personal background, and you can
greet them warmly and confidently by name and exchange some
personal words between you.

Then there are others you recognise, but only by reputation or
acquaintance, you may or may not know or remember their names.

Some will approach you, and introduce themselves, reminding
you of some previous encounter or connection. You may politely

acknowledge them, and maybe even make a note of their names and promise to make contact again.

Yet others, you will accept as welcome faces at your gathering, but you do not know them, friends of friends perhaps, yet you may nod or shake hands in greeting but it is not necessary for you to know any more than that. They will be breezing through your life and out the other side, as if they never where at all. They anyway leave a positive and beautiful energy in their wake and so that, is all you need to know.

Occasionally a stranger will approach you with such illumined determination and purpose that you will make a point of spending time with them, hearing their story and determining your connection. You may feel an immediate resonance and know that you will not lose touch with that one.

My experience of the angels is similar. There are those I recognise immediately and from afar, and those I am merely acquainted with for the time we undertake our work together. Some are just momentary fragments of connection. I do not develop neediness or attachment to any of them, not even the most beautiful!

It is not necessary for me to know the name of each one that passes through, in fact it is really none of my business. They often remind me of this fact when I get too inquisitive.

The moment when an angels name is shared is very precious; once the name is expressed to a human soul, that angel may be called upon at any time.

The relationship between human and angel is very profound and not to be diminished through idle curiosity. As the names are unpronounceable, they will give a "name by which I may be known", this may be something very unglamorous or seemingly ordinary and often human expectation requires something altogether more "angelic".

My advice is to put all pre-conception aside and allow whatever you are given to settle. You may find that the name crops up several times over a few days or so, on TV, in a magazine article, an introduction to a new colleague or you will hear it called out in the street. This will be a confirmation, don't dishonour it by wanting something fancier. The higher the vibration of the angel, the harder it is for them to integrate in our dense dimension and so a good solid name is an anchor point which helps them to hold the energy in order to be with you.

We have to find ways of meeting them halfway.

They lower their vibration; and we must raise ours proportionately.

Another way the angels introduce themselves, or certainly introduce their energy, is through crystals. Crystals help them to meet us more comfortably.

Michael had already shown me the importance of the crystal for his own vibrational growth and there were to be a few more crystal acquisitions along the way as the angels revealed themselves to me.

Sometimes, the angels went to great lengths to get me where they needed me to be in order to "receive" and so when I got the directive to attend a Colour Therapists Conference in Oxford I should not have been surprised.

I am not a colour therapist, so I blagged my way in and paid a rather considerable amount for the privilege. There was an impressive list of guest speakers, although to this day I have no idea who they were or what they talked about.

At registration, in the foyer of the Conference Hall, there were a few interesting tables including one selling crystals.

My focus was absolute as I approached; I could see a piece of crystal that appeared to have a bright violet/blue light running around it, almost like an electric current. The main part of the crystal was a dull solid looking brown mass but the interesting part was a milky whitish pearlescent violet with flashes of green and red and blue. I had never seen such a thing. My hand reached out for it, and almost simultaneously my other hand reached out and picked up a small solid copper ball.

The sensation of the crystal was like an electric shock running up my arm and branching off at the shoulder into all the other parts of my body, the copper ball seemed to counteract this sensation and stop me exploding!

I asked the vendor how much the beautiful crystal would be, expecting to have to pay a fortune for such a thing. *"Oh, the opal, . . it's £12. The copper ball is £7. Would you like to buy them?"* I must have nodded agreement because I wasn't really capable of stringing words together in sentences. The pieces were packaged up and handed over with a word of warning "You won't sit with those on your knee all day will you? That opal is really powerful." Of course, I sat with the crystals on my knee all day.

My consciousness had shifted and I was no longer in the seminar. I have no recall of what was said or who spoke. By the end of the day I knew I had to ground myself before I got in the car to drive 2 hours home. A strong cuppa and a cake usually does the job nicely.

The new crystal was kept close at hand for the forthcoming days. It felt necessary to be in its presence and to pay attention to it. We were getting to know each other.

I was inspired to begin work on a series of four watercolour paintings. They were pretty much my usual style and nothing out of the ordinary in terms of materials. However, as I began work on the fourth one, I had a sense of something massive. . . . something significant and huge.

On the paper the angel looked no different to the other three, but energetically they were like chalk and cheese.

The energy was so overwhelming that I needed to go out of the house whilst the angel came in. I went into town for the afternoon and amused myself around the shops.

When I got back, I was aware of a presence of great majesty and magnitude. Cautiously, I opened the door to my studio and peered in. I felt I needed to ask permission to enter my own space.
Three beautiful, gentle angels sat with heads lowered whilst the fourth angel bristled and vibrated like a large annoyed tomcat who has been brushed up the wrong way.

There was certainly no aggression or anger but something else, which seemed to be of an urgency and immediacy to "get on with it".

Cautiously, I had to ask what was required of me and without hesitation, a directive came to send the painting to Mrs G's friend, know to me only as "The Master". Let us simply say "I knew" what had to be done.

As I had no personal contact details for The Master, it would fall to Mrs G to deliver the angel, so I gave her a call to warn her of its imminent arrival. The answer machine was on, so I just left a brief message. There was no time to waste, the angel had to be packaged up and posted off that very afternoon and I was chivvied and harried until I got my coat on and scampered down to the post office.

I felt such a sense of relief once the painting had gone, although that feeling was to be short lived. When I got home, the energy of the angel was still very present and palpable. Although I never usually ask their names, I felt I needed to know this one, and so sought permission to be availed.

"METATRON", a voice seemed to boom in my head, with a resonance only produced in human form by the classical actor Brian Blessed. Sorry, but I had less than no idea who Metatron was, and could barely pronounce his name, and so I had to resort to my "A Dictionary of Angels" bought on a whim some years earlier.

According to the trusty tome, Metatron is commonly known as "The Voice of God". He is a powerful Archangel who project manages and delegates to the other Archangels. He is always aware of their activities and reports directly on all doings to God.

As the voice of God is too brain shatteringly awesome for mortals to hear without instant death and annihilation ensuing, Metatron is given the task of delivering the messages to mankind, or delegating them to other angels to do so.

Within my own experience of Metatron, in this current time, he is also sent by God to heal the wounds inflicted by man; upon man in ignorance and fear. Much of his work is with the abused and broken, particularly women.

I felt it only fair to call Mrs G again and let her know who was due to arrive through her mailbox. Again, the answer machine was on so I left a short, to the point message *"The angel says his name is Metatron, and I think he is probably right!"*

When Mrs G called me the next day, she was shaken and a little stirred. She had received my somewhat anxious messages, so had been lying in wait for the postman .

Once Metatron had arrived safely, she had undertaken to deliver him immediately to "The Master".

Upon opening the package, there had been an immediate sublimation of energies between angel and human, as Metatron and "The Master" were reunited.

Mrs G had described the moment as quite touching and emotional for all concerned. It would seem that this moment had been long awaited and "The Master" had almost given up wondering just how Metatron would get to her. Now they were together again.

I do love a happy ending . . . or beginning!

I understand that I really am only the delivery girl, the facilitator and channel. The work of the angels goes beyond my limited comprehension and it is perhaps as well that I do not know the magnitude of it. The responsibility at times can feel overwhelming and I must confess, in the early days, I felt less than adequate for the job.

Metatron was not finished with me yet. I was subsequently to bring him in several times over the next few years. Each time his energy became stronger and his appearance more defined and physical. One incarnation, channelled in January 2006 is absolutely magnificent, and this resides in my husband Martins workplace.

His message rather challenging.

"*There are hearts who, as yet, feel untouched by the hand of the Divine. Hearts who shrivel when kindness and love are offered, turning like the dog who bites the hand that feeds it, though starving. The hunger breeds fear and the fear brings more hunger. Deprivation of the soul is the cruellest way to live and the hardest way to die. The heart is the fountain centre of Being. Feed the heart before the belly! Mankind can endure much of physical deprivation before the Soul chooses to leave, but when the heart is deprived and allowed to become a withered and empty husk the Soul cannot be sustained. I come to you now and ask, in all humbleness, that you feed your Soul and keep your Heart full and warm. There is no Divinity, nor Grace in hollowness. Look around you. . . . . offer your love and warmth especially where you see the lack in another. Do not be embarrassed that your offer will be spurned, or mocked, you will touch that heart anyway, at the Highest level. It may be a small kindness, a loving gesture or a gentle word, but it will make its way home carrying the Light of Source which illuminates and succours all. I hold your Heart as my own, and in Love, blessed be*"

Previous versions of Metatron always seemed to find their way to the people who understood his work and were not afraid to embrace his energy.

I have come to understand that part of my work is very much about getting these angels to where they need to be to undertake their work. The energies can imprint again and again, there is not, one; definitive, version. Each time they come they deliver a slight adjustment, a recalibration, another aspect of themselves, or they raise their energy level, depending on who or what they are destined for.

Over the years, Archangel Metatron would become one of my closest angelic allies. I no longer feel his prickliness, and he no longer bridles.

I experience him as a HUGE presence, broad of shoulder, he is dressed in a type of armour, styled rather like a Samurai with a helmet and full face visor always in place. He has a very dark violet blue energy, with a holographic silver metallic "skin". He pulses and flashes as though his very being contains bolts of lightening. His fragrance is rather like an electrical discharge as it has hit the earth.

Every so often, I will be on the verge of losing my patience with someone who is simply not "getting it", and I will be aware of Metatron, standing behind me, whispering into my ear *"Hey Alison, remember, There are hearts as yet untouched by the hand of the Divine"*

"Yeah, yeah, I know". . . and everyone deserves to be treated as though they do understand, but sometimes it can be so hard!

Then our relationship deepened.

One night, not so long ago, I was sleeping an unaccountably troubled sleep. Tossing and turning, my discursive mind playing monkey tricks with me. I was in some self inflicted torment. Martin, my husband, was getting up very early to drive to an appointment, and of course I was anticipating the alarm rattling me into wakefulness around 04.00am . I was feeling as miserable as it was possible to feel.

Somewhere within the torment, I was aware of a large masculine presence standing beside the bed, peering down at me with great compassion and concern. I heard my name called, and I looked up to see this huge angelic presence beckoning me.

"*Come here, come here,*" he entreated, holding out his huge arms ready to enfold me.

I was ungraciously suspicious.

"*Why?*" I demanded.

"*Come here*" he invited a third time, beckoning like a father to a child.

Despite myself, I felt myself arise, and enter his great embrace.

As he held me close he told me "*I love you; I love you: I love you*"

Still ungracious, I told him not to be so silly, as he didn't even know who I was.

He looked at me with eyes of unfathomable colour, set deep within a face of such extraordinary, brutallly broken beauty, it made my heart weep. That face and those eyes had seen it all, been there, done that, and lived to tell the tale, and now he was holding me, and telling me that he loved me. . . . and I was denying him.

Holding me ever closer, he declared; soft "*I do; I do; I do*"

Relaxing now a little within this unconditional embrace, I turned my attention to criticise his hair. "Please, tell me this is not your real hair? It must be a wig!" I was looking at a thick shock of wiry, unruly hair, not unlike a horses mane, but vibrant peacock blues with a metallic sheen unlike anything I had ever seen before. The fringe and crown hair stood on end like a crazy Mohawk, and there was a large jaunty swag tied loosely at the nape, and slung heavily over his shoulder draping onto his chest. He seemed to be wearing some sort of casually styled oriental pyjamas, made of a soft warm cloth I had no name for.

Abashed, he took my hands and placed them in his hair; I felt the warm, wiry, waxiness of it through my fingers, and in that moment, I became one with him and everything else, sublimated by Light, and then delivered, in the same moment back to my bed.

The alarm went off, as I invariably knew it would, and I awoke with a start.

All my fears were gone, but I still felt the warmth and texture of that strange hair in my hands.

I must have dozed off again, and just about recall Martin kissing me goodbye as he tootled off to his early appointment.

Later that morning, still feeling very much "held" I went about my day to day stuff, and took the dog for her morning walkies. I parked the car in our usual spot, and as I unloaded my dog and her two best doggie mates, I noticed a van parked next to me, and upon the tailgate of the van was emblazoned a word which made my heart sing.

Pa'az

Unaccountably, I knew this to be the name of my wiry haired visitor. The knowing filled me with such unbounded joy, I had to call the name out loud as we went about our dog walk.

Each time I said it, the deeper it touched me.

When we returned to the car, I took another peek at the van. The tailgate actually read "Ford Topaz". Sometimes, the angels hijack what exists and supplant it with what they need us to see. It bears no logical scrutiny, but the feeling is indelible.

A day or so later, a client called me asking about some random angel they had been in communication with. I confessed I didn't know, it wasn't one of mine. However, I offered to look it up in my faithful dictionary.

The page opened at the letter "P".

The first name on the page was PAZIEL; another name by which Archangel Metatron may be known.

I nearly passed out.

Now fumbling to find the angel the caller had asked about, but to no avail, I apologised for my ignorance, and went straight back to letter "P" as soon as possible.

In that moment I understood, my relationship with Metatron had entered a new level. He had effectively revealed himself to me, by removing his usual protective headgear, and wearing only his more "at home" clothing. I felt I had been entrusted with this experience. To see his face, in all its broken glory, was a real privilege. I knew he carried a softness. I loved him all the more for it.

The name Pa'az, is a diminution, a "nickname" if you like. It has to be pronounced in a very specific way, that way he knows it is me who calls him.

As a final gift, I was permitted to paint his portrait, exactly as I encountered him that night. The actual canvas is modest in size, but that is typical, the physical size is no real indication of the power within them.

It is not a "pretty" picture, but it is exactly him.

ARCHANGEL AZRAEL~

This mighty Being, presented himself on 27.7.07 as a large painting (100cm x 100cm) wearing wearing a patina of what I can only describe as verdigris.

Azrael looked like a bronze statue left outdoors to weather in the elements. The colour vibration of greens/blues/violets illuminated by shimmering gold. (He hi-jacked my new twinkly eye shadow from Superdrug and insisted it be spread over his wings). He also asked for a rather beautiful blue opalite crystal heart to be set within his own Heart Centre.

His reputation does him no justice .. often referred to as the angel of death he is in fact a facilitator of change and transformation.

Working as an ally to Michael and Raphael, who are often called upon as bringers of healing and release, Azrael will contribute and help the process when invited.

Often however, we just want the problem "sorting" we don't want to engage in the messy business of changing the way we live our lives.

Azrael encourages us to take responsibility, instilling a level of acceptance within us that we may embrace change, and integrate the necessary process of transformation from one state of being to another with grace and ease. We may, of course, continue the painful struggle, to fight and balk: change will happen anyway, it must, it is the way of things.

Change creates the Circle of Life.

As is often the way with my angels, he showed me a kind of cinemascope film in my head, in which he held out his hands and presented a collection of small coppery coins.

Peering into his great open hands, I was puzzled.

"What is it?" he asked *"What does it represent?"*

"Erm,. . . money? Wealth? Abundance?" I proffered.

Patiently, he showed me again.

"What would you call small coins?" he asked encouragingly.

"Change?" I cried delightedly. . *"Change!"*

Yes, Change, that is who I am and what I represent. People are very suspicious of me" he stated *"they always expect that change will bring less than they had before"*

Once his energy was fully integrated into the painting, I was able to include Azrael in my workshops and he always insisted that I found some small coppery coins to offer as tokens to the participants. I had to offer the opportunity to accept change . . and once that small token was taken, change would be imminent!

ARCHANGEL SANDALPHON ~

Showing up on 09:09:09, he gave me a little puzzle to work out too.

I found myself staring at my feet and watching in amazement as my footwear transformed and segued from delicious bejewelledness, through to strong sturdy leather, then flimsy cotton, and rough hopsack, elegant velvet, to inflexible wood and thousands of other styles and forms of shoe before settling on the image of a pair of well worn, simple, honest soft leather thonged sandals. I could almost feel the grit of the road between my toes.

(I do so love it when they play these games with me.)

The angel who had presented himself was extremely tall, a glorious sight in shimmering pearlescent silver and pinks, I could almost have mistaken him for Uriel or Gabriel but his size was so much greater and his fragrance was so distinctively different, he emanated the fragrance of the rose.

Within his great Heart there beat a glorious rose pink crystal surrounded by a garland of clear bright shining stars. I was made aware that these stars represented the gathered prayers of the faithful, which may be granted if you have the courage to ask for one, and then to allow it to be released without condition to be returned as an answer to your own Heart.

In the painting which held his energies, he is an exceedingly tall, magnificent and compassionate being who offers his Heart as a weapon of Light in the eternal battle of Love over Fear.

Sandalphon, is often recognised being as the twin brother, or "co-brother" to Metatron. Sandalphon is said to have walked the Earth as the prophet Elias whereas Metatron walked as Enoch. They both have a distinct advantage over other angels as they have existed and experienced the human condition and therefore have a greater empathy for what we have to deal with.

I do appreciate an angel who has a fancy for fine shoes and necklaces!

ARCHANGEL RAZIEL ~

Sometimes angels can take a bit longer than others to declare themselves, and so it was with RAZIEL.

I had a rather intriguing painting perched above my workstation for quite some time. He was soft in colour, with distinctive bronze/gold wings and a well defined body. He had never spoken or made any demands, other than to be created in the first place, and so I allowed him to remain in his spot above my desk without interference. I found him to be a rather quiet and thoughtful angel.

Thus we rubbed along nicely for some considerable time.

One day I received in the post a rather sweet certificate from a lovely lady named Angelina who has a newsmag "Angels World". I had made a contribution of an article which she published, and by way of thanks she had sent me this document. The message on the paper was from the Doreen Virtue Archangel Oracle cards "Spiritual

Understanding". Touched by her considerate kindness, I laminated the paper, and found a place to pin it right next to this silent angel.

Sometime later in the day, I paused in my work for a nice cuppa, and sat on the sofa in the bay window of my studio. As I sat and sipped, the sun broke through and delivered a bedazzling display of light on the wall opposite. I felt the energy from it. Intrigued, I got up to have a look at what was creating such an effect and realised it was the laminated sheet from Angelina. The light was merging the angel and the script together, and in that moment I understood that this was the introduction I had so long waited for. The certificate bore the name of Raziel. I had initially missed that bit!

Raziel brings esoteric knowledge and Truth. He reminds us that once we ask to be availed of information, we cannot then "un-know" it. He is like the keeper of Pandora's box.

I didn't take Raziel out with me to the MBS events, he was very much a "stay at home" type, but one night he made it clear he wished to accompany me to a talk that I was delivering to a spiritual group in Derbyshire.

Perched casually on a chair beside me, throughout the whole session, he flirted outrageously with a lady on the front row .She insisted that she had to buy him from me as she knew they had work to do together. Who was I to argue?

Reader, of course I had to let him go!

♥ **According to my angels: A miracle is a shift of perception.**

I was increasingly able to commune with the angels in a very direct way.

It felt miraculous.

My acceptance of their funny ways, and lack of neediness to hang on to them, or to prod and probe into areas that were frankly none of my business, made it so easy for them to work with me.

I no longer became quite so irritated and overwhelmed. My perception had shifted. Our relationship had softened to something more equal, more intimate.

I felt quite honoured at the trust and faith they placed in me and my ability and willingness to be of Service.

We were definitely making progress together.

Chapter 25

~ EARTH ANGELS ~

"An angel can illume the thought and mind of man by strengthening the power of vision, and by bringing within his reach some truth which the angel himself contemplates."

- Thomas Aquinas ("Bliss of the Way")

Angels are primarily messengers, they are here to help us achieve our souls purpose and to guide us, as best they can, as we go about our day to day business.

I have already shared with you my experiences of the angel at the hospital, and the grey faced angels who forced me to sit on my hands, and the angel who hi-jacked me to save the man from the beating at the roadside.

Angels can hold human form in order to get their message across. It doesn't make then human though.

It's up to us to get the message, and in so doing, we get to see the angel.

I don't believe you can walk away, fundamentally unchanged, by an angelic encounter.

Here are a few of the most popular of my angel encounters, as shared, and re shared over the years.

CRIMSON WING ~

I have a series of 7 small watercolour paintings which depict the angels relating to the chakras. They were originally created for my T shirt project, and now live in the happy chaos of my studio, pinned on a high cross beam. I like to know they are there, they are very much of part of the family.

One day, a lovely friend of mine, Sue, came for a cuppa and a bit of a chat. She was going through a really miserable time of things with her (now very much ex) husband, and had felt unloved and undesired for quite some time.

Sue is one of my dearest and most enduring friends, we were colleagues when we were in the fashion industry together. Sue was there for me through my redundancy, my cancer, and my shamefaced exit from the terrible job in London. She was one of the first people that I "came out" to after my Reiki experiences. I know how hard it was for her to feel part of what I was going through. It was hard enough for me to understand, and I don't think I always made a very good job of explaining it to her. However, there are some people who stick by you whatever, because they are a very different kind of "family" to the one you were born into.

Anyway, there she was, in pieces, sipping tea in my kitchen.

I had asked her to pop up into my studio with me, as she wanted to choose a couple of angels from my box of cards This is unusual, I rarely ask people into my studio space, mainly because of the indescribable mess, but also because the energy has been so carefully calibrated to accommodate me and my work, it can be quite difficult for anyone else to be in there.

Sue was welcome.

She sat in my big swivel chair, as we talked and picked through the angels.

Suddenly, she went very giggly, red faced, squirming in the chair, gripping the arms .To be honest I thought she was having some sort of spasm.

When she had recovered herself sufficiently, she picked out one of the angels, the bright red, crimson winged one, representing the base chakra, passion and LOVE in the most powerful context.

She told me that this angel had "zapped" her.

Was she OK?

I was very worried.

Yes, she assured me she was fine, it had actually felt very nice, most unexpected though!

Right, I was taking no more chances in the Studio, so we went back downstairs for another much needed cuppa.

To be honest, I forgot all about the incident until some months later when Sue called me in great excitement to tell me about an extraordinary encounter she had just had.

Apparently, she had been attending a training course in Leatherhead. Arriving early in the pouring rain, she had parked the car and headed down the high street, looking for a coffee shop. (Being ever the practical one, Sue had worn a really old pair of shoes from under the back seat of the car, not wishing to ruin her fabulous footwear selected for the training session) for some reason, despite the torrential rain, and her increasing sogginess, she rejected all the immediate coffee shops in favour of one that attracted her at the end of the street, merely because "it looked so nice".

It seems no one else was prepared to brave the rain on that basis, and the place was empty when Sue finally made it through the door. She ordered her cappuccino, and found the perfect cosy seat near to the door. She was now soaking, and by her own admission, she had looked and felt better.

The café door opened again, and in walked a man of such striking good looks, Sue could not take her eyes off him. She watched him, agog, as he ordered his coffee, then with increasing horror and embarrassment as he headed straight for her, in her soggy puddle.

He asked politely whether he may share her table.

Why? . . . the café was empty. . . he could have any table he wanted.

He obviously wanted to sit with her.

Sue merely nodded, feeling mortified, and a little over whelmed as she had been gawping at him quite hard.

She tried to hide her soggy old shoes beneath the chair.

Mr Gorgeous, un phased by her damp coyness, introduced himself as "David" and engaged in chit chat about their respective children until Sue realised she was now in imminent danger of missing her training course. She had to drag herself away.

David, insisted that she take his mobile number, and call him after the course had finished, he assured her he didn't usually do this, but for her, he would make an exception. He really wanted to see her again.

Sue is not usually given to such shenanigans. Although she was undoubtedly in a miserable marriage, she was not a fanciful romantic, and had certainly not been looking for anything other than a cappuccino in the coffee shop.

However, apparently, the training course could not end fast enough, and before she knew it she was back in the coffee shop to meet David, wearing her nicest, driest shoes.

She and David "clicked" as they say, and despite some minor obstacles like her tricky (very soon to be ex) husband, and David's ex wife and their ready made family of kids (Sues daughter and Davids two sons) to integrate, they gently embarked on a long term relationship together.

Sue reckons that the red winged angel which she found in the box in my workroom prepared her at some deep soul level for the potential meeting with David.

The "zapping" had somehow awakened her to his energy, so that when that moment happened, she would not dismiss it on the basis of her temporarily battered self esteem.

If this still sounds a bit far fetched, then let me share this; David's business (just recently sold out to KPMG) was called "Crimson Wing".

THE ACROBAT ON THE TUBE ~

It was a few days before Christmas and I was travelling on a packed London Underground tube train to take part in an LBC Radio programme about angels. From my squashed seat in the corner, I observed the other passengers, all desperately trying to keep to their own space and avoiding any unnecessary contact with others. Noses were buried in newspapers or magazines, and eyes averted to look at anything other than someone else.

I only had a couple of stops to go, when the carriage seemed to clear, there were no longer any standing passengers and the remaining seated ones seemed to have breathed a collective sigh of relief.

A striking looking man, of perhaps early 20's boarded and strode with jaunty purposefulness down the carriage. He was dark skinned, with a dazzling smile and wearing typically casual clothing, baggy jeans and a hooded sweatshirt style jacket and designer trainers. He seemed to be humming a little tune, and as he walked, he was reaching up and testing the overhead handrails with a series of investigative tugs.

The other passengers palpably shrank as he approached, and once again retreated into their own silent spaces. Heads down, eyes averted. As he passed, there was relief, as he approached, tension and anxiety. What on earth was he going to do?

He stopped, just beside my seat where there was now clear space in the aisle, and proceeded to pull himself up onto the handrails and execute a perfectly elegant gymnastic move which ended with a little flourish and a small bow as he landed, with catlike ease on his feet again.

The silence was deafening. The communal in breath held. I was applauding inwardly, because it was such a random act, and yet so perfectly considered.

I could not resist asking him, "*Have you always been such a show off then*?"

Grinning broadly, the impromptu gymnast bounced over, pointing at his own chest "Who me?" he asked incredulously.

More shrinking and breath holding from the passengers around me.

"*Yeah, you . . . the only bloke hanging from the ceiling of the train*" I laughed in reply.

In response, he simply grinned even more broadly, hoisted himself back up onto the rails and did another twirl for us. "Only when I'm happy!" he confirmed with a twinkle, as he landed once again, with perfect timing, directly in front of me.

The train was now at my stop, so I gathered myself up and as I left, I caught his eye and in farewell said to him "Stay happy!", and he returned my salutation with continued good spirits.

It struck me as I fought my way out of the busy station, had that joyful young guy grown wings and a sported a bedazzling halo, the response from those passengers would have been no different. Eyes averted, hearts pounding in misplaced fear, they would not have seen the angel.

"Fear not; I mean you no harm. . . I bring tidings of great joy"

I seem to remember reading that somewhere . . . . I think that message was delivered was around Christmas time too!

MARTIN and ARCHANGEL MICHAEL ~

My personal relationship with Archangel Michael had also evolved, and flourished as we worked together at the various Mind Body Spirit events, always drawing a small crowd of attention and admiration whenever he was with me.

I was feeling very comfortable with him, we suited each other and enjoyed the work.

Often, if I was at home perhaps in the kitchen engrossed in some cooking or washing up or whatever, I would mistake his presence for that of my husband Martin. I would engage in a conversation with "Martin"; without looking up from my task, and be very much aware of his proximity, even at times a warm hand on my back or a fond ruffle of my hair. Eliciting no verbal response to my chatter, I would turn around and of course Martin was not there, just a bluish flash and a faint fragrance of bitter coffee, it had in fact been Michael.

How could I confuse the energy of an Archangel with that of my lovely husband?

The angels are quite happy to temporarily hi jack a human vehicle, and for a few moments, connect with us in a more direct way. Whether we always notice what is happening, is another matter, and I suspect we miss many such moments.

Michael and Martin had merged energetically many, many times. I had become used to seeing a more powerful, more present and other worldly version of my husband sitting at the kitchen table reading the Financial Times.

Martin rides a motorcycle, a KTM Duke (for those who need to know!) a large, powerful machine, and when he is dressed in his protective clothing, the angelic energy is even more visible, really he would only need the wings to complete the picture.

Sometimes, Martin would drop into my MBS events and more often than not, he used the opportunity to have a run out on his bike. The sight of him approaching my table looking for all the world like he just stepped out of one of my paintings had been noted by more than a few surprised visitors.

I assure you, this is not just my fanciful mind running riot, I do not make any leading comment about him or our relationship, folk just see it for themselves.

Or not!

The other giveaway is in the voice, I hear a slightly unfamiliar inflection in the delivery. Often he would ask me the kind of questions a stranger would ask, as though he had only just met me for the first time, not as a husband of thirty odd years. He would come out with profoundly startling statements and observations and quite take my breath away with his inherent knowledge of "stuff".

Perhaps when the angels are able to hold physical form with us for a while, it gives them the opportunity to experience some of the limitations and joys of being human, to be able to taste food in the mouth; to touch things; to hold things; to feel laughter in the belly and grief within the heart. It is part of their ascension process, to know and meet physicality, as ours is to increase our Light.

We are here to help each other grow. We must raise our vibration; they must lower theirs.

We meet each other on the Bridge of Light, and that is where our Unity begins.

WHITBY ANGELS ~

This experience was one of my first; just a couple of years into my awakening.

Whitby is one of my most favourite places for a brief sojourn by the sea.

Martin was away for a few days, and I decided to take myself and our old dog Minnie up to Whitby for a bit of a break.

If you know Whitby at all, you will recognise the walk along the beach from Whitby up to Sandsend.

One morning, Minnie and I walked that beach together, enjoying the solitude as we bimbled along, pausing every so often to pop some bit of interesting driftwood, an exquisite piece of glass disarmed by the waves, or a particularly attractive shell, into my burgeoning carrier bag.

I love collecting these "treasures" and enjoy making wall hangings from them. The process is very therapeutic, meditative, and they capture the essence of particular moments in time. They are totally unique.

We sent off mid morning, and I had promised myself a bite of lunch at the cute little roadside café, just before Sandsend proper. I knew Minnie would be welcome as there was a little patio area and it was sunny enough to want to sit outside.

By the time we reached the café, it was only just gone 11.00 am. Funny, because I had felt we had been walking for hours. I re-checked my watch, as I had planned to have some chips for lunch, but my own self imposed seaside rule was "no chips before midday". Pah ... I would just have to make do with a snack and a cuppa.

The café was quite busy, but we managed to find a table outside and I made Minnie comfortable with a bowl of fresh water and a nice bit of shade, before going inside and ordering a cuppa for myself.

Refreshed, I was just considering making a move when a large red "superbike" pulled up, all throbbing engine and shiny metal bits. It caught my attention and the attention of Minnie who always relates the sound of a motorbike engine to the appearance of Martin, he being an avid biker and all.

Two men dismounted. The rider was unusually tall and well built beneath his full set of leathers, and when he pulled his helmet off, he revealed a handsome dark skinned face with cropped brown hair and the most extraordinary twinkly eyes.

The pillion passenger, was by contrast, very short in stature, fine boned and pale almost white skinned. This man had very blonde hair, again it was close cropped, and he wore a grin that almost wrapped fully around his face.

Beaming, the pair made their way over to my table, pausing to acknowledge Minnie, (who was beside herself with joy at the attention), and they asked permission to join me.

I glanced around, other tables were now free. Why did they want to sit with me?

They seemed decent enough guys, and they had a nice bike, so I shifted over a bit and made room for them.

The taller one, offered to buy me a cuppa and a cake, I heard a distinct Northern accent, but couldn't place it.

I accepted.

Whilst the taller one was in the café, I had chance to look more closely at the pillion. He was almost transparent in the sunshine, and he had the same extraordinary twinkly eyes as his friend . . . yet they could not have been related, they looked too dissimilar in all other features.

I would describe one as "fine" and the other as "weathered".

The tea and cakes had arrived, and the two guys settled down to enjoy a nice break in their journey. They were vague as to where they had been, or where they were going, so I didn't pursue that line of conversation. Martin can be just the same when it comes to his bike adventures! They however, had many questions for me, regarding my sojourn in Whitby, and seemed to be able to elicit quite a lot of details without much effort. We talked mostly about the "treasures" in my carrier bag. Pieces would be lifted out, examined, and discussed in terms of their colour, beauty, and potential purpose or meaning. It was great fun.

We chatted, and cooed over my haul, whilst sipping hot tea and scoffing yummy cakes. The moment was suddenly shattered by the shrill ringing of a mobile phone. In those days, it was much less common to hear the trill of a mobile in public, so I was startled somewhat. Muttering, the darker guy got up, and began rummaging in his jacket pocket to retrieve the insistent and intrusive device. Shrugging by way of apology, he walked off, leaving his companion to entertain me whilst he took the call.

I realised, the café was now empty except for us.

Something jolted my attention bringing me back into the moment again; and I felt it was time to make a move.

Gathering up my things, and persuading a reluctant dog to join me, I made ready to leave.

The darker guy was still occupied on the phone, so I took my leave of the still beaming blonde, thanking him for their company and the interesting chat.

In those days, I used to keep a little stash of pewter coins, embossed with the image of an angel, in my capacious handbag. I liked to share them with people who did me a favour, or just touched my heart in some way. I felt these two guys qualified for one each.

Scrabbling into the depths of the bag, I managed to find the last two coins, and proffered them to the young man who was now tickling my dog and whispering gently to her. I have no idea what he was saying but she was loving it.

Beaming, he accepted the pewter tokens, with a simple "Thank you". I made it clear that one was for his friend, and he nodded acknowledgement, but didn't ask me any questions.

Taking my leave, I walked away, dragging a reluctant little dog with me.

After a few yards, I turned to wave.

They were gone.

The café was empty.

I had not heard the bike start up, and I know from experience how long it takes to get all the protective clothing back on. It was just not possible in that few seconds it had taken me to walk that short distance.

Curious, I looked at my watch.

It was only just after 11.30 am.

How was that possible? It seemed we had been talking together for hours.

It was still too early for chips!

♥According to my angels; the human vessel may host the angelic light, that does not make us angels, but for a while, angelic.

These two guys were "Emissaries".

An Emissary is a person (or angel) sent on a Diplomatic mission, a representative, a legate, or even . . . a spy!

They had come to check up on my progress, to see how I was doing, how I was looking at my world.

They would be reporting back to whoever had sent them!

Their interest in my bag of bits, and my experience of my stay in Whitby had been a gentle inquisition.

The angels are very respectful of the human condition, and the fact we have free will. They present us with opportunities to "see" them, and if we are not ready or willing, then no harm done, they just back off and disappear into the environment like they never where.

They use familiar things that are a little out of context to catch our attention. Here, they chose to use the motorbike as their "familiar". Had I not been married to a biker, and hold a full motorcycle licence myself, perhaps I would have been a bit standoffish with them. Bikers, are part of my experience, and so it was easy to welcome them.

My dog had seemed to recognise "friend" when they arrived. Minnie could be very vociferous if she didn't like someone, and whilst not ever actually ripping someone to shreds, I am sure she often thought about it for her own amusement. She was very taken with these two.

My recognition of the unusual eyes was significant, as this has become a clear indicator to me that the face I am looking at is not what it first seems. It is a way of the angels differentiating themselves from human, without resorting to deploying the wings and trumpets!

The sense of those two angels stayed with me for the rest of my time in Whitby, and of course I looked out for them on every corner. Every rumble of a motorbike engine had my head swivelling to look for them, but of course, it never was.

When I got back to the hotel, after the "time slip", I did take the trouble to check the correct time against my own watch. It was perfect. I had simply experienced a little warp in my time line, so we could share what needed to be shared together.

I am not usually very sentimental regarding my angels, but I will let you into a little secret of my heart.

I do believe, absolutely, that one day, my little pewter angel tokens will be returned to me, by those same angels, but dressed in another guise, and in another circumstance.

AN ANGEL IN THE GUTTER ~

It was around Christmas, and I had been shopping in Nottingham with my sister Gaynor.

The city centre was cold and crowded, and we were heading back to the car park, and the promise of a lovely hot cuppa at home.

As we dodged the pedestrians and traffic, I spotted a young woman sitting on the side of the road, in the gutter. She was visibly shaking, and all I could see was the top of a very blonde head held within the folds of the collar of a thick, slightly grubby, black coat.

I went over to her, and kneeled down beside her.

Not wishing to interfere, but needing to acknowledge her plight I asked, "I can see you are distressed about something, can I help in any way?"

She didn't even look up, but sniffled into the folds of her coat and tried to explain her situation.

It was a garbled, incoherent mess of circumstances which had left her fearful and depressed, and for the want of £23.50 to get into a Hostel refuge, she had nowhere to go to feel safe.

I don't usually do this, but I checked in my purse, and there was just about that amount, plus a bit for the car park. I offered her the money she needed.

Without looking up, she accepted, still sniffling and shaking.

I put my hand on her shoulder, and encouraged her to stand up with me. As we stood together, something extraordinary happened.

The dirt and grubbiness of the gutter dropped away, and the woman standing before radiated a beauty and light which belied her pathetic situation. She seemed to grow taller, before my very eyes, and her energy expanded so it enveloped me totally.

She held out her hand, and I placed the money in it. She drew me to her and we exchanged a hug, an embrace that told me she was no guttersnipe.

I asked her name.

"*Claire*" she replied.

"Ah, Claire means Light in French. . . did you know that?" I proffered.

"*Yes,*" she replied "*I did*"

With that she smiled, a beatific smile, and she merged into the crowd, and was gone.

My sister Gaynor suddenly appeared, a bit cross, having lost me at the traffic lights.

"Where have you been?" she demanded.

I began to tell her about Claire.

"Oh my goodness" Gaynor declared "*I hope you didn't give her any money! There are far too many of that type about!*"

I saw no point explaining further, so I just shrugged, picked up my bags and continued to the car park.

The sense of Claire stayed with me.

Later that afternoon, Martin called me and asked if I'd had a good day with Gaynor.

I told him, I thought I had met an angel in Nottingham. I regaled my experience.

I felt it had been another test.

Martin heard me out, then laughed "Of course, it was a test" he chortled "*The angels wanted to see if you were willing to hold the Light!*"

Ha ha . . . of course they did!

♥ **According to my angels: I must acknowledge my own kind before I may engage with angels**.

This was indeed another test.

The Light had been carefully dressed in a layer of grot and grime, would I be willing to embrace that???

Only in the acceptance, and willingness to engage with the "human" could the angel reveal itself through "Claire"

I often wonder if the girl who held the energy of the angel "Claire" ever worked out how she came to have £23.50 in her hand . . . just when she needed it most.

I feel £23.50 was a very fair price for my lesson.

THE IMMACULATE MAN ~

As you know, for a few years I juggled my time between the working with angels and my Design Consultancy.

I admit it was not always easy, and there were times I felt like it was all just a bit much, but I was in too deep, and what is known, cannot be "unknown" and there is no going back.

One morning, long before before dawn, I found myself making the seemingly interminable drive down to Stanstead Airport to catch an early flight to Florence, Italy. It would be a one day trip, literally a "flying visit", I needed to check on some fabric designs which would be available at an International Textiles Fair in the City.

Arriving at the airport, at what felt like an ungodly hour, feeling exhausted and seriously questioning "Why?", I caught sight of myself in a mirror. There was no escaping the vision of grumpy misery and dishevelled weariness, as the mirror extended the full length of the Departures check in area. At every turn, I was confronted with myself.

In those days, I wore my hair short and spiky, dyed a harsh black, and it took some effort and products to get it looking just right. This morning, it looked dreadful. I needed to buy something to sort out the hair.

At that early hour, there were very few airport shops open, but I spotted a branch of "Body Shop" and felt that would do very well.

I ventured in, and stood surveying the well stocked products on the shelves. What did I need? Where would I find it? Aaaargh, too many choices!

I became aware of someone standing behind me.

Turning, I almost backed straight into a very tall, well dressed and well groomed man. He was black skinned, with cropped short hair, greying a little at the temples, he wore a pink shirt with a cutaway collar and a tonal but darker pink tie with a Windsor knot. His suit was a silvery grey, and to my trained eye, a very fine cut and cloth indeed. He wore a delicious fragrance, far more refined and subtle than Body Shop products. I would describe him as "immaculate".

Recovering myself, I apologised for nearly stepping on his toes, and he assured me no apology was necessary.

His voice was as delicious as his fragrance.

He asked if I was looking for anything in particular?

Could he help?

Pointing to my wayward hair, I explained that I was searching for a "miracle" .

"Ah" he said, pointing over to the far side of the store, "*the miracles are over there*".

Grateful, I thanked him and went to find the hair product .

At the till, the cashier was dull eyed and sleepy, she took my money and we barely shared a word.

As I left the shop, the Immaculate Man, was standing by the door.

Gently, he accosted me, touching my arm with his hand. It stopped me in my tracks. I turned around to meet those familiar eyes, the ones full of unnamed colours and depth, the ones which are the dead giveaway. In this dark skinned face, they look particularly jewel like and stunning.

"Do what you love: and love what you do!" he advised.

Stunned; I walked out of the shop, pausing seconds later to acknowledge what had just happened.

I turned to thank him for his wisdom.

He was of course, gone.

Despite myself, I had to go back into the store and look for him. I had to ask the cashier if she had seen him, and if she knew who he was.

Of course, she didn't know, and no one of that description worked at the shop. She had seen no one.

I caught my flight to Florence with his words singing through my heart, on repeat play, I felt a little dazed.

Somehow, I completed my contracted work really quickly, and efficiently. I had the rest of the day to myself in Florence, my flight back was not until quite late. I chose to spend my time simply walking, across the Ponte Vecchio, along the banks of the River Arno, popping in to the various little churches and gardens en route. It was blissful, just being, not doing.

Alison Knox

♥ *According to my angels: I must love what I do, and do what I love*.

I now realised, that my work as a Design Consultant was no longer fulfilling me.

It was earning me a good income, but I didn't "love" it.

The angels had raised the bar exponentially as far as "loving it" goes, and I was starting to resent the time I had to spend away from them.

I had already allowed most of my contracts to expire, un renewed, and now I only had this one client left.

Funnily enough, in recent times, the Management of the company had changed, and my original contacts had left, I felt no connection with the new team.

It felt like a good time to make the "leap of faith", to exit the fickle world of fashion, with grace and gratitude, and wholly embrace EVeRYDaY ANGeLS.

AN ANGEL CHORUS ~

The date was 16th September 2001.

Our friends Simon and Denise had invited us to their wedding in San Gimignano, a small, walled medieval hill town in the province of Siena, Tuscany, north-central Italy. We were to stay at Villa Magiori, the birthplace of Mona Lisa.

On September 11th, 2001, terrorists had hijacked four U.S. airliners carried out deadly attacks, destroying the World Trade Centre in New York and damaging the Pentagon,. . . the rest is as you know is imprinted on history and within our souls.

To fly to Italy, was a challenge indeed under the circumstances, but we all made it!

It was a time of true appreciation, celebration and joy. The wedding and the party were glorious, and the setting was perfect.

On our last night at the Villa, Martin and I went down into the vineyard around midnight. We took a bottle of the Villas own wine, made from the grapes of that same earth upon which we now sat, and gazed up at crisp bright stars. It was truly beautiful, awe inspiring.

We felt blessed and happy.

As we sat there, a thin, high melody drifted on the air, like a wisp of smoke. It ebbed and flowed around us, drifting in and out of our consciousness, leaving us wondering just where the sound had come from. It was a chorus of a multitude of angelic voices, beautiful and extraordinary, ethereal and exquisite.

Of course, we wanted to know where such beautiful singing had come from, there was no obvious point of source; we were miles from anywhere, at night, in a vineyard!

We drank our wine, and made our way back to our room, and slept a deep and sated sleep.

Next morning, as we checked out, we asked the proprietor about the singing. They could offer no explanation, certainly not at that time of night. It was a beautiful mystery.

♥ *According to my angels: Grace comes unbidden within the ordinary moments.*

Martin and I both felt we had witnessed something other worldly, although wc had no words for what it might have been, it would give us an anchor to a moment of Grace, shared at a time of world crisis and great uncertainty.

I would hear this again, at a future date, under very different circumstances.

VILLA PHISI ~

Even though I work with angels, I still need a holiday from time to time.

It is lovely to just slip into some semblance of "normal" for a couple of weeks, soaking up the sun, and sipping chilled wine with a good novel.

In the September of 2006 Martin and I had booked a little house on the Pelion Peninsula in Greece.

(Pelion or Pelium is a mountain at the south eastern part of Thessaly in central Greece, forming a hook-like peninsula between the Pagasetic Gulf and the Aegean Sea)

It was a random internet "find" and we loved the name of the place "Villa Phisi" . . "Natures House" . Situated down a virtually inaccessible track, surrounded by pine forest and wild flowers, it promised bliss.

Typically, I had become a little fraught prior to the holiday. I was attending so many Mind Body Spirit fairs, I barely had time to replenish my stocks between events, and of course clients were asking for paintings and angels were omnipresent demanding attention. . . as ever.

I decided to banish them all, just for the holiday.

No offence, but I needed a break, a bit of clear space . . thank you!

It felt a little odd, but I appreciated the opportunity to have a little "me" time.

Martin had been rather bemused, he wondered if perhaps I hadn't been a little harsh? Banishment of the angels had felt a bit brutal.

I explained, if you give them an inch, they take a mile. The angels have no concept of boundaries, they just move in and take over.

He looked at me askance, I knew he wasn't convinced.

So, we arrived at Villa Phisi. It was as beautiful as we had hoped, and more than magical.

I relaxed a little.

Our first night was celebrated by finding a lovely bar with comfy seating on the beach, twinkly lights, ambient music and a great cocktail menu.

Our order was taken by a Mermaid.

OK, it was a gorgeous girl in a mermaid costume, but still, it made me smile.

Our first drinks were delivered by a fairy.

OK, it was another gorgeous girl in a fairy costume, but it made me smile.

Martin smirked and said "You thought you had escaped eh?"

I sipped my Retsina and giggled.

The bill was brought by an angel.

OK, it was yet another beauty in an angel costume, but I had to laugh at the persistence.

There was no point keeping up the charade, the angels were on holiday too, so I may as well let them in. . . normal angelic service was resumed.

The little house was delightful, peaceful and otherworldly. The elemental nature of the place was very beguiling and embracing. We loved it.

One afternoon, Martin declared he was going to the shops to buy a loaf of bread. In our current world, this was indeed a declaration, and so armed with the keys to the Jeep, he set off down the dry, stony river bed to the village bakers.

I stayed, languishing in the garden, lulled and soothed by the incessant song of the cicadas.

I must have drifted .

The song had changed, from a trill thrumming chirrup, to a soft ethereal chorus of a million tiny voices all woven into one. It was beautiful, expansive, enchanting.

I have no idea how long I was held in that glorious state, within that sacred song, but the moment was broken by the sound of tyres on the track.

Martin was back; and so was I.

It was impossible to describe what had just happened, or where I had been, but I was infused with a sense of heightened awareness, a magic and beauty that felt "other" than my angels.

Martin and I had heard that same celestial chorus before, under very different circumstances and a different sky, but it was indeed the same thing. Remember the vineyard in Tuscany?

The little house had a guest book where visitors were invited to write a few notes about their stay.

I found myself writing this.

"When the soul seeks the solitude of the secret places, and the heart longs for the silence, borne on the song of a million tiny voices. . . come to VILLA PHISI.

Be held in the gentle pulse that beats in time to that of the Universe, and know, you are home.

Let the spirit of the place come to you, and touch you deeply; reaching in and opening up the spaces, long forgotten, within.

Celebrate the slumber of indigo night, bringing dreams borne on wings of gold and violet.

Dawn is the herald of the song of the mountains, as each small life re-awakens, and you, struggle to emerge from slumber so deep, you wonder whether you are still within that subtle dream world.

You exist here in Kairos time.

Days meet seconds and melt together; hours flow liquid into weeks and ebb back to days before yesterday was even thought of and after tomorrow long slipped by.

Do not seek your agendas here; they do not exist.

Feel your breath return you; whole and sated, in sun kissed languor, with every cell of your body vibrating to the same note of bliss.

This is VILLA PHISI and you are as one."

Alison Knox

♥ According to my angels: time does not exist.

Time is an interesting concept and construct; I have found that since working with angels, the linear time I have been used to, means very little.

There are two different types of time. Chronos time is what we live in. It's regular time, it's one minute at a time, it's staring down the clock time. Chronos is the hard, slow passing time we often have to bear. Chronos time, is time tamed, and dictated by man to keep us all under control.

Then there's Kairos time. Kairos is God's time. Kairos time has no size or shape, it is wild and free-fall, it is gentle and embracing, it is whatever we need it to be. It's time expanded outside of time. It's metaphysical time. It's those magical moments in which time stands still. I have a few of those moments each day.

I truly cherish them.

A friend had made me aware of the work of an artist; Jim Wilson who had created an extraordinary piece of music called "Gods Cricket Chorus.

This recording contains two tracks: the natural sounds of chirping crickets, and the crickets played several octaves lower and slowed down to emulate a human lifespan of 3 score years and10.

You can find the track on http://www.youtube.com/ watch?v=of90IEoE-IM

When Martin and I heard this recording we were amazed, it was exactly the same as our experience in Tuscany, and the same sound I had heard in the garden at Villa Phisi.

In more recent times, we attended a Norwich Theatre art event "Walking" set over a three mile stretch of the Holkham estate, a major collaboration between the Norfolk & Norwich Festival, in collaboration with *Theun Mosk* and *Boukje Schweigman*, and the internationally acclaimed American director and artist *Robert Wilson*. *(funnily enough not the same Wilson just the same name!)*

It qualifies as "immersive theatre". Part walk, part theatrical experience, punctuated by gigantic architectural installations along the way, "Walking" was designed to heighten the senses and thrillingly alter your perceptions of space and time.

This same track was used as part of the experience, played through a sound system in a glade amongst the sand dunes, it felt and sounded as hauntingly magical as the previous, totally natural experiences.

I am just astounded at how anyone, would even think to render the sound of crickets in this way.

It must surely have been a divine inspiration!

Chapter 26

~ SPIRIT OF PLACE ~

"There is a language beyond human language, an elemental language, one that arises from the land itself!"

Linda Hogan ~ Chickasaw Writer

In the late summer of 2006, the same year that I stayed in the magical house Villa Phisi in Pelion, I was delivered another delightfully unexpected gift.

Whilst flip-flopping down to our local post office one hot summer's afternoon, I had a revelation.

A full screen cinema presentation played in my head, showing a series of twelve photographic images which were drawn from nature. As they were shown to me, they magically embroidered themselves with details and light, as though their hidden secrets were highlighted and revealed by an invisible hand. The sense of them was so tangible and clear, and I almost felt with each one, that I was somehow within the picture itself.

The images refused to go away, even as I stood in the queue at the post office counter, and it was all I could do to complete my business and scamper back home.

I burst into my studio, and grabbed a sheet of paper, scribbling down the images as best I remembered them, fearful that if I didn't act immediately they would be forgotten or erased from my memory.

♥A beautiful pink rose dressed with dewdrops
♥A woodland scene with two large rocks and a waterfall into a pool
♥A fast flowing stream, crashing and thundering over rocks.

♥An eagle rising in flight over an open ocean
♥A white dove ascending
♥A pile of three standing stones
♥A forest glade filled with golden light
♥A rainbow across clouds in a blue sky
♥A winding path through an oriental garden
♥A walkway across a golden beach into an invisible horizon
♥A group of beautiful red candles with golden flames dancing
♥A pure white feather

What was I supposed to do with these? I didn't feel competent enough as an artist to be able to replicate the detail I had been shown, nor was I confident enough as a photographer to be able to capture these images for myself.

A stiff cuppa was needed!

Fortified by the tea, I then got the rest of the message, and was given the working title for these images "SPiRiT of PLaCE ARt".

"Upon entering into SPiRiT of PLaCE; become as one with the world as seen through angels eyes.

The ordinary becomes extraordinary, taking on a magical quality that is indefinable yet undeniably tangible.

To become lost in the connection between self and place is to experience "kairos time" where seconds feel like days, hours fold back on themselves as though mere minutes have passed, and time as we know it means nothing.

Only the moment is real.

Only the place exists for you.

To honour the spirit and feed the soul with beauty and grace is our commitment to Self.

Relax into your special place and embrace that spirit as it eases you into balance, stillness and wholeness.

Know, the place your heart calls Home is here."

I understood that although these images were not overtly of angels, they certainly carried the same positive and emotionally challenging energy and would offer another "vehicle of convenience" for the angelic energies to be made available to others.

Since I had returned from the magical holiday experience, I had spent an equally magical day in the company of Vanessa, a Feng Shui expert and very much an appreciator of my angels.

Vanessa and I had taken a rather beautiful walk through the fields near where she lives, we had embarked on the jaunt dressed merely in summer frocks and flip flops, so hardly expecting anything too taxing by way of exertion. There was something intangible, alive and frizzante in the air as we approached the gate of the first field, the entrance to which was guarded by a tall coral coloured holly hock, standing sentinel. Big fat bumble bees busied themselves in the blooms, adding to the buzz already building up around me like a static charge. We commented on the tallness and beauty of the hollyhock, and as we admired the plant, we seemed to get smaller, or the plant got bigger. . . it was rather an Alice in Wonderland moment. A shift of perception.

Giggling like children we made our way through the overgrown brambles and shrubbery, pausing to scavenge some luscious blackberries from the heavily laden bushes, eating what we could, staining our mouths and hands purple in the process.

Rabbits scampered across our path, looking more like pets than wild creatures, kind of "super real" glossy bunnies.

A herd of alpacas came trotting over the field to investigate what we were up to. They gave us a giddy twirl like a gaggle of naughty teenagers, all false eyelashes, long legs and tumbling blonde locks. They were a delightful and unexpected sight!

The whole afternoon slipped easily and gently into that extraordinary state of Kairos time, and before we knew it we were back at Vanessas house, grubby, sunburned and berry stained, but happy and exhausted, and we had been out for hours! The experience had been very other wordly and I felt we had been strongly connected to the elementals and nature spirits.

I do feel this was a snapshot, a sneaky peek into a twighlight world between worlds, a view through angels eyes.

An augmented reality.

I knew that this latest gift of Spirit of Place Art, was related to these recent experiences, and needed to be expressed as art in some way. . . but how?

My brother Steve has a print business, so I made call to him, to ask about resourcing the images I needed. Did he know where I could get such photos from?

Of course he did, and better yet, he had an account with an online photo gallery. He invited me to browse and select whatever I needed, he would pick up the tab for the images. He told me they had thousands to choose from! Gulp . . . I only wanted 12.

It was actually much easier than I ever imagined to find the exact prints I needed. They stood out from the crowd, somehow more vibrant and visible amongst the many.

I had chosen the images, I needed to better understand their purpose.

I called Vanessa.

As a Feng Shui practitioner, I knew she would be able to give me the deeper meaning of each of my images, to help reveal them in their Truth.

It seems each image had a very specific relationship to the Feng Shui principles. Vanessa patiently explained each one to me, and I duly made note.

Feng Shui is the Chinese art or practice of creating harmonious surroundings that balance yin and yang within an environment. In a home or office, there can often be imbalances which effect the energy of the place, and consequently effect the mood and energy of the people who live or work in that environment. By addressing the imbalances, and placing positive images and icons, it is possible to influence the environment and improve the energy. If you would like to find out more go to www.fengshuisociety.org.uk

My brother Steve undertook to print the images onto canvas for me, then I worked on them with my paints and twinkles to bring out the previously unseen magic. It was never a question of painting things in to the image, but drawing out what was already there.

Each of the images came with a channelled message, underpinning the Feng Shui principles in a most beautiful language, undoubtedly delivered on the breath of the Nature Spirits. The words just arrived fully formed in my consciousness, ready to be written upon the page, no editing or struggle to "correct", it is an amazing experience and process to be able to do this.

Once I had the canvas's completed, I was able to offer them on a specially designed website, separate to the angels, and to produce a range of related cards and prints too.

I am extremely grateful to Vanessa, who embraced these images within her own work, and freely advocated my work to her own clients.

Vanessa had a regular client, a young man, a high flier earning a six figure salary, who had recently hit a bit of a temporary career slump. He was already familiar with my angel work, but she felt he needed the "Magical Waterfall" in order to get his "flow" moving again. Without hesitation, Vanessa called him and recommended he invest in a canvas, to place in his "career" area. Such was his confidence in Vanessa, he committed to the canvas sight unseen. I sent him an image by e-mail, just so he had something until his canvas was ready. He used it as a screen saver. This had the immediate effect of influencing his "flow" and before he knew it, a valuable contract had been signed and a big bonus was in the pipeline! I am advised that the painting continued to positively influence his financial flow and it was only when he chose to reposition it in an unsuitable place that the flow stopped. It didn't take long for him to reinstate the painting to its most effective position!

Another client had a house that had not sold for 3 years. She was getting very fed up about it. Vanessa recommended the same "Magical Waterfall" to her, to help the energy "flow" to help to sell the house. Within days she had a cash buyer!! Amazing!

Of course, I never make any guarantees with my paintings as outcomes are influenced by so many factors, intention being one of them. It is always inspiring to hear of the successes and to know that my work has been part of some ones growth and spiritual development in some way.

♥*According to my angels: Nature speaks to us beyond mere words*

Nature has many voices.

The voices are not always audient, and our ears are not always the means by which we hear it speak.

Sunlight breaking through a canopy of trees and dappling a golden path before us, has a message for those who are ready to hear.

A crashing waterfall playing over rocks has a song to deliver, if we are able to simply pause to appreciate it.

A magnificent vista which takes our breath away, has spoken already without a single word.

A brilliant, starlit, velvet night embracing us beneath its awesome majesty and infinite endlessness has whispered to our soul.

Birdsong at dawn, awakens the heart to a new day, we are rebalanced and vitalised.

Sunset in all its smouldering beauty settles our energy, rendering a sense of peace and calm within.

Nature has many voices, we would do well to listen to her more often.

The Spirit of Place Art, showed me how to look at the world differently, through angels eyes, to see the magic and the subtlety, to connect with nature in a more direct way and to appreciate the hidden realms.

To further illustrate the point, I found rather intriguing photo in a copy of New Scientist (31/03/07) It is what is known as "hybrid imaging" is a process which digitally breaks down spatial frequencies by filtering images so one retains only gross details whilst the other retains only fine details. Superimposed, the result is a single blurry image which seems to "switch" depending on how it is viewed.

The hybrid imaging example typifies how the world can be viewed in terms of gross and fine details. When we choose to view the world "through angels eyes" we tend to see more of the fine detail.

If you are familiar with the "Magic Eye" art, where a series of seemingly meaningless dots suddenly realign and form a scene or image. This works when the eyes are allowed to become soft, and relaxed. The harder you stare, the harder it is to see the hidden images. So it is with angels too!

The time I spent in Greece in that magical garden, and the subsequent adventure through the fields taken with Vanessa held a new level of connection for me. Awakened to another level of awareness, a heightened level of consciousness, I consider the experiences to be no less than a natural attunement; rather than this being delivered by a Reiki Master, it was delivered by Mother Nature herself. This is why it is so important to take time out in nature, to allow the body and the mind to rest in silence and stillness.

I have never been very textbook or orthodox in my practices, I like things to be simple and uncomplicated. What does it for me is a simple walk with my dog, a run in the rain, washing dishes at the sink, a long silent drive in the car, . .. the list goes on. It is always ordinary, everyday, accessible stuff. It does not have to be in a formal meditation or retreat, but anywhere where you can find time and space to simply "be".

NB: In very recent times I was introduced to a wonderful book "The Gentleman and The Faun" by R.Ogilvie Crombie. It is a true account of an Edinburgh scientist who in 1966, through an encounter with a Faun at the Royal Botanical Gardens, was introduced to the great Pan. Roc, as the gentleman was known, was instrumental in the founding of the Findhorn Community and his direct and grounded connection with the Nature Elementals helped Findhorn to create the environment in which nature could thrive. In reading this book, I understand better my own experience with the Nature Elementals, and find the descriptions and experiences described by Roc, to match many of my own. To date I have never had the privilege to meet Pan, but I have met many other beautiful beings.

Chapter 27

~ THE ANGEL AT THE CONVENT ~

There is a point at which everything becomes simple, and there is no longer any question of choice, because all you have staked will be lost if you look back. Life's point of no return.

Dag Hammarskjold

Easter weekend 2003 saw me arrive at a place of religious spiritual retreat in North Wales.

I had been concerned for some time that I needed to be "doing something" or "going somewhere" and despite the best suggestions of well intended friends and spiritual contacts, nothing felt right.

Talking to my ex Franciscan monk friend Sean one day, he happened to mention a place he used as a personal retreat, my heart woke up and paid attention, I needed to find out more.

It felt so right.

Sean, very generously, gave me the details of the Convent, but felt it only fair to mention that this was a closed community and I would have to be prepared to find my own answers to whatever my question might be. The Sisters simply provide the space and the peace .

The Call, had been powerful and I had followed my heart, to what had initially seemed the most daunting and unpromising choice for me; a woman of no religious background, certainly non-Christian, definitely non Catholic, about to enter a Convent.

Had I been asked to unicycle to the North pole wearing only a thong and a smile, it could not have been more of a challenge.

At this juncture, my spiritual journey had barely begun.

I had only been channelling and painting angels since 2001, yet already I had been blessed with some incredible gifts and insights.

Now I had a question.

I hoped for some kind of answer.

"What is my relationship to God?"

Early on the Saturday morning, I arrived at the Convent of the Sisters of The Poor Clares, complete with a vast selection of my tools; canvas's, paints and brushes, etc fully intending to undertake some painting during my stay.

The Sister who showed me to my quarters was warm, bubbly and gracious. She seemed completely un phased by my lack of religious fervour, reassuring me that my time with them was my own, and Gods, and they would leave me to get on with whatever it was I had come to do. Should I need help, at any time, there was a little bell to ring, and someone would come and attend to me. Once installed, I was on my own.

The guest apartment was very simple, clean, neat and humble, with a cosy bedroom, sparkling bathroom and a dinky little kitchen. The main sitting room opened out through French windows onto a small walled garden which was full of spring flowers and warm sunshine.

The day was bright and soft.

Making myself at home, I found the kettle and made a cuppa, then went about moving the dining table out into the garden. There I began work on a large painting, about 40" x 60" and a series of small canvas's of 5" x 7". I often work on several pieces at a time, it is just the way I do things.

Alison Knox

The work, as ever, absorbed me totally and I was truly lost in the process of creation, quickly and easily losing sense of time and place. I worked through the morning and well into the afternoon.

Eventually; I had to pause, my painting palette was congested and I desperately needed another cuppa.

Turning back into the apartment, I intended to go straight through to the kitchen, but something stopped me in my tracks. I was entranced by a tiny pattern of vivid, golden light dancing in the top left corner of the room.

My natural curiosity demanded I find out where this beautiful dancing light emanated from, but I simply could not work it out.

I just stood there, gawping, captivated.

As I looked, it appeared to grow, to open out rather like a fan, or a wing, it was very tangible and pulsating with a light of pearlescent luminosity.

Then; a second pattern of light appeared directly opposite the first, and now it looked as though two great wings had unfurled right in front of me.

Then; a head and a body manifested, and standing before me was an angel written in living light.

Absolutely.

Of course, I was astounded.

Even though I was now regularly painting angels, this was beyond my experience or comprehension.

Why was I not afraid?

The revelation was extremely beautiful and graceful, in no way "spooky" or scary. It had unfolded so gently before me, so perfectly, from a little patch of nothingness into full Glory. Had I felt, at any stage unwilling to "see", then I am sure the whole thing would have just faded out or disappeared and that would have been that. End of conversation. I would have simply got on with the coffee making and palette cleaning.

The angel was not a static projection, it was totally fully dimensional, alive, constantly moving, changing position and size, sometimes appearing much taller and sometimes quite small, but mostly it held a size similar to my own. I felt it was trying to "meet" me, not to make me feel overwhelmed.

The energy felt entirely feminine, and so I will now refer to the angel as "she".

When I had regained myself, I asked the angel my question "*What is my relationship to God?*"

She replied "*God is being*"

This was not an audible sound, heard by my physical ears, but an absolute implicit knowing, heard by my heart. The answer was delivered whole and intact directly into each cell of my body. I vibrated in bliss with the knowing of it. I surrendered to her.

Then, by playing a kind of video film, projected through my memory, she reminded me of another message delivered to me just after 9/11.

This is what had happened.

My friend Andrea, who at that time was a popular TV personality, had invited me to join her for a chat programme with Kilroy. Andrea was invited as a guest speaker, and she wanted me to be there as support in the audience.

The panel were discussing the part that psychics play in the predicting of such catastrophes. It was not really my sort of thing. I felt like a fish out of water.

For me, the event had been a disappointing shambles. I had given up a whole days work, taken the peak travel (expensive!) train down to London, and at the critical moment, my throat chakra had clamped tight shut, so I couldn't speak a word! I had been unable to make any contribution to the discussion. Even Andrea had wondered why I hadn't spoken up.

Disappointed at my own ineptitude, I had returned home on the late train from London wondering "Why? What was that all about?"

Sitting there on Midland Mainline, sulking into my copy of "Hello" magazine and morosely munching a soggy packet of sandwiches; I had then been guided to write a channelled message to myself, which ended with the words "Being is enough"

On that occasion, it seems, it was enough that I had simply been there. That, was my contribution. I didn't need to speak.

So, now I had "God is being. Being is enough"

I thanked the angel from my Heart.

She then surprised me further, by asking that I take some photographs of her.

As it happened, there was an old APS camera in my handbag with a partially used film. I rummaged around in my bag, got it out and did as requested, took a series of photos until the film ran out. I have no idea what setting was used, I am not sure there is a "best setting" for photographing angels! The last couple of shots were distinctly different as her light had changed and become a more intense white rather than the soft golden. Without further ado, she was gone, melted into nothingness.

Once I had recovered my sensibilities sufficiently, I could go and clean my palette (an old dinner plate) and to make that much needed coffee. I then returned to the garden to my work on the paintings, which were finished by the end of the afternoon. I was astounded at how much I had achieved since I had arrived at this sanctuary.

It must have been around 4.00pm. I had felt guided to go down to the small chapel which was just along the corridor from my rooms. I had no plan as to what I was to do there, as I have already told you, I am not a religious woman, and so praying was not really my thing. I am not educated on the protocols.

As I walked through the heavy wooden door, a shaft of bright sunlight seared through the window and hit a pew, very directly, and in a way that I could not ignore. I swear, it was just like a movie set!

I sat in that place which had been so beautifully highlighted for me. It would have been rude not to.

This light had a very different quality to sunlight; a milky, pearlescent fullness, a charge of energy that seemed to gently fizz and pop around me.

The angel came again. This time I did not see her, but felt her presence behind me as she asked a question of me.

"Ask for what you truly need?"

I heard myself say out loud, and unhesitatingly, "Please; let me be sustained in my work".

As the last syllables left me, a tiny bird flew in through an open window, it landed on the pew in front of me, looked me straight in the eye, and sang its little heart out. When its song was ended it simply flew away. It was a wren.

All I could do was say "Thank you".

No embellishments.

No prostrations.

Just "Thank you".

I then turned to leave that beautiful humble place.

As I closed the door to the chapel, I noticed just to the side, a wire stand of postcards, all created by one of the Sisters, an artist. (I confess, I had not appreciated just how spiritual and creative this particular Order were. It never occurred to me to ask)

These handmade postcards and little leaflets were charmingly simple, illustrated depictions of passages and quotes from the Christian bible.

I picked up a small booklet entitled "God is. . ." and opened it at random to a page upon which the first line read "God is enough"

So, now I had "God is being. Being is enough. God is enough."

I realised that to be delivered such a message, in 3 words, 3 sentences and 3 phases was indeed Divine.

Those words resonated within my heart in that moment, and have never left me. It was all I needed to know.

My time was done in that beautiful place, to stay longer would serve no purpose and it would be rude of me to expect more.

Rather than utilise the bedroom, I enjoyed a good nights rest, sleeping on the sofa in the same room where the angel had appeared, surrounded by the paintings I had created. In the morning I was able to take my leave of my gracious hosts with a full heart.

Before leaving, I shared my experience with the Sister who had been charged with my care. She listened quietly, without comment or interjection. When my story was finished she told me simply "You are truly blessed"

I acknowledged, "I know that I am"

Before I packed my things up, I offered the Sister one of the small paintings, as a token of my gratitude to the Convent. She selected a little angel very carefully, assuring me it was to be shared by all, and not just for her personal enjoyment.

Reciprocally, she then proffered an A4 sheet, a simple crayon drawing, a depiction of the Crucifixion, with Mary at the feet of Christ, and a small red fox as witness, and upon the cross; a small bird. . . a wren. This had been created by the Sister whose artwork had already touched my soul as a little booklet.

Did you know, the wren is beloved to the Franciscans and in Celtic Pagan lore it is regarded as a vessel of hidden Sacred Wisdom. On St Stephen's Day (26th December) wrens were traditionally hunted by druid's apprentices, who would consider finding one a sign that they would be blessed with wisdom and inner knowledge in the coming year. (I am not sure what they did with the wrens once they had found them, maybe we better not ask!) Wrens are tiny, and elusive, almost invisible in the wintry hedge rows, so actually very hard to find. A successful wren hunt was a metaphor for finding the elusive divinity within all life. It is allegedly, where the old saying *"A little bird told me . . ."* comes from.

Well, it seems a little bird had told me, too!

By the time I had driven back home to Nottingham, the local supermarket was still open and I knew it had a one hour film development service. Just an automated system, but I thought it would be worth seeing if I had managed to capture anything of the angel on the film.

I had.

The girl on the photographic counter asked me "Are those photos what I think they are?"

I asked her what she thought they were.

She replied "An angel"

I confirmed she was absolutely correct.

The images were clear, the sense of them exactly as I remembered the experience. The angel was moving around the room, and changed her position and stance. The last couple of shots showed the change in the light before she left.

I showed the images to my husband Martin, he was incredulous, and demanded to know how I had "done" it. I assured him, as I assure you now, there was no digital skulduggery, intervention or clever camera tricks. I do not have that kind of technical skill, and anyway the camera was quite limited to an "idiot proof" operation. This was way before the days of commonplace digital wizardry.

The images I have, are absolutely untouched and authentic. You may make of them what you will. http://www.everydayangelsart.com/angel_story.php

There are several practical factors which must be borne in mind in relation to this account.

I was open; with a question in my heart, but without specific agenda.

I was very much outside of my own "comfort zone".

The moment of connection and subsequent unfoldment, required present attention. How easy it would have been to miss that tiny shimmer, if caught up in my personal agenda of needs.

The large painting I created "The Angels of Here and Now" speak of the importance being present in the moment. (They now live at Gorton Monastery in Manchester.)

My camera was a basic APS using a pre-packaged film, already partially used up. I had no high tech settings available.

The development of the film was a commercial automated process, with no digital alteration or human interference.

The experience, the delivery of the message, was absolute. With or without the recorded images of the angel, the experience would live within me as a Truth.

My Truth, is that I met with an angel.

My Truth is unalterable.

This was possibly the most significant thing that had happened to me since the advent of the original angel connecting, to awaken me to my purpose, way back in November 2001.

Although at this stage I had no idea what I was supposed to do with these images and this experience, I knew for sure what I was not supposed to do. This was not an occasion for selling "proof" to the highest bidder, or showing off, informing the press that an angel had been seen in a Convent in North Wales.

No, this felt very much like the blue eggs experience, a test of trust, tender, transformational, and a true blessing.

There was one person I really wanted to share this with; of course, my beloved teacher and mentor, Mrs G.

Bursting with excitement and joy, I drove up to see her, to share the experience, and to show her the amazing photos.

I went through the whole thing, verbatim.

I am not sure what I was expecting, but her response truly knocked me sideways.

I was, deluded, according to my Beloved Teacher.

Mrs G was adamant; this revelation was not what I thought it was, and if I persisted in my delusion, then everything I had done so far, would come to nothing. I would be made to look a laughing stock. My credibility would be in tatters.

I was stunned.

Valiantly, I went back into the fray, explaining that even without the photos, the experience still stacked up and held great insights for me. Mrs G was unmoved.

I felt as though I had been kicked in the guts.
There was nowhere to go with this but home.
I arrived in a state of shock.

When I told Martin, he was quite outraged on my behalf, what was Mrs G playing at?

We had both loved and trusted this woman with our spiritual development, indeed our souls. Now she was adamantly denying what felt like my greatest gift ever.

Of course, I couldn't let it rest there. I had to go back. I tried to phone her several times, but each time I was rebuffed, simply told that I was wrong.

Eventually, Mrs G simply refused to take my calls, leaving me pouring out my heart into her answering machine.

Very soon after, I had the opportunity to speak publicly about this experience, at my favourite local Mind Body Spirit event. It went down really well, and I had asked Athena to come, to be in the audience and to let me know if I had talked a load of rubbish. The audience had been really warm, receptive, and respectful, no one had thrown cabbages or walked out. The photos had been respectfully inspected, and returned with thanks, and not a few tears. I felt truly vindicated.

I called Mrs G to tell her the good news.

She now went into an absolute fury, and far from accepting my account, she pretty much told me she wanted nothing more to do with me and my crazy fantasies. What was I thinking of? Had I gone mad?

Athena calmly reassured me that I had not gone mad.

I now had a choice.

I could either capitulate to Mrs G, as my wise and beloved teacher, and let go of my own experience and my truth. . . or . . . stand in my truth, and risk losing Mrs G.

I chose to stand.

We seemed lost to each other.

It was a painful time.

I loved Mrs G, and so did Martin. I had absolutely expected her to embrace my epiphany as she had, each step of the way, so many times before. A period of grief and mourning followed and I had to cut myself free from my relationship with her.

This was a point of no return.

I had staked everything. There was no going back.

♥ According to my angels: It was time to stand in my own Truth and fly free.

I truly believe that Mrs G's response was not all it first seemed.

You may wonder whether it was jealousy or some dark evil forces that made her behave this way towards me, but no . . . I swear she did it out of love. There always comes a time when we are called to stand in our Truth. I had to be tested on where I stood with mine.

If I had denied my experience, in order to please Mrs G, then I could not be writing this now. My story would have taken a very different path .

It was necessary for Mrs G to cut me free, to allow me to fly on my own wings, and the sacrifice we had to make was our relationship.

Over the years, since that break up, I have occasionally had people come to find me. They are bright eyed and vibrant of energy, mentioning that they had been advised to find me by a friend of mine. That friend, they tell me, has a little cottage up in Yorkshire, and some beautiful paintings of angels on her walls.

That friend, was always none other than Mrs G.

I realised that had she truly not believed in me, she would have destroyed the paintings, and never spoken my name again, let alone given it to her clients. Mrs G, did me the greatest favour ever and I am eternally grateful.

Easter 2010, saw me driving up to one of my favourite Spiritual Centres, Gorton Monastery. Sitting in Bank Holiday traffic on the motorway, I was given an insight .

It had been exactly 7 years since my experience at the Convent. During that time I had been learning to be an Exemplar of all I know about angels, to walk my walk, talk my talk and deliver my Truth as best I can.

From time to time, I had shown my original photographs to those who needed to see them, not as "proof" but as confirmation and inspiration. I had always been diligent and protective and mindful and discerning.

Now, it seems, the time was perfect to declare myself and to publish the photos with my written testimony on my own website. I now had enough experience behind me, to be able to stand my ground, and to understand what that gift had been.

As an angelic challenge, they do like to keep me on my toes, I was instructed to produce 100,000 cards (printed postcards) to share with the world. They didn't have to all be produced on day one . . it could take as long as it takes . . but that was the deal.

*I know this was in deference to my favourite CD "**One hundred thousand angels**" by Bliss.*

Chapter 28

~ PACK YOUR OWN PARACHUTE ~

The greatest gifts you can give your children;
are the roots of responsibility,
and the wings of independence.

Denis Waitley

Some many years ago, when I was still in Corporate world, I took up parachute jumping. It was not for any altruistic reasons, no charity fundraisers, simply to get the adrenaline rush that forced me to confront my mortality and acknowledge that I was indeed still alive.

One thing I learned was the importance of packing my own parachute.

If you leave it to others, you cannot ever be sure that it will be done correctly.

There was a funny cartoon in the airfield café, which depicted a parachutist pulling the rip cord and deploying a bag of dirty laundry! Oops!

It can be so tempting to simply sit back and let someone else "do" for you.

It can also be very tempting to take over and "do" for another.

There is well told story of a man who every day took a home made sandwich to work for his lunch. Every day he complained to his friends and colleagues that he didn't like the filling. Eventually, after witnessing continual disappointments with regard to his lunch, a friend asked why he didn't simply ask his wife to fill the sandwich with something he liked. Mournfully he replied "*My wife doesn't make my sandwiches . . . I do!"* So, we wonder, what part of taking responsibility did that man have trouble with?

This means, you must take responsibility for what you need with you for this journey.

Take responsibility for yourself, and allow others to take responsibility for themselves too.

You get to choose the tools and the sandwich filling!

That way, when you take the leap of faith, off whichever precipice you find yourself poised, you will be able to deploy a "parachute" that will support you, rather than a bag of dirty laundry which will simply disperse to the four winds.

When you land, you can be sure of a tasty edible snack to sustain you whilst you get your bearings!

Conversely, do not try and take responsibility for the choices of others. Whilst good intentions for the best interests of others are admirable, you must respect that this is their journey too, and if you take away the opportunity for others to learn, for them to do what they have to do the way they have to do it, then you are actually dishonouring them.

For example, to watch a left handed child learn to use a sharp knife safely and adeptly is painful indeed for the observer and sometimes for the child, but it is only through the struggle that the child learns how to do it, safely, adeptly, their way. Eventually the child has a confident if ungainly skill which will serve them well; but not if the experience is taken away from them before the skill is learned. Without that experience, the child remains dependent even into adulthood.

I well remember as a small child, asking my Dad to let me borrow his penknife to cut something. He refused, saying it was too blunt, and he went and found me a sharp Stanley knife for the job. I was fearless because Dad was fearless. He supervised but did not take over. I still have all my fingers and I am a dab hand at bladework! There is a song by the Girl band, Bananarama which has a title "*It ain't what you do, it's the way that you do it*".

Your thoughts, your actions, your choices, your exchanges with others are all dependent on your intentions and your Truth. Whatever choices you make right now must serve you well.

If you opt out of taking that responsibility then please do not be surprised if you are continually feeling disappointed or short changed in some way.

No one cares about your well being as much as you do. . . however much they may try to convince you otherwise.

Above all else, be authentic, be courageous in that authenticity, and whatever you pack in that bag for the journey, make sure it is the best you have available to you, this is no time for just making do!

♥According to my angels: We have wings to carry us beyond our own limitations.

I love learning.

I love giving it a go.

I love being allowed to fail, it makes me stronger.

Being allowed to try; risking failure, has given me a confidence in my own resources and ability way beyond my classroom education.

Everything I know about angels, about my work, my purpose, my journey and my life has been taught by experience.

I thank all those who ever stood by and allowed to feel my way forward.

Epilogue

~ SO FAR . . . ~

"She flew like an angel to the stars . . .
she didn't realise she had her dress
tucked into her knickers though"

Edward Monkton

What can I tell you?

I have had to take a risk here, not just with writing this book, but with everything I have done so far.

Sometimes it has felt as though my dress was indeed tucked into my knickers.

Maybe it was.

This work with the Angels has changed my thinking, my being, my life.

I cannot possibly go back to "normal" . . . why would I want to?

What is "normal" anyway?

My work has allowed me to create a richness within my life. It is nothing to do with how much or how little money I may have, but everything to do with how I feel about the gifts I have been given, and how I choose to use them.

It is about being; not having.

Alison Knox

It is not dependent on status, or positioning in some construct of hierarchy.

It is about gratitude, appreciation.

I am truly grateful.

Working with angels is a form of wealth. I feel my life is incredibly abundant.

I am rich.

Whatever I think I may have had to give up, in order to do this, has already been forgotten as inconsequential by comparison.

I would rather spend just one more day in the company of angels, than eternity without them.

This is how it is.

This is not the end.

I have barely begun.

How can a story such as this, ever end?

Even my physical death will not stop the story.

The story is an living organism born of light and love, it can only survive and thrive in the telling and retelling.

Those of you who know me, and are perhaps already part of this story, and knowing of my work may be forgiven for throwing your hands in the air and saying "*Aahhh, she has forgotten to tell us about the time that .. . .*"

Well, no, she hasn't forgotten anything, she is merely pacing the unfoldment, so we can all keep up with each other.

I have so many more stories to share, and already the angels are forming an orderly queue around the block to remind me of what needs to be done next time.

Remember the questions I asked you in the first chapter?

♥Can you be open of heart and clear of vision?
♥Can you commit to the path, no excuses, forever, whatever?
♥If it looks like it needs doing; can you do it.?
♥Can you embrace the stranger?
♥Can you leave your comfort zone?
♥Will you look for the open doors and check which way they swing?
♥Will you do your best?
♥**Discern. . . discern . . discern.**
♥Will you ask for help if you need it?
♥Do you love what you do; do what you love?
♥Can you accept that Spirituality is not a race or a competition?
♥Can you accept that once you know; you cannot un-know?
♥Can you accept that much of this defies rational explanation, nevertheless, it is?
♥Are you prepared to meet your detractors with alacrity and compassion?
♥Do you understand that the road less travelled is that way for a reason?
♥Can you accept that you cannot take everyone with you?
♥Are you ready to pack your own parachute (and lunch box)

So, how did you do with them?

Maybe you have found some of your answers within these pages, or at least some more questions, to challenge and inspire you.

One of my favourite writers Kahlil Gibran, wrote, in his epic The Prophet

"*I cannot teach you how to pray in words... and I cannot teach you the prayer of the seas and the forest and the mountains.*

But you who are born of the mountains and the forests and the seas can find their prayer in your heart."

I unashamedly paraphrase his words to say to you "*I cannot teach you how to meet with angels; but you who are of the offices, hospitals, schools, shopping centres and financial institutions, will find them within your own environment, or not so very far from it. You will find them as they will find you*"

That which you seek is probably right where you are; right now.

Are you open to that possibility?

Do you believe it to be true?

What are you expecting?

My angels came through my familiar brushes and paints, via my own heart, despite my ignorance and resistance.

Courageous multitudes.

We are walking into the future; awakened.

It is a privilege to have walked this far with you.

Keep your twinkle bright; you never know when you might need it.

So far . . . so good!

~ ABRACADABRA~

"I create what I speak"

Aramaic: Avrah KaDabra

I speak of angels. Through my work, the Light of Humanity and the Light of The Divine are unified.

When you meet my art, you have the opportunity to experience something extraordinary, to meet the energy of the angels in a tangible form.

I; am a bridge between worlds.

Part of my undertaking is to bring in colour which does not exist in this dimension, although many of us have seen glimpses in meditation or during healing sessions, especially those who are familiar with Reiki. I trust, that although I only have materials which are commonly available in most shops, my practice delivers into them something "other" over and beyond the gross pigment range of a mere 7 colours, sublimated into a feeling of the limitless possibilities of the full spectrum of Divine Light.

Colour is a living Creative force.

In recent times, I was guided to have a very special violet coloured paint mixed. My obvious recourse was to nip down to the local DIY store and use their digital mixer service. The particular colour specified has a very high vibrational constitution of magenta and cyan, so that at times the human eye perceives a distinctly pink element, and then at others a more blue tone. How you see it, depends on where you are within yourself. The paint has the potential to "open" the 3rd eye and facilitate Creativity. It is a simple, yet wonderful tool of direct and divine connection. Paint! From a DIY shop.

So how do I create what I speak?

I feel I ought to share something of this process with you, as so many people ask me about it.

The truth is, I don't quite exactly know how my paintings become what they are as I am merely a channel for them.

I sense my angels as a feeling within my canvas' and paper, although I cannot physically see them at all until they have emerged and shown themselves.

If you saw my studio, you may be shocked at how small and messy it is. I work as though I am at the helm of the Starship Enterprise; everything is more or less at fingertip reach and despite the mess, I usually know where things are in the moment I need them (unless someone has borrowed something and not put it back!)

My brushes paint many things, always gloriously God given images, beings of Love and Light in the purest sense. They are not always depictions of angels but they invariably carry that high, light vibration within every brushstroke. We can speak of these ones another time, there will be another time, I assure you.

I'll keep it simply to the angels for now.

I have two preferred ways of working, watercolour on paper, and acrylic paints on canvas.

My first ever angel painted was a watercolour.

When I work in watercolour, the angel form has to be laid down first. To do this, I use a special textile glue called Appliglue which comes in a variety of fabulous holographic twinkly finishes and is applied directly from the tube onto the paper. It is important that the gluey stuff is 3D and not just water based glitter glue which does not hold form or energy very well.

I never sketch anything out, or measure anything, I just go straight into the process. The gluey stuff has to be formed with fingers or a cotton bud, it depends on the size, fingers are often too clumsy. The initial form, which I think of as an embryo or chrysalis, has to be left undisturbed for at least a few hours to dry properly, but even more importantly, the angelic energy has to be integrated and I have to trust my sense of feeling on that one. I just simply know when it is "hatched".

Mostly, the "hatching" happens in our guest bedroom where I can lay the angels down in comparative safety and quiet, away from inquisitive pets or clumsy humans. If you have ever been a guest in my home, you will have slept in the bed that has birthed in thousands of angels in the last few years, and probably will host a few more thousand yet to come. We work in a very domestic environment, never too far away from a cuppa.

In the early days, I would hold my hands over the painting in a way that my thumbs and forefingers formed a triangle, and through this I would direct the Divine Light to bless and empower the angel. These days we can dispense with that formality as I am constantly in touch with Source and anything I touch is touched by it anyway, by default.

Once the angel is ready for its colours to be delivered, I just use a basic tap water, with a pinch of sea salt and I will sloosh a generous puddle around the angel. Into this I add watercolours from my old tin palette and sometimes a dab from my special palette of pearlescent paints. I may use 3 or 4 colours to get the right balance. Then, using an ancient old toothbrush head, I dip it dry into the "twinkle powder" which is an aluminium coated silica at 40 microns, and flicky flack the powder into the puddle of paint around the angel. Somehow, it finds its way to where it needs to be.

When the paint dries, and it has to dry naturally, not hurried up with a hairdryer or fan heater, the colours will have naturally merged and evolved into something really quite beautiful and ethereal.

When I offer my "Sitting Room" sessions, my client is able to see this process in action as I create an angel for them, in their presence, exactly as described. It is always a surprise and always totally individual. There are often tears.

The process with the canvas is quite different.

I buy a good quality but basically off-the-shelf canvas from any good art suppliers. Even though they are primed with a white base, I prime them again, often using an element of my special violet paint in the primer mix, as in the process I create a portal or opening through which the angel has continual access. Imagine a celestial catflap.

I paint the space which the angel is to inhabit, and this is very much a stream of consciousness exercise over which I have very little or no control. My hand is guided in its actions. The paints are often applied directly from the tube and worked into the surface of the canvas until they feel done.

I will use anything really, but I do love to use the Daler Rowney Interference range which has a very pearlescent iridescent quality, like butterflies wings. It is exciting to use it in conjunction with more ordinary paints and see what magic happens. I also like to use a brand Pebeo which has gloriously vibrant pigments. Sometimes we go a little crazy and use "Barry M" eyeshadows which I buy from Superdrug when they are on offer as they have amazing pigments and vivid sparkling colour. It mixes well with my more traditional paints as bases.

Once the created space is ready (and I may have to wait for a few days for it to be useable, even if the paint is dry!) I can bring the angel in. Again I use the Appliglue straight from the tube, and the angel(s) seems to guide my hand to show me exactly where it needs to be.

In the early days I felt I should measure things, try and get them centralised or balanced in the space, but they actually don't seem to like that "precision" and appreciate a more organic and intuitive approach.

The angel will anchor itself energetically into the Appliglue and I will now get a strong sense of who it is. The personality shows through, and I can see certain characteristics form within the body and wings which tells me something about the nature of the angel and at this stage it may also indicate whether it wishes to wear a crystal embedded in its Heart Centre. Some do, some don't. Some can demand the ring off my finger or stones from a necklace! They are not shy in the asking. I always have a good selection of high vibrational crystals with flattish backs, on standby for any angel who needs one. They are very fond of Swarovski crystals, especially the type known as Aurora Borealis.

So, we now have to wait for the angel to get its act together before we can move on to the finishing stages. I may be guided to play some high vibrational music, such as Ian Richmonds Soundscapes, perhaps spray a little of a special Crystal Essence spray or use some Bach Rescue Remedy. They appreciate it if I burn some fine incense such as the Hare Krishna temple incense or Nag Champa or a naturally fragrant candle to scent the room. None of this is necessary, it is just nice to do it.

In due course, I can finish the artwork with a top coat of a very fine pearlescent ink, which is watered right down and applied as a radiance. Then, the final layer of paint which is a very fine holographic glitter glaze to seal everything and provide a multidimensional aspect to the whole thing.

Sometimes, the angel requires an additional finish using a metal foiling process. This is very challenging as it has to be applied with a hot iron, and one false move and I have burned a now activated angel. It looks easy, but trust me it is nail biting stuff!

When the work is finished, I just know.

It kind of closes off to me.

WE ARE DONE!

Nothing I use is particularly special, not even the reflective twinkle dust which is, after all, only an industrial product used for safety clothing. The angelic energy renders all my standard materials to something truly magical.

I cannot readily explain why people react to my work the way they do. It is absolutely due to the angelic energies which have chosen to reside within them.

Even if you view my work simply as beautiful art, it is often unexpectedly and inexplicably able to touch you in a way that nothing else can.

When I was still doing the Mind Body Spirit circuit, I had to load and reload my van on a regular basis; my angels have to be robust and fairly thick skinned to work with me. We can't be too damned precious.

Some of my most powerful angelic artworks, known collectively as the Archaeons, are 6ft x 2ft. They are incredible works however you look at it. Their whole process of creation was so subtly orchestrated it can never be replicated. Yet, I have to be easy and comfortable to allow those who come to me to work with them, access to engage at a very personal level. They have to travel to our workshops stacked up in my van, wearing their red "pyjamas" to afford a degree of comfort and protection while in transit. We have the whole travel thing down to a T these days, and the journeys together are often very interesting! Someone once asked me how much they were insured for. I had to laugh out loud, as they are essentially uninsurable. If I were to put a price on them, I could not even work with them myself. I prefer to declare them of "no commercial value", and trust that they can look after themselves, as they so clearly can and do.

If you want to find out more about these unique artworks go to http://www.archaeons.com/ as theirs is another story for another time.

From time to time I run workshops and encourage other artists to make their own connection with the angels. The results are often amazing and we have great fun.

If you have any inclination whatsoever to have a go at painting, to connect to your spiritual purpose, then please DO IT.

Let go of your embarrassment, judgement and coyness, remember, my first angel nearly ended up ripped asunder in the waste paper bin!!! I thought it was rubbish!!

Allow your soul to show you what needs to be done. Enjoy the process of creation. It is a wonderful thing. The world needs more courageous artists, in all their many guises, and it needs more angels too. I have just laid my soul bare for you, shared my secrets of my creation process, so maybe now it is time for you to do your part, grab your tools of light, whatever they may be, jump in, make a mark, give it your best.

ABRACADABRA . . . create what you speak . . . in love and twinkles.

Appendix 2

~ A "SILENT VOICE" ~

Silence is medication for sorrow.

~Arab Proverb

We are backtracking a little bit here.

On Sunday 6th May 2001, (before any angels had yet showed up) a gloriously sunny Bank Holiday weekend, I was delivered of a gift.

Martin was away for the day.

I had amused myself by painting our back garden wall a magnificent shade of vibrant blue, and was just contemplating a nice cup of tea at around 3.00 o clock when I was overcome by a need. . . a compulsion. . to write.

Quite what I was to write was not clear.

I was not usually given to such bizarre behaviour.

I raced upstairs to find a notebook and pen.

With my cup of tea in hand, and my writing materials ready, I settled myself in a comfy garden chair up by the top pond.

Silence!

It took no time at all for the pen to start flying over the page, and words pouring out, effortlessly and perfectly. Scribble,. . scribble,. . scribble; until I was done.

Three thousand words, without pausing for breath.

The cup of tea lay on the grass, untouched.

I was not actually consciously aware of what had been written, and so it was necessary for me to read the whole thing. It was as though I was seeing it for the first time.

The actual writing was appalling, a loose script with many slightly dyslexic mistakes and shocking use of punctuation, but beneath that a very powerful piece of writing.

It was entitled "*The Child And The Woman*".

This; was my Souls own story to myself.

The simple Truths within it were quite shocking to me, its honesty and clarity, deeply moving.

I had to just sit with it for a while.

More silence.

, I felt moved to go and transcribe this onto my computer as the handwriting was so appalling that I feared might lose the meaning of the words over time.

This was harder than I could have imagined.

With each word re-written I felt as though my heart was being ripped asunder.

I battled on fighting my emotions every step of the way.

Just as I was finishing the last few paragraphs, Martin came home and I heard him bounding enthusiastically up the stairs. As usual, he came over and kissed my neck as I worked on the keyboard, and cast a crafty peek at what I was doing on the screen.

"That looks interesting. . . what is it? Can I have a read?" he enthused. To be honest, I really hate it when he does this "peeking" and my inclination was to tell him to bugger off.

I was still trying to understand what had happened, and what it meant.

However, I heard myself agree that he could indeed have a read of it, so I printed off a copy, settled him down on my studio sofa and left him to it. My gut feeling was, he would find it quite harrowing in some ways, maybe even upsetting and I did not want to intrude on whatever emotional reaction he might have. What he was now holding and reading, was an aspect of myself that I did not even know existed.

When he was done, he came downstairs and found me bimbling around in the kitchen.

I looked up, and could tell he had been crying. Wrapping me in his arms, he hugged me really tight to him and told me it was one of the saddest things he had ever read; he had no idea I had felt like that.

Well, truth be known, neither did I.

I understand, it was an acknowledgement of Self through the eyes of my inner child, as the woman I had now become.

The process had been a true stream of consciousness with no influence from "me". The heart had dictated all. In the writing of this piece, something had opened and broken apart, releasing some trapped part of me.

To date, I had only experienced this "silent voice" once before in this way, when I wrote the message for Tish just before she died. Now, the experience of writing in this way is very familiar to me.

It still takes my breath away at times.

So: I have included "The Child and The Woman" at the end of the book.

When you read it, please bear in mind that it was written at the very start of my awakening, and so when you compare (as you will!) the words from this book, with the same events recorded in that version, you will of course find subtle differences. I have resisted editing and "correcting" the original.

~ THE CHILD AND THE WOMAN ~
(a Souls story)

"The woman that I am looks back from the safety of 41 years of life to the child that she was.

The child I was and the woman I am now are not so very different. We share the same outlook on life. A blind optimism tinged with a healthy cynicism and an implicit belief that things will always work out, no matter how impossible, or far-fetched.

My love of frog spawn is undiminished by age or experience.

A new packet of crayons or paints still excites me.

My hair is still mad and impossible!

I still hate getting out of bed in the mornings.

At 41 I am still waiting to be "caught out". Exposed as a fraud, nowhere near as good as people think I am. The woman that I am and the child that I was both share the same fear and are incredulous that we have got away with "it" for so long.

Somehow, the stuff that comes naturally and feels effortless, the stuff I enjoy and am good at, seems to require more proof of effort to qualify as "real".

At 41, I am better placed to make my own decisions about my choices, my life.

The child that I was remembers with a sense of shame some of the choices which were foisted on her. Clothes were often second hand, and entirely unsuitable even if clean and pressed. Playing always at friends houses; because our house was always full of its own screaming inhabitants, with no respite. Walking miles to school in shoes that didn't fit; because we needed the bus fare for a loaf of bread. Borrowing other peoples dogs because Mum wouldn't let me have one of my own.

The child I was, is creative, inventive of necessity. Whole new worlds, lives, people come alive and very real in a fertile imagination. Sometimes it is hard to remember the difference. What is real and what is not. Then the child becomes disappointed. The fantasy continues because it feels better. Others don't quite see that and the child is admonished for her lies. She is not a liar. She just sees things quite differently. Now, the woman that I am gets frustrated because I can't always remember what was real and what was not.

Does it matter?

Maybe not?

Probably not!

On a "bad hair day" I see the child that I was peering, anxious, hard, into the mirror. Wishing for what she does not have. The thick dark unruly stuff with which I am bestowed is not what I would have chosen for myself. The hair I should have had was bestowed upon my sister. My sister has perfect hair. As a child she had the finest, blonde white tumbling curls which glowed a golden halo in the sun. So pretty, so sweet and angelic was my sisters hair that the Nuns begged my Mum to let them adopt her. They thought she was an angel on account of that hair. So, when I peer despairingly into that mirror now, and run my fingers through the mad thatch it is a gesture made a million times already in my life.

I am not beautiful. I have an interesting face which can look quite striking in a good light with the right make up. Eyes that are so dark they are almost black at times, now beginning to settle a few bags and crows feet in the corners. When I am truly happy, joyful, they can dance in the darkness and I can almost feel the sparks they give off. In anger or displeasure they freeze over and burn. Most telling is when I lose myself in fear or pain and the eyes simply fade, giving and taking nothing. It is a mobile kind of face which has been described (not unkindly) as a walnut. It screws up into a tight wrinkly ball, especially around the forehead and chin, when I am deeply concentrating or fighting off pain or boredom.

This face has the wrong ears. They are sticky outy and spoil a reasonable shaped outline. My husband twists them in fun, little realising the humiliation I feel.

The child that I was promised that those ears would be fixed as soon as age and finances permitted. They would be pinned to perfection, neat, flat. I still have the old ears, so perhaps the woman that I am never grew up enough or became rich enough to fulfil that promise.

The teeth came into a similar conversation with promises of improvement in later life. The teeth are gappy tombstone things capable of accommodating a sixpence between each. In their favour, they are strong and white requiring minimal dentistry. I never got my wisdom teeth and I was rather relying on them to fill those gaps. You see, its like the hair, if I really wanted to I could become as blonde and angelic as my sister. But I really can't be arsed!

As I write, at 41, I have a small irritating rash on my top lip. Just an irritation but enough to remind me of the afflictions the child suffered. Who the hell knows what it was, but family legend has it that I was allergic to a tortoise, which I had insisted on acquiring. The subsequent rash disfigured my face and hands so dramatically that Mum was forced to insist on re-homing the tortoise. The rash was dealt with by application of a vile thick paste which made me look and feel like a clown. I have no thick white paste available today, so I look like I have been sucking on a particularly synthetic red ice lolly and the frozen stain has blurred my lips until they are out of focus.

The child that I was grew sun browned and skinny limbed. Always outdoors, riding a bike, running wild on the building site which was our estate and playground, or haring madly through fields of grasses and corn as yet unspoiled by the developers. The child was unconcerned and incurious about her body. It was simply a vehicle and as long as it continued to function as it always had it was given very little thought. The woman I am now wishes it could be so again.

How many times has offensive flesh been squeezed and threatened with expulsion?

How many days have passed when I have not asked "Should I eat this?" Then the child speaks up and asks, confused "Why not?" . The child has no concept of calories or fat units. Never did, never will! That responsibility lies with the woman I am now, the grown up me, capable of self torture on a grand scale. Sometimes when the dissatisfaction reaches a point verging on self loathing I will do some exercise, join a gym, buy a mountain bike, go running. For a while I feel free, daft, light headed and light hearted. The child and I enjoy ourselves, we could conquer the world not just my thighs! Really. . . all it is, is a bit of physical exercise, getting the blood circulating again. So, how come I stop it, give up, let it go? Back comes that fat, floppy, frumpy feeling and we start all over.

The child that was me (despite her shameful clothes, thickly anointed rashes and the wrong hair) often thought she was the most beautiful and dazzling person in the world. Unbelievably, . . yes!! She was often seen standing on the railway embankment throwing pebbles at the windows of the passing Manchester to Liverpool express train just to let travellers admire her loveliness as they hurtled onwards. She thought nothing of riding her Triumph 20 bike down the centre of the main road, weaving elegantly in and out of the white line markings, just so people could admire her incredible control and skill. Cars often tooted horns in appreciation and drivers waved (sometimes, with only one finger raised) as they careered by. Yes, the child often felt loved by the whole world – as her right!

The woman I am now, knows this to be true. The child was well loved, and still is, and so it is in my interests as the woman to encourage the child and let her be.

How do I know this?

If I, as the woman that I am, met the child today, what would I tell her?

That her life will be wonderful, and she will be everything she dreams of being and more?

Would that be true?

Would it be fair?

Has it been?

Is it now?

Will it be?

I cannot really tell her that everything will be perfect because much of this life has been hard and there have been times when I wondered if I would indeed make it through. I would not want to dampen her enthusiasm but I would not want to mislead her either. All I can tell her is "I tried my best for you"

The woman that I am has made some good choices for the child and they have been constant for the woman.

The child was good at art, and so she went to art school and learned to put her creativity to practical use. She became a designer – a good designer. At art school, she met a boy who was destined to become her husband and life partner, the love of her life. She married him, and still has the same passion for him now all these years later. She believes him when he says he feels the same about her.

She got her education, and her love, and over the years she got good jobs earning good money. She was well paid for doing something she was passionate about and enjoyed.

The woman worked hard.

Very hard.

One day, she realised that she was no longer doing what she loved or was good at and that she was losing herself because she did in fact hate her work. When she failed to comply with company policy and diktat, she lost her good job with the good pay packet and she felt she had lost herself too.

For quite some time now she had not seen or felt the child that she was.

The child that was her.

She had been too busy.

When the initial pain and shame of losing the job and the good salary had lessened, the woman could hear a child singing somewhere inside her head. The child that she was needed attention, she was coming back to her. The child continued its singing, tuneless, off key, jumbled up words (she was always" cloth eared") but she is joyful because for the first time in ages she has the full attention of the woman.

So, the woman listens to the child, desperate for approval, to be loved as she was before, confused at the rejection. The child wants to buy things, for the fun of it, a new car, new clothes, holidays, start a business, and so she does. The woman lets her. She knows she owes it to indulge the child, to make her happy, see her smile again, she had forgotten how that felt.

When the money is all gone, spent on foolishness, the woman blames the child.

Scolded.

The child is ashamed and retreats back to where it is safe.

Away from the woman.

Now, the woman has to find a new job. Not so hard, she is well qualified and able. She finds a job easily.

Before she can start the new job, she has to see a doctor. Just straightforward procedure – for the company records.

The doctor is not happy.

The woman has cancer.

The woman is in shock! She feels fine, she is not ill, she has no symptoms.

The child is very frightened, she knows what cancer is, she doesn't want to die.

Neither does the woman.

When she goes into the hospital, the woman must become the child she was. She has no control over what may happen to her. She must let others do the thinking, make her decisions for her. There is little dignity and she knows only too well how shame feels. The fear that lies in her belly, tightening and growing is like the cancer itself. They think it is operable but they are not sure. She will have the operation then wait 10 days to know if she will live, or die from it.

All the mad hair has been cut off, the lipstick has been forgotten and quite honestly the woman doesn't even think of the calories she will save by not eating for almost two weeks. She knows that just to survive this, will be enough. She promises the child she will never push her out again. Never tell her to "shut up" this is too important.

When it is all over, the woman finds it hard to believe that this happened to her. It feels like the 3rd person, someone she knew of – once.

Once upon a time . . . .

Anyway, the scars remind her that it was her. Visible scars, across her stomach, hip to hip and the backs of her hands where the drips went in.

The woman feels old, broken, useless.

Her husband, the love of her life, tells her she is beautiful.

She is to him.

Every night she can hear the child crying herself to sleep.

Small, animalistic, raw.

It gets on the woman's nerves a bit, because she never cries.

So, the woman healed her body and was proclaimed to "have done marvellously".

The woman went back to work, taking the child with her. As she promised she would.

After a while, the child got bored and disappeared again. She visited a few times, unannounced and taking the woman by surprise. On those occasions the woman found herself enjoying life, having fun. She learned to ride a motorcycle, took up watercolour painting, went on holiday with the love of her life, made some new friends.

In those next few years the child that was me tried to help the woman I am now. To keep the woman open minded, free thinking, curious and proud.

Proud of who she was, what she had achieved, how far she had travelled.

When the woman was called to take a job with a Company she already knew she hated, she didn't listen to the child's protestations. She coldly told the child to "shut up" just like she had promised she never would again. The woman was the adult, she knew what she was doing.

The woman didn't know what she was doing or why she had done it. She only knew she had made a big mistake. All the things she had grown to be proud of, to enjoy about herself, including the child that she was were held up for criticism and ridicule by people she had no respect for and disliked intensely.

The woman's' husband, the love of her life, did not really see what had happened until one day when he took the woman to the sea.

The woman hardly spoke the whole time, not daring to for fear of criticism. The child picked up stones and shells from the shoreline, dancing with sodden shoes in the waves that washed ever more precious shells for her to collect. The child wanted chips and ice cream and hot chocolate and cakes with jammy bits and, and... and!!! The husband laughed, crinkling at the corners with joy, "you are back!!" he cried

"Where have you been!?"

The woman was confused, because she had not said a word all day, she had just sat back and let the child play on the beach. She was too fearful, too distressed to enjoy herself. The child that she had been had taken over, it was her day, nothing was going to spoil it.

The woman smiled a slow smile of realisation. The husband, the love of her life, loved the child too!

When the child was re-united with the woman once more they took each other in their arms and promised "No more!"

When the woman left the job she hated so much, they gave her a surprising gift. The chance to consider what she really wanted to do with her life, how she should work, to question what she really valued.

It was hard. The woman often felt scared because the path she was choosing was untried by her and solitary, but the child she had been saw thing differently. The road ahead was clear and full of possibilities, she was keen to explore!

The woman had learned that she was the instrument of her own success and destiny. The person she was held valuable knowledge and ideas which people would pay for. The woman need not change or leave herself behind to fulfil her commitments. She was all she needed to be.

Over the next few years the woman and the child that she was, worked together. They enjoyed each other's company and enjoyed the work that they did. They were well paid and realised that they had much value.

When she was 40, the woman that I am, found herself taking a different course in life. She began to learn new things, things which surprised her, intrigued her, delighted her and filled her with such incredible joy.

She felt exactly like the child she once was.

When she was given instructions for a job which needed to be done, by her and her alone, she didn't really understand the request. The instruction was in itself clear enough, but she realised that all she was, wasn't enough to fulfil it.

The woman that I am, needed to know more and had no idea how to find that knowledge.

The child that she was, knew.

She asked the Universe.

The child that she was knew that nothing is impossible, that all things happen just as they should do, and that we only have to ask for the help we need to achieve that.

When the Universe answered, the woman was amazed, but the child took it all in her stride.

The Universe smiled at the woman in her awe and amazement and reminded her that she had once been the child that she was, and so could trust her entirely. The woman listened, (intently; with her face screwed up, like a walnut,) to the Universe as the child that she was.

At 41, she began to understand.

~ IN OTHERS WORDS ~

I am so grateful to all my clients and friends who offered to contribute their own stories, of their own experiences, in their own words.

Thank you x

♥TWINKLE TWINKLE ~

"My friend Jo has a little boy Henry who has Rubinstein Taybi Syndrome and has spent a lot of time in hospital, with his Mum Jo by his side.

I wrote and asked you to choose a card for me that Jo could take into hospital with her when she had to go with Henry to show that the angels were with her.

You sent a Angel card called Twinkle, Jo thought it was lovely and showed the card to Henry later that night. Henry communicates with sign language and at the time was not very old.

Henry signed Twinkle Twinkle, when Jo looked on the back of the card she was amazed that the Angel was called Twinkle and phoned me straight away. There was no way that Henry could have known the name of the Angel.

Jo has always carried the card with her Henry when they go to hospital and it sits by his bedside and still calls on the Angel for support when she needs it."

Love hugs and light Karen xxxxxxxx

♥ MARIAS STORY ~

"I haven't known Alison that long at all.... It was one of those "accidents". I was looking up something else on the web and up came the website about angel readings.

I'd been coming to terms with a number of significant events in my life and also trying to make sense of some really unusual experiences when I came across the site and so decided to pick up the phone and book a reading. I left a message and later got a call back. When Alison spoke to me on the phone we booked the time and she chatted about how the reading took place and gave me directions on how to find her, but I had this strange feeling that I was speaking to someone I already knew. I can't explain it. It felt right somehow.

I turned up, at what from the outside seemed like an office or industrial unit, but once inside opened up into a magical place full of character and art. It was as though I'd entered a really special place. It kind of reminded me of the programme Mr Ben and/ or Narnia when you go through the door what you find is so unexpected...

Alison made me feel at ease, again that feeling of having known her for a long time....

Once in the space Alison realised she'd forgotten her special pen and wanted to return to her home to fetch it and invited me to go with her - she was so trusting and open.

Once at her house she showed me her garden, her bees, her Mary Magdala rose which immediately took me to a candle someone had bought me from a visit to a monastery that was of St Theresa and stated: "Pick me a Rose from the Heavenly Garden and send it to me with a message of love" and that, through her angel messages is literally what Alison does.

It also bought to mind "The Little Prince" by Antoine De Saint-Exupery and the journey to protect his rose and the saying from there that "what is essential is invisible to the eye".

The pen collected, garden visited, beautiful rose imprinted on memory, we returned to the reading room. We began with the angel card reading and then the channelled letter and painting. The message was amazing and reached that invisible, essential place...

It was as though I had been directed/ guided to Alison, to understand the strange experiences of the last 12 months, to give them a form and a voice and to realise I was not going crazy, I was not alone.

Alison is an Earth Angel with a very special gift. Her pen is that of a ready writer. To my mind comes an Ancient message of the Sons of Korah:

My heart is stirred...my tongue is the pen of a skillfull writer...your lips have been anointed with grace... Gird your sword on your side you mighty one; clothe yourself with splendour and majesty. In your majesty ride forth victoriously in the cause of truth, humility and justice...All your robes are fragrant with myrrh and aloes and cassia from palaces adorned with precious stones. Listen and pay careful attention my beloved I will perpetuate your memory through all generations through the work of pen and the images I bring to you.

With Love, Maria xxx

♥ WINGED MESSENGERS ~

"Having connected with the Angelic Beings through my own personal journey, I was invited to attend a workshop, run by a lady called Alison Knox. I followed my instinct with an open heart and trusted there was a reason for me to be there. Wow! The Power and Magnificence emanating from these beautiful Illumined Beings was breath-taking. To stand in their presence was Mighty. I knew something on a deep level was happening.

Since that day, 5 years ago my connection with Winged Messengers has become much stronger. My friendship with Alison, has grown to that of a trusted Earth Angel. I consider Alison as a truly gifted

Messenger, her artistic talents are evident right to the finite details of specks of angel dust. I regard Alison as trusted friend, someone who has integrity, passion and strength."

Kam x

♥TOUCHED BY GRACE ~

I have known Alison for a good many years, I first met her at a Mind, Body, Spirit event In Newark Nottinghamshire, a mutual friend introduced us, I was still reeling and recovering from a tumour and losing a baby and the possibility of cancer occurring in any of my major organs within the next year. A regular client of Alison took me by the hand (knowing that Alison had recovered from illness in a similar area to myself, she told me that it would be really good if we could swap stories) I was led to a stall which lit up as though heaven had just shone its Holy Spirit onto both her and her channelled angels and whilst Alison was twinkling away on her stall, she still found the time to sit me down and chat to me with the promise of us meeting up and sharing in quality time.

A little while later we did exactly this, Alison very kindly allowing me to meet at her home, it was as though we had known each other a long time and were very much at ease; talking the same language and sharing our story, she was very warm and generous and her journey thus far amazed me. When she shared with me the photograph of the Angel at the Convent, well, it touched me on such a deep level, I cried, Alison is so blessed and is as though she see's through the eyes of an angel.

Another time, I saw my own Angel very similar to Alison's in the Convent. It just so happened that one of my children Andre' was off school sick and was upstairs, suddenly a warmth came into the room, followed by an apparition of an angel which levitated in all of its shimmering glory in my living room. I asked permission for Andre to see and she nodded (I refer to as "she" as there seemed to be a certain feminine energy), I shouted Andre "*to come downstairs and meet an angel"*, he ran down and stood agog at the bottom of the stairs "wow" he declared, *"look at its crown chakra mummy, it has all the colours of the rainbow".*Oh, it was glorious, all opalescent and smiling away at my son. I will never forget it, Although, I have seen other beings to include Angels since I was a baby, I have never seen one so colourful and that others have been able to share. I got down on my knees in awe, whilst reaching my hand out to this most radiant being and prayed. Of course, I just had to telephone Alison, I was all of a quiver and a positive emotional wreck, I left a garbled message on her answer machine, I was almost apologising for sounding so batty as to see an Angel, well you can imagine her wonderful response, she told me to never apologise for being given the Grace of seeing an angel, I feel so blessed, now and always.

My clients who come for angel card readings are always touched by one of Alison's channelled Angel paintings that shares my workspace and even when I was in hospital giving birth to my miracle twinkly baby last year, I was handing out her miniature picci's to the nursing staff – who were totally entranced by my mini painting on its easel sat next to the crib, her work touches people on such a deep level.

Alison and I had a shared Angelic experience through dream, here is my dream: I was walking up my pathway to my house, named "Riverside Walk", in my dream Alison was my next door neighbour and I could hear shuffling around in the shrubs which divided our houses, as though a small animal was in them, so I got down on my knees foraging around to see what was in the foliage when all of a sudden I heard the flapping of some very large wings, wafting very loudly on the breeze until it was very close indeed, I knew that a large winged something had landed in Alison's garden, I climbed over the fence and into her garden. Well, I was in awe of the vision that stood before me; the most beautiful black Angel, it could have been either male or female as it was very beautiful but felt slightly more masculine, I felt very drawn to him, his wings were black with a red edging to them – I walked towards him and kissed him (non-sexually on the lips) I then awoke, I contacted Alison and told her of my dream, she had also dreamt the same night of a black Angel similar to mine (Alisons had bright red wing tips) and she had kissed him too – I believe we were both touched by the same Angel the same evening in our sleep state – what amazing Grace was this?

Alison may I share with you this message? which I feel and know is from the Angelic realm, the start of which came to me only a few days ago: *"Oh illumined One, you shine so bright, your soul is evolved, you are indeed an Earth Angel, you walk the path with souls who wear flesh and walk the earth plane, you have endured what the flesh has to endure and know what pain and suffering is as well as the pleasure and high frequency of joy, you ARE indeed a chosen One, we wish to thank you for your service to us, your dedication to our work, you are a vehicle for which we impart messages and divine wisdom to others, oh vessel of light please know that we are no closer to god than you are, but we serve his purpose in a way that you would judge to be more direct. We bear the very essence of unconditional love, and yet we have the power to direct this and place it where god would have us do so. We seek earnestly to raise the human understanding, to bring it to a sufficient level where through our channelling - answers may be found, you my beloved one may continue to outpour through your art and your heart, please know that you are truly loved and give love, you are now evolving at a different frequency than before and must wear armour, you are more sensitive, however, we do protect you my beloved child – oh, children of the earth know that we are with you now and always, work in love and light, do not give way to those who will knowingly or not may serve to tempt you from your path, they do not know that they may serve the dark side, do not sway from your path - your current journey, we do not come from a place of ego, only love and only light, a struggle is taking place on the earth plane, of which you serve to assist and to spread the holy word, we will lift you and inspire you in your work ahead, we say a fond farewell for now with knowledge that both you and we are likewise children of god serving his divine purpose.*

In Love and from Light always X Jo

♥THROUGH ANGELS EYES ~

You helped me when I came to one of your workshops (*Through Angels Eyes*) . You guided us through a meditation, during which you took us into a room. Then you told us to feel the energy of the person who was in the room. I could feel a beautiful soft, safe and loving energy. You then told us that we were looking into a mirror, and that we were really feeling our own energy. Thank you so much for that moment. It has had a profound effect on me, because until that point I was not able to believe people when they told me how lovely I am. I still sometimes struggle with self-love issues, but I often think back to that time and remember, and it really helps.....

With love and hugs, Anne (Animal Healer) xxxx

♥TRUE LIFE CALLING ~

"Each of us has a destiny, a purpose and True Life calling - we all of us are on a journey toward our whole-istic self, and once fully embodied, we are to enjoy living that true self in our full potential and divine bliss.

Alison and her Everyday Angels have played a big part in my 'journey home to self', to finding that true soul self, and now that I have, they continue to guide me along the way toward truly living that self as 'spirit being' intertwined and balanced with 'human being' - the whole-istic self of which I speak. Alison, and her Everyday Angels, have played an integral part of my journey. Messages have always arrived just at the perfect time with wisdom so perfect for the moment. Those most poignant to me and my journey adorn my walls or sit in frames around my home, being, and writing space. Mini angel cards often accompany me in my daily activities in my purse. I could write a full book on my experiences since meeting Alison and becoming acquainted with her angels - to mention one particular channelled line written would render it 'less than', and no one word, nor angel that comes forth, is ever less than. They are not angels with harps singing sweetly to the heavens, they are angels with an attitude who are very aware of their purpose. They are true, honourable, and totally responsible of their purpose, offering a soft shoulder when right to do so - just as they offer a hobnail boot if, as, and when required. If asked to choose a moment in time, of which there have been so many when Alison and her angels remain most memorable to me, it would be the weekend that I was to experience 'an everything all at once' experience.

Attending a workshop at which the Archangels made it clear to me, through direct channelled messages that they were an embodiment of me and that I was an embodiment of them - that I was able to do on Earth what they were unable to do. The following day I had a 'sitting' with Alison during which I was to meet my own Angel and spirit self – in relation to which, in a later workshop, I was to receive her spirit name.

Here is what I wrote as a testimonial: *"How does one express the joy you 'feel' on meeting with your 'angelic and spirit self' in the birthing of an angel portrait channelled and birthed by you, your essence, heart and hand...Your work is priceless, YOU ARE AN ANGEL, and I cannot thank you enough for what was, as precious an experience to me, as life itself. I would urge those that have the same inner knowing that I had, as and when it feels right, to embrace time with you in the Sitting Room. The tea and biscuit, atmosphere and music are all a part of this magical experience...,and when the angel comes....well, those who come to see you will know just how that feels, as although I have used words here as a way of expressing my gratitude, the experience itself surpasses words. With deep appreciation and eternal gratitude for helping me to bring my angel into this world – she and all the other angels that you paint are birthed into this world for great reason. With love and gratitude, . . .*

Susanne xxx ...

When you meet Alison and experience her work, through her book, paintings, channelled lines or in person - you will indeed have been touched by an Everyday Angel .

Susanne x

♥ANGELIC ADVOCACY ~

Alison's artwork has always had a life and language of it's own in the holographic expression and layering of the form. In my experience when you invite one of her pieces of art into your home and surroundings, it becomes equal to sharing your space with a living BEing.

I have freely advocated Alison and her work to many of my clients over time as a tool to magnify and enhance their aims and intentions, and have always been really delighted to hear their ongoing stories of success and achievements."

Cascades of Rainbow LOVE and TWINKLES

Vanessa XX

♥ANGEL FEATHERS ~

Dear Alison,

I love getting your letters and follow you avidly angels and bees and of course your time at Gorton Monastery which I do hope to get to sometime it looks wonderful and sounds amazing which you bring to life when you write about it.... I first met you at a MBS at Elsecar Heritage centre not long after my husband died, I think it probably would have been 2002 I got so much comfort speaking to and buying my beautiful Angel friends. I also wrote to you and you sent me an Angel feather....Since my husband died in 2001 after a wonderful marriage and a week after celebrating our 40th anniversary with a family party I have received so many angel feathers from him in the most unusual places...all are pure white and very beautiful, I have kept them in a special box which is half full. At the time I wrote to you I sent you a photo of them...I get so much joy and a lovely comforting feeling knowing he is around. Something quite funny happened yesterday....I have got a new puppy following the death of my faithful dog Molly who died 3 weeks ago. I felt so sad without her and my son bought Pippa a very pretty black Cocker Spaniel and when I called her in from the garden she looked so startled as there on her nose was a little angel feather which I took as approval from Molly and Leslie hope you think the same......

all my love and twinkles, Dee x

♥KATIES MUM ~

My partner and soulmate of twelve years, Mike, had passed away from cancer two years before I had my angelic experience. One weekend in July 2010 my eldest daughter Katie came to stay with me as she was doing a skincare products stall at a local healing event in Somerset. On the second day of the event I went to help on her stall. Katie said that she had met Alison of Everyday Angels on the stall opposite selling amazing angel art. She said that I would be drawn to one of her pictures or cards. I must admit I was very sceptical, but when I looked at the images, I was drawn to a card and bought it. I looked at the back of the card and it said this was of the Archangel Michael - what a coincidence! Later that day I went to a friend's birthday party and during the evening this lovely man, Morris started talking to me and we really clicked together. His wife had died of cancer and we had a lot in common. I never thought I would meet someone again after losing Mike, but Morris and I are still very happily together and enjoying life again.

Hazel

NB: Archangel Michael is the angel that helps cut us free from that which holds us back. He is a liberator and freedom fighter ! In this experience, Archangel Michael allowed Hazel to feel she had permission to move forward in her life.

♥THE PHOENIX RISES ~

Sometimes you feel like you need to start again and rise from the ashes like a phoenix. Deciding to make some major changes in my life I chose the phoenix as a symbol for my fresh start and new beginnings. It evoked strong powerful internal images and gave me strength and courage to go in a new direction. Unknown to me Alison had painted a picture in celebration of this new start. Imagine my surprise and joy when an amazing Fire Angel revealed herself in Alison's gift, sparkling, passionate, dazzling and fiery like a beautiful Phoenix. Alison had no inkling of my totem yet had created an amazing work of art that still stands proudly in my studio and reminds me that when we are brave enough to make changes the Universe is there to support us

X Rachel

♥YES!

The arrival of the 'YES' angel, in all its amazing other wordly colours (impossible to create on canvas unless a divine influence is at work), changed my life.

This angel made me realise that, when we are ready to say 'YES' to all and everything in and around our lives, we step into a very different experience.

We move into the stream of pure potential, and our soul merges with our physicality.

The 'YES' angel asks us to be courageous in the face of true destiny. Miracles become the norm and best of all, we actually notice them.

The 'Yes' angel opened my heart to love the life I was meant to live, opened my eyes to see where that lay and dissolved the edges of my resistance.

X Trish

♥ ~ WITH GRATITUDE ~ ♥

I am so very grateful to all those who have walked this journey with me, so far, through time, space and consciousness, with whom I have shared the magic and the mystery, the miracles and the miles. My beloved nearest and dearests, my friends, teachers, colleagues, my adversaries, challengers and detractors; I love you all for *everything* you have taught me.

I appreciate all the "cuppas" over the kitchen table, the off road adventures, the advice, the encouragement, the honesty and the occasional kick up the backside. . .all good stuff! Most of all I appreciate the love, in all it's many splendid guises.

♥I offer special thanks to my steadfast Beloved; husband **Martin Knox** who has absolutely encouraged the writing of this book, and has put up with some very random domestic arrangements as I immersed myself in the process of writing, editing and rewriting.

♥To my parents **Margaret and Brian Lewis** who taught me independence and values and allowed me to become who I am.

♥BIG gratitude to my dear friends **Annie Jones and Raphael,** who found each other and in so doing, facilitated the publishing of this book.

♥To my trustworthy "reviewers", **Flo Aeveia Magdalena, Thrity** and **Meher Engineer, Tina Bettison,** and **Maria Poyser**, who delivered honesty over flattery, to ensure this book held what they know of my voice, my truth and my passion.

♥To **Marianne Gunn O Connor** for believing in my writing, taking me on, and guiding me through the scary part.

♥To our generous hearted friends **Julie, Mike and William Hanson** who offered us the use of their beautiful holiday home in Turkey, so

I could finish the first manuscript without distractions, in a peaceful and inspiring environment.

♥Thanks, to **all those whose stories are woven into this book**, the named and the un named, the dots that became joined, the missing links that became found. I appreciate the open hearted generosity of each of those who contributed to **"In Others Words"** it means a lot to me to have you here.

♥To my **Angels** and **Illumined Ones**, for their dedicated patience and unfailing love; for their willingness to meet me as I am, and in doing so, make me more than I was.

I feel truly blessed to even have such a story to share with the world, and I thank **YOU**, beloved reader, for choosing this book.

Lightning Source UK Ltd.
Milton Keynes UK
UKOW04f1104161215

264820UK00002B/77/P